7/15/15
$34.99

The Daily Show and Rhetoric

Arguments, Issues, and Strategies

Edited by Trischa Goodnow

LEXINGTON BOOKS
Lanham • Boulder • New York • Toronto • Plymouth, UK

Published by Lexington Books
A wholly owned subsidiary of The Rowman & Littlefield Publishing Group, Inc.
4501 Forbes Boulevard, Suite 200, Lanham, Maryland 20706
http://www.lexingtonbooks.com

Estover Road, Plymouth PL6 7PY, United Kingdom

British Library Cataloguing in Publication Information Available

Library of Congress Cataloging-in-Publication Data
The Daily Show and rhetoric : arguments, issues, and strategies / edited by Trischa Goodnow.
    p. cm.
  Includes bibliographical references and index.
  ISBN 978-0-7391-5002-3 (cloth : alk. paper) — ISBN 978-0-7391-5003-0 (pbk. : alk. paper) — ISBN 978-0-7391-5004-7 (electronic)
  1. Daily show (Television program) I. Knapp, Trischa Goodnow.
  PN1992.77.D28D35 2011
  791.45'75—dc22   2010047748

The paper used in this publication meets the minimum requirements of American National Standard for Information Sciences—Permanence of Paper for Printed Library Materials, ANSI/NISO Z39.48-1992.

Printed in the United States of America

For Mary Louise and Bill DeMarco

For always making me laugh

Contents

Acknowledgments

As with any undertaking of this magnitude, there are a myriad of people to thank. First, I want to thank the authors who contributed to this volume. Your patience and diligence in producing this work is greatly appreciated. Rebecca McCary at Lexington provided thoughtful and patient guidance throughout this process. You're the best. Thanks! I'd also like to thank Robert Iltis, Gregg Walker, the Department of Speech Communication, and Oregon State University for providing encouragement, support and a sabbatical to create this volume. In addition, I extend my thanks to Mark Moore who postponed his sabbatical so I could take mine to work on this book. Additional thanks go to Lee Rianda and Melissa Weintraub for answering questions during the editing process. My friends and family have been great in listening to me whine during this project so many thanks to you all (especially Lee for making me leave the cabin every now and then). Taliesin Mihacsi, Jonathan Smith and Nikki Roberts had the underappreciated job of citation checking. Thanks, guys—may the graduate school gods smile kindly upon you. Finally, thanks to Jon Stewart and the cast and crew of *The Daily Show* for providing such interesting fodder for this rhetorical study.

Introduction

The Daily Show and Rhetoric— Arguments, Issues, and Strategies

Since its inception in 1996, *The Daily Show with Jon Stewart* has amused, bemused, confounded, and angered audiences and critics alike. *The Daily Show* is not easily categorized as it is part news and part entertainment wrapped in a healthy dose of critique and cynicism. One thing is certain: host Jon Stewart, with the help of his staff of writers, can be considered a master rhetorician. Why, you might ask, does this definitive label matter? Rhetoric concerns the ability to persuade an audience. What may seem like harmless entertainment may contain powerful persuasion.

Rhetoric, like *The Daily Show*, often confounds its students and critics. Plato's (1959) interrogation and ultimate denouncement of rhetoric in *Gorgias* exemplifies the age-old debate about the nature and purpose of rhetoric. Today, it is common to hear politicians and reporters cast a seeming slur on political statements by labeling a statement "mere rhetoric." However, as scholars of rhetoric can attest, there is more to rhetoric than empty words.

Aristotle (1954) defines rhetoric as "the faculty of observing in any given case the available means of persuasion" (p. 1355b). He meant by this that rhetoric is a skill through which the user discovers the best means to influence an audience. Jon Stewart certainly has a skill in using humor to shed light and, thus, potentially influence his audience's perceptions of political happenings and political statements. The purpose of this book, The Daily Show *and Rhetoric*, is to examine and uncover the rhetorical dimensions of *The Daily Show*. This examination of the program will allow the reader a better understanding of the power to influence evident in this popular culture phenomenon.

Scholars have undertaken recent study into *The Daily Show* as an important source for information and critique. Perhaps the most cited example is

Baym's (2005) examination of the program as a reinvention of political reporting. Baym asserts that *The Daily Show*'s mix of humor and critique, "is a quite serious demand for fact, accountability, and reason in political discourse" (p. 273). Such assessments are common in scholarly essays on Stewart's show. This type of assessment is seen in the works of Borden and Tew (2007), McKain (2005), and Brewer and Marquardt (2007). Of course, the impact of *The Daily Show* is also examined. Baumgartner and Morris (2006) consider how the program impacts American youth, ultimately concluding that the show may increase cynicism toward politics and politicians in an already disaffected youth. Cao (2008) concluded that programs such as *The Daily Show* may provide viewers with information that they may otherwise not receive. These studies and others (see for example, Morris 2009, Baumgartner and Morris 2006, Feldman and Young 2008) lay the foundation for legitimizing *The Daily Show* as a reasonable subject for scholarly study. Perhaps there is no more an appropriate area in which to undertake such study than rhetoric.

The Daily Show *and Rhetoric: Arguments, Issues, and Strategies* seeks to fully engage the idea of *The Daily Show* as rhetoric. Consequently, the book is divided into four sections: The Nature of the Beast, Arguments, Strategies, and Issues. The book begins by examining *The Daily Show* in relation to traditional news and how the program itself makes news. Jon Stewart, the host of the show, has been called "the most trusted man in America." Barbur and Goodnow uncover how Stewart's credibility arises out of an Aristotlean notion of ethos, thus justifying this labeling of Stewart. In the next chapter, Spicer considers *The Daily Show* as political satire and the implications of said satire for the viewing public. Compton's essay dissects Stewart's feud with CNBC's *Mad Money* host, Jim Cramer, to discover both how Stewart uses other programming to make news, and how others use *The Daily Show* to advance their position.

Having established *The Daily Show*'s nature, the next chapters consider the political arguments that Stewart makes. First, Self conducts a close-textual analysis of *The Daily Show* to assert that the program provides a new form of political communication through the use of satire. Wilz then picks up the mantel to argue that the form of argument in which Stewart engages is a rehumanizing discourse that provides a model of democratic deliberation. Hess's first essay is an exploration of specific arguments that Stewart makes against the mainstream media to conclude that the carnivalesque and self-parodic nature of *The Daily Show* disallows the mainstream media to respond to Stewart's biting critique. McGeough also takes up Stewart's feud with Cramer. However, in this essay McGeough uses the exchange to illustrate Stewart's use of dialectical vernacular as a method of holding the media and politicians accountable to their constituents.

The book then turns to specific strategies *The Daily Show* uses to inform its audiences. Wiesman excavates the notion of framing to uncover the comic frame by which Stewart steers the audience's perceptions of the media and politics. In his second essay, Hess looks to *The Daily Show*'s use of irony, parody, and satire to force audiences to rethink their perceptions of mainstream news programming. In the final essay in this section, Mullen considers the visual rhetoric evident in *The Daily Show*. He examines how Stewart mocks mainstream news media through the presentational style of the program.

Finally, the book considers how *The Daily Show* handles specific issues including religion, race, and sexual preference. Buerkle's opening essay utilizes Burkean frames for determining either the positive or negative outcomes for *The Daily Show*'s coverage of GLBTQ issues. Kaylor then takes up the program's stance on religious satire. This essay asserts a new way of looking at religious rhetoric in light of contemporary humorous prophetic discourse. Finally, Purtle and Steffensmeier undertake an analysis of the rhetorical homology between President Obama's speech in response to the Reverend Wright controversy and *The Daily Show*'s coverage of the controversy, ultimately concluding that both speech and program share the comic frame.

Taken as a whole, the works in this volume make a strong argument that *The Daily Show* is more than just a comedy program. As several essays suggest, the humor evident in Stewart's use of satire and parody provide more than just a few laughs. Indeed, perhaps as the audience laughs they are learning as well. *The Daily Show* mocks mainstream media news and in so doing offers a different view of events of the day, a view that challenges viewers to analyze the bill of goods the mainstream media are selling. In addition, these essays suggest that *The Daily Show* should be considered as a game changer in how viewers approach the media, politics, and public issues. Through the strategies used in the program, the arguments advanced, and the issues approached, *The Daily Show* is, indeed, a rhetorical force to be reckoned with.

The essays in this book shed light on a program that is itself enlightening. Rather than *The Daily Show*'s "Moment of Zen," consider this your "Moment of Rhetoric."

REFERENCES

Aristotle (1954). *Rhetoric*. (W. R. Roberts, Trans.). New York, NY: Modern Library.

Baumgartner, J. and S. Morris (2006, May). *The Daily Show* effect: candidate evaluations, efficacy, and american youth. *American Politics Research, 34*(3), 341–367.

Baym, G. (2005). *The Daily Show:* Discursive integration and the reinvention of political journalism. *Political Communication, 22,* 259–276.

Borden, S. L. and C. Tew (2007). The role of journalist and the performance of journalism: ethical lessons from 'fake' news (seriously). *Journal of Mass Media Ethics, 22*(4), 300–314.

Brewer, P. R. and E. Marquardt (2007, November). Mock news and democracy: analyzing *The Daily Show. Atlantic Journal of Communication,* 15(4), 249–267.

Cao, X. (2008). Political comedy shows and knowledge about primary campaigns: the moderating effects of age and education. *Mass Communication and Society, 11,* 43–61.

Feldman, L. and Goldthwaite Young, D. (2008). Late-night comedy as a gateway to traditional news: an analysis of time trends in news attention among late-night comedy viewers during the 2004 presidential primaries. *Political Communication, 25,* 401–422.

McKain, A. (2005, December). Not necessarily not the news: gatekeeping, remediation, and *The Daily Show. The Journal of American Culture, 28*(4), 415–430.

Morris, J. S. (2009). *The Daily Show with Jon Stewart* and audience attitude change during the 2004 party conventions. *Political Behavior, 31,* 79–102.

Plato and Dodds, E. R. (1959). *Gorgias.* Oxford: Clarendon Press.

I

The Nature of the Beast

Chapter One

The *Arete* of Amusement: An Aristotelian Perspective on the Ethos of *The Daily Show*

Jonathan E. Barbur and Trischa Goodnow

Once upon a time, there was great trust in the news media establishment. Though the American media has always produced both partisan and yellow journalism, it was also shaped by individuals such as Edward R. Murrow and Walter Cronkite who stood for courageous and probing investigations into the powerful, practiced civility and fair-mindedness, and envisioned the role of journalist as a public servant. Television news was shaped by such attitudes during its first three decades, and Murrow and Cronkite's most prominent successors (e.g., Dan Rather, Peter Jennings) seemed to live up to their standards.

Thus, even if it was never perfect, for many years national television news at least aspired to high ideals. Early broadcast journalists "saw their profession as a mission," filling a critical social and political role by functioning as "a *searchlight*—a light of public inquiry and political accountability, dedicated to providing citizens the informational resources they needed to participate in a political public sphere" (Baym, 2004, p. 2). But all Golden Ages end, and in contrast to the ideal of yesterday, "today's television news, absorbed into the portfolios of the giant media conglomerates, has become a *floodlight*—a hyper-mediated, theatrical light of exposure, a commodity packaged to sell" (Baym, 2004, p. 2).

There are undoubtedly many reasons for this change—though as the passage above notes, a major factor has been consolidation of ownership and the new media conglomerates' treatment of news as a commoditized, profit-centered business rather than a unique, public-centered profession. Today, the news is expected to turn a profit. Meanwhile, an explosion in the number

3

of competing radio and television channels, and the birth of the twenty-four-hour news cycle (i.e., CNN and the Internet) act to pressure journalists to run stories without time for adequate investigation and background research (Baym, 2005). Moreover—particularly since the terrorist attacks of 2001—the news media has increasingly abandoned its role as "watchdog"—that is, as a critic of government and corporate abuse—functioning instead as a defender of the powerful, or at the least as an uncritical conduit for powerful institutions to spread their messages (Holbert, et al., 2007); indeed, McKain (2005) notes that three-quarters of the content of most news broadcasts originate from government statements.

But these trends have coincided with—arguably, they have caused—a severe decline in viewership for traditional news media, particularly among younger viewers (Morris, 2008). In rhetorical terms, in other words, these trends have caused the traditional news media to lose its *credibility* as a legitimate source of information, while at the same time they have given citizens other options to get information about the world. Increasingly, people find little of merit in either the traditional news' content or its judgment, and cynicism about the media is rampant.

In contrast however, shows that mix news with entertainment, such as late-night talk shows, have gained viewers (Baym, 2005; Coe, et al., 2008). Such "soft news programs are those that package political information in an entertaining form, often through the use of an interview format wherein the interaction between host and guest provides ample comedy or conflict" (Coe, et al., 2008, pp. 201–202). Besides the entertainment factor, such programs avoid accusations of bias because they never claim to be objective or serious; they never aspire to the calling of a "journalist" in the mold of Murrow or Cronkite, and thus they lose nothing if they fail to reach journalistic ideals.

The Daily Show, Comedy Central's "fake news" show, is of course one of the best examples of this hybrid genre, mixing entertainment with an insightful critique of the media. Baym describes it as an experiment in journalistic practices in that its hybrid of parody, satire and serious discussion presented in an entertaining way moves beyond the limits of traditional television genres such as "news" and "entertainment," forming a "profound phenomenon of *discursive* integration, a way of speaking about, understanding, and acting within the world defined by the permeability of form and the fluidity of content" (2005, p. 262). And despite concerns that its comedic approach to news would negatively affect its audience's understanding of the world, *The Daily Show's* audience is actually among the most informed segments of the population, though also typically quite cynical about both media and government (Long, 2004; McKain, 2005; Baumgartner and Morris, 2006).

Moreover, *The Daily Show* (and particularly Jon Stewart as an individual) has emerged as a source that its viewing audience *trusts*—it has developed credibility even as the "serious" media has lost it. The show has garnered

Emmys, Peabodys, and numerous other accolades for the quality of its coverage ("Awards," n.d.); and Jon Stewart tied with Dan Rather, Tom Brokaw, Anderson Cooper, and Brian Williams as the most admired and trusted journalist in America—a significant achievement for someone who repeatedly insists that he is not a journalist at all (Pew, 2008).

Presumably, *The Daily Show* has not achieved this status simply because of a vacuum in credible news media, but rather because the show exhibits qualities that lead its viewers to see it as trustworthy in its own right—in rhetorical terminology, qualities that lead its audience to judge it as possessing *ethos*, a trait that "brings to mind a person's moral character, [and] communal existence," exhibited through their skillful use of rhetoric (Hyde, 2004, p. xvii). Over the rest of this chapter we briefly review the concept of *ethos*, then turn to consider how *The Daily Show* exhibits its ethos.

ETHOS

From the earliest discussions of rhetoric in classical Greece, persuasion has been understood as centered on "a speaker's knowledge of the varieties and complexities of human character," such that "this knowledge enables the speaker to project a favorable self-image and to shape arguments in ways that accommodate differing audiences and occasions" (Baumlin, 2006, "Ethos" section). In more modern terminology then, rhetorical effectiveness might be seen as grounded on a practical application of psychology as the speaker makes judgments about and adapts to their audience's outlook, prejudices, and emotions.

For some classical theorists, such as Isocrates and Plato, the projection of self-image seems inherently interwoven with the speaker's *actual* moral character and role in the larger community (Hyde, 2004; Baumlin, 2006). But ethos is most commonly associated with Aristotle's theory of rhetoric; for him, what is of interest is the *audience's judgment* of a source's character and the strategies that the speaker uses in order to be perceived positively (Hyde, 2004; Baumlin, 2006).

For Aristotle, ethos is "persuasion [that] is achieved by the speaker's personal character when the speech is so spoken as to make us think him credible," and it fits with *logos* (the evidence and arguments advanced by a speaker) and *pathos* (the speaker's evocation of emotions) as one of the three basic means by which a speaker can seek to persuade (Aristotle, 1954/1984, p. 25). It is, however, the most powerful of the three artistic proofs because

We believe good men more fully and more readily than others: this is true generally whatever the question is, and absolutely true where exact certainty is impossible and opinions are divided. . . . [The speaker's] character may almost be called the most effective means of persuasion he possesses. (Aristotle, 1954/1984, p. 25)

The Aristotelian concept of ethos can be considered as composed of three elements exhibited by speakers during their rhetorical acts: *phronesis*, or good sense, intelligence, capability, and practical wisdom; *arete*, or excellence, virtue, and good moral character; and *eunoia*, or benevolence and goodwill towards the audience (Aristotle, 1954/1984, p. 91; Baumlin, 2006, "Aristotelian ethos" section).

Good sense encompasses all knowledge and capabilities that are relevant to the topic the speaker is discussing. This includes sound reasoning abilities, knowledge of theory, science, history, and other fields, practical and technical skills when relevant, and so on; as Smith summarizes, "what is clear from early on in the *Rhetoric* is that a public speaker must know a great deal to be successful" (2004, p. 10). *Phronesis*, however, goes beyond any specific list of knowledge to encompass "a capacity for discerning in the sphere of action the intermediate point where right conduct lies in any given situation" (Smith, 2004, pp. 10–11). In the end, it is the speaker's overall capacity for judgment that matters, and specific knowledge is merely grist for the mill of a soundly reasoning mind.

Beyond good sense, a source must exhibit sound moral character—they should be an excellent person. While it is beyond the scope of this chapter to discuss Aristotle's ethical theories in great detail, it is useful to note here that—in keeping with the general classical Greek notion of the Golden Mean—he articulates virtues as *character traits* that consistently exhibit a happy medium between two undesirable extremes (Kraut, 2010).

For example, when describing someone as "courageous," one is speaking of how a person routinely deals with experiences of fear and danger. A cowardly person is ruled by their fear, while a rash individual tends toward taking unnecessary risks; but a courageous person overcomes their fear to take reasonable risks as the situation warrants them. Aristotle's ethics are primarily concerned with such *habitually* exhibited traits, such as courage, honesty, friendliness, and generosity, rather than with rigid rules that dictate whether to consider a given act right or wrong. Such balanced and consistent virtues are the "character traits that human beings need in order to live life at its best" (Kraut, 2010, "Preliminaries" section, para. 1): to exhibit excellence in their endeavors (*arete*), and to live in such a way as to promote their own and others' happiness (*eudaimonia*) (Kraut, 2010).

The final element of Aristotelian ethos is benevolence or goodwill directed towards the audience. This can be considered something like friendship, in that the speaker's behavior conveys that they have the audience's best interests in mind and that they are on the audience's side. It differs from friendship, however, in that it does not imply reciprocity or the expectation that the audience will necessarily care for the speaker in the same way (Smith, 2004).

As a speaker exhibits (or fails to exhibit) these three elements, they interweave to shape how the audience will likely judge the speaker's overall character and trustworthiness—their ethos. Aristotle notes that they build on each other because

> Men either form a false opinion through want of good sense; or they form a true opinion, but because of their moral badness do not say what they really think; or finally, they are both sensible and upright, but not well disposed to their hearers, and may fail in consequence to recommend what they know to be the best course. These are the only possible cases. It follows that any one who is thought to have all three of these good qualities will inspire trust in his audience. (Aristotle, 1954/1984, p. 91)

Moreover, the three elements function to reinforce each other, as when a speaker's apparent practical wisdom suggests to an audience that the speaker also possesses a virtue of fair-mindedness, because to exercise good judgment implies the capacity to weigh all the available information and consider all reasonable viewpoints (Smith, 2004). Conversely, a source that seems fair-minded to an audience will be more likely to seem to have good sense, because their willingness to consider others' viewpoints is likely to lead to more well-reasoned decisions.

In the following pages we will consider some of the ways in which *The Daily Show* exhibits these traits of good sense, good character, and goodwill. Before doing so, we pause to reflect again on the loss of trust in traditional news in light of the constituent qualities of ethos. The profession's traditional mission to serve as a means of informing a nation so that it could function effectively as a democracy seems to mirror the quality of goodwill toward the audience, while traditional journalistic ideals such as objectivity and the questioning of sources parallel the quality of good sense. Conversely however, the commercialized spectacle of modern broadcast news and partisan punditry is the antithesis of ethos: in failing, for example, to investigate a government statement before airing it to the public it fails to express wisdom and good sense; and it pursues profit at the expense of sound information, indicating a lack of concern for its audience's interests. Thus, most attempts to recapture viewers by increasing the spectacle are likely doomed to failure so long as they ignore the basic nature of what makes a source credible. In contrast, although *The Daily Show* may also be an entertaining spectacle it *has* gained its viewers trust, and in the next section we turn to examine why.

THE ETHOS OF *THE DAILY SHOW*

The Daily Show is first a comedy, and the audience is in their seats because they expect to laugh. Whether on or off the show, Stewart adamantly maintains that he is not a journalist, nor a social or media critic, but a "comedian who has the pleasure of writing jokes about things that I actually care about. And that's really it" ("Bill Moyers interviews Jon Stewart," 2003, n. p.).

Yet, unlike other hybrids of news and entertainment—e.g., late-night variety show monologues or *Saturday Night Live's Weekend Update*—the show's discursive integration of news and entertainment clearly involves more than just punch lines that happen to be based on current events. It is frequently referred to not only as one of the funniest shows on television but also as one of the most *intelligent* and *intellectual*. For example, Smolkin (2007) notes how the show has become a favorite among media scholars and professional journalists, Trier claims *The Daily Show* is arguably "the best critical media literacy program on television" (2008, p. 424), and Colletta calls the show's "informed satire . . . some of the most bracing and engaging commentary on the television landscape" (2009, p. 872). Moreover, the show arguably "not only assumes, but even requires, previous and significant knowledge of the news on the part of viewers if they want to get the joke" (Pew, 2008, n. p.).

In addition, the show's approach is typically *ironic* and *satirical*. Colletta reminds us that

> Traditionally, irony has been a means to expose the space between what is real and what is appearance, or what is meant and what is said, revealing incoherence and transcending it through the aesthetic form and meaning of a work of art. (2009, p. 856)

Satire, moreover, differs from the strictly comedic because it uses humor not merely as an end to itself but as a "weapon," "hold[ing] up human vices and follies to ridicule and scorn" in an attempt to improve society (Colletta, 2009, p. 859). We can thus begin our assessment of *The Daily Show* by keeping in mind that much of its display of good sense, good morals, and goodwill will revolve around the manner in which it uses humor intelligently to expose the gaps between reality and appearance, and the way in which its strategies critique follies and attempt to improve society.

Good Sense

The first element of Aristotelian ethos is intelligence and good sense, and in this section we consider four key ways in which *The Daily Show* exhibits this trait: first, through the type of news that it covers; second, through its strategy of remediating clips drawn from other media; third, through its exaggerated parodies of news reports and journalistic conventions; and fourth, in its interview segment, particularly its selection of guests.

Turning first to its selection of stories and the content of its news coverage, we note that as a proportion of its airtime *The Daily Show* incorporates roughly the same amount of "substance"—actual information—as does mainstream broadcast journalism (Fox, et al., 2007). A key difference, however, is that where the remainder of *The Daily Show's* content—the non-substantive portion—is humorous, in conventional news broadcasts the non-substantive content tends to be "hype"—i.e., political election coverage that focuses on the horse race or on candidate image over issues (Fox, et al., 2007).

In common with mainstream broadcast journalism, particularly the network evening newscasts that it parodies, *The Daily Show* focuses most heavily on U.S. foreign affairs, national elections, and politics; it differs from them, however, in that a significant portion of its coverage focuses on the media itself (Pew, 2008). Moreover, *The Daily Show's* coverage is more heavily concentrated on these subjects, and it tends to entirely ignore subjects that consume a significant portion of the content of conventional news, such as crime and disasters (Pew, 2008).

Perhaps most important, although *The Daily Show* offers a more focused selection of news that arguably sacrifices breadth, it also tends to devote far more time to each story. Conventional news, as well as comedy like Jay Leno or *Weekend Update*, emphasizes a "now this" format in which each story is given very little time (Baym, 2005). For the comedy shows, each topic serves only as the premise for a quick punch line, while for network news broadcasts brevity is an ostensible necessity as it allows the inclusion of more topics; but in either case, it is rare for any topic to be dealt with in detail. *The Daily Show*, in contrast, tends to develop stories to much greater depth even as it incorporates humor throughout the delivery—in some cases, single stories consume up to eight minutes of a broadcast, far exceeding most conventional news (Baym, 2005). Moreover, its segments include far more extensive discussion of an event's background than would ever be present on a network or cable news broadcast, situating the event within a historical context (even if this context is often presented through parody) (Baym, 2005). Finally, not only is the subject matter more completely contextualized in terms of individual stories, it is also (in the case of events that are part of major ongoing stories, such as the Iraq War, often constituted as part of a long-running series of stories (e.g., *The Daily Show's* "Mess-O-Potamia" series discussing Middle East affairs) that further imply continuity and contextualization.

When we put together these aspects of the show's selection and treatment of news, we can see the first element of *The Daily Show's* *phronesis*. The show suggests superior judgment and thoughtfulness in comparison to conventional news simply because it develops context for its stories, a practice that is enabled by its more selective choices about what to cover. At the same time, by replacing hype and sensationalism with humor, it performatively criticizes the conventional news' emphasis on non-substantive material even as it entertains its audience.

Next, we turn from the show's subject matter to its strategy of using clips drawn from other media, particularly network and cable news, congressional hearings, and press conferences. McKain (2005) labels this an example of "remediation," the constantly self-referential practice of media borrowing and re-contextualizing each other's content and formal practices. Ironically, in its heavy emphasis on directly showing politicians' soundbites, the show hearkens to an earlier era of broadcast journalism, but *The Daily Show* has developed its use of clips into a new art form, with "its choices of soundbites turn[ing] contemporary conventions on their head" (Baym, 2005, p. 264).

By placing a politician's statements—often a dozen or more statements stretching over months—directly next to one another, contradictions and hypocrisy are made self-evident. By playing clips drawn from many different news or punditry broadcasts, it becomes easy to observe the otherwise subtle way in which the media's self-referencing enables the chaining out (in the sense used by Bormann [1972]) of simplistic reactions or calculated issue framing—i.e., it becomes easy to see how, somehow, nearly *everyone* on television uses the same language and assumptions to discuss issues.

McKain (2005) describes an example that highlights this technique's ability to effectively demonstrate the government's attempts at "message control" (i.e., spin or propaganda), when the show compares footage of National Security Advisor Condoleezza Rice and White House Press Secretary Scott McClelland speaking separately to the media about Bush Administration war plans. By cutting back and forth between them, *The Daily Show* reveals that both speakers are using almost exactly the same (rehearsed) phrasing, with the segment "culminat[ing] in 'the money shot': an interyplicing of the two voices as they recite the same line, 'at the meeting it was a map of Afghanistan that was rolled out on the table'" (McKain, 2005, pp. 421–422).

The Daily Show does not rely only on juxtaposition of clips. Sometimes simply playing a clip that would otherwise be edited for brevity and clarity places its subject in an entirely different light. For example, Baym (2005) considers the coverage of George W. Bush's statement at the resignation of CIA Director George Tenet. In the *New York Times* and on ABC News brief quotes are drawn from Bush's speech, which, in and of themselves, suggest clear speech and thought. In contrast, *The Daily Show* plays a lengthy clip that shows Bush speaking haltingly and searching for something positive to say about Tenet. The news media's conventions demand clarity, but without the full context of the delivery such conventions produce a misleading image (Baym, 2005).

The use of clip remediation, in its various forms, thus serves as both a direct way of holding the powerful accountable for their statements and actions and as a central element of the show's effectiveness in terms of media criticism. The strategy "consistently disrupts government officials' cultivated images of assurance and knowledge" (McKain, 2005, p. 419), while also laying bare the illusions created by, and the limitations of, the news media's professional conventions. Moreover, simply by making use of publicly available clips from other media *The Daily Show* positions itself as an intellectual (and possibly moral) superior in relation to other media. In principle, any news or editorial show could use clips in the same way. That they do not (despite the ease of doing so and the abundance of material that illustrates, for example, a politician's direct contradiction of previous statements) suggests, in and of itself, that the conventional news media are either lazy, inept, or intentionally colluding in the concealment of the truth—and that *The Daily Show* possesses the good sense to be able to recognize and demonstrate this effectively to its audience.

The third aspect of the show we treat in this section is its parody news segments—skits, sketches and discussions with its "correspondents." For example, many of these sketches involve green-screened reports with backdrops that suggest on-the-scene reporting from the White House to Baghdad to outer space. In these parodies, the show mocks and deconstructs the news media's long-standing practice of sending reporters to read statements in front of the White House or at the scene of a crime, a convention that aims to create the illusion of immediacy and construct the news media as a (falsely) transparent medium that enables viewers to experience the reality of a situation (McKain, 2005). In the show's self-evidently fake on-the-scene reports

> the satiric payoff is that calling attention to . . . the clichéd use of "on the scene" reporters demonstrates how ludicrous they are as gestures of immediacy. After all, that ABC News's John Gibson stands in front of the White House when he recites news about the president does not mean that he has particular, unique, or even useful access to the president. Most likely, the news he delivers came down through the same channels of gatekeeping that it did for the other News networks. (McKain, 2005, p. 418)

Perhaps the most ubiquitous aspect of the show's parody of news media conventions are the absurdly inflated (and constantly varying) titles borne by the comedian-correspondents and the arrogant, condescending tone struck by most of them—*every* correspondent on *The Daily Show* is a "senior correspondent," whether Senior Baghdad Correspondent or Senior Black Correspondent. Like fake on-the-scene reports, self-important titles and demeanors undermine the traditional news' claim of authority; in claiming obviously unfounded expertise, the show is suggesting that conventional broadcast journalists likewise lack such expertise. *The Daily Show* thus highlights how merely appearing on television *confers* the appearance of expertise, rather than expertise *justifying* one's appearance, and thus

> The ultimate target of *The Daily Show's* parody pieces, then, may be the myth of the contemporary journalist as a credentialed professional who commands some specialized ability to determine the truth of a situation. (Baym, 2004, p. 15)

Guest interviews constitute another critical element of *The Daily Show*'s *phronesis*, but rather than focusing on satire or parody, the interviews are typically played straight. Humor during the interviews emerges mostly from Stewart's self-deprecation and quipping asides; indeed, "the interviews are entirely incongruous with the 'fake news' portions of the show" (McKain, 2005, p. 425). The interviews' core, instead, is substantive discussion of public affairs. With the occasional exception of a Hollywood celebrity, the majority of guests are politicians (recent guests included Tony Blair, Sept. 14, 2010, and Bill Clinton, Sept. 16, 2010), non-fiction authors, historians, social critics and others who would rarely (if ever) appear on other late-night talk shows. Stewart invariably engages with the substance of the book being promoted, or pushes a politician to move past spin and give straight answers to questions.

The interview segments, therefore, function directly to emphasize the show's *phronesis*, first by constructing the show as a place where serious discussion can occur—and where books on classical history can co-exist with high elected officials; and second, by demonstrating Stewart to be a thoughtful, widely-read and articulate individual committed to the serious exploration and consideration of wide-ranging topics. Thus, the mere presence of guests of the caliber that *The Daily Show* routinely garners, and the manner in which Stewart engages with them, grant the show intellectual authority.

Much of the literature discussing *The Daily Show* has focused on how these characteristic elements innovate in terms of integrating previously separated genres of discourse, or in dissecting media norms. But through the lens of Aristotelian ethos, we can also understand these practices as strategies that illustrate the show's reasoning ability, its broad knowledge base, its cleverness and its good judgment. Through satire and parody, *The Daily Show* not only deconstructs the traditional media's claim of authority and holds the powerful accountable, but also actively constructs itself as an

> authority predicated on knowledge—knowledge of what actually lies outside the window, of what the reporters/producers of what is going on cannot say, of the immediacy that their remediations obstruct. (McKain, 2005, p. 427)

At the same time the guest interviews take an entirely different tack, positioning the show not merely as a national court jester using humor to expose absurdity and folly, but also as a forum for serious discourse. We will return to this last point when discussing how the show conveys its sense of goodwill; first, however, we turn to the show's exhibition of virtues and good moral character.

Good Moral Character

In this section, we focus on two key virtues exhibited by *The Daily Show*: wittiness and good temper. This is hardly an exhaustive discussion of the show's exhibited virtues, and equally strong cases can be made for its exhibition of those virtues labeled by Aristotle as friendliness or honesty about oneself, among others; but limitations of space and the primacy of wit and good temper in establishing the show's overall ethos lead to our focus here.

First, and most obviously, the show is centered on the exhibition of wittiness. In his discussion of the virtue of wittiness, Aristotle defines it as the golden mean between the excess of buffoonery and deficiency of boorishness. At first glance (or if one does not find its humor to their taste) *The Daily Show* might be accused of buffoonery—of "striving after humour at all costs, and aiming rather at raising a laugh than at saying what is becoming and at avoiding pain to the object of their fun" (Aristotle, 1925/1998, p. 103). But its nature as a comedy show, and its deployment of humor for the purposes of social improvement through satire should alleviate such criticisms; certainly, the show cannot be accused of a *deficiency* in its attempts at humor.

Aristotle also distinguishes between types of humor suitable to the educated and the ignorant—for example, innuendo to the former and indecent language to the latter—and *The Daily Show* practices the entire spectrum, from the most immature to the sophisticated. Indeed, its use of (bleeped) profanity and crude humor plays an important role because it deconstructs the conventions of television and implies that the show is willing to say even that which has been condemned by the conservative standards of government and network censors (McKain, 2005)—it thus conveys a sense of casual honesty and lack of concern for the limitations imposed by social convention. Conversely, the fact that so much of its humor comes from, for example, nothing more than the juxtaposition of politicians' contradictory statements and Stewart's raised eyebrow, or from parodies that cleverly highlight faulty media conventions, means that the show operates at least as much (actually, more so) at the level of educated, intellectual humor.

Next, there is the virtue of gentleness or good temper, terms that Aristotle uses primarily to refer to one's demeanor with regards to the emotion of anger. An excess of anger is irascibility or irritability, while the undesirable deficiency is spiritlessness, the failure to feel anger even when sufficiently provoked. Indeed, in Aristotle's phrasing, "to endure being insulted and put up with insult to one's friends is slavish" and "those who are not angry at the things they should be angry at are thought to be fools"; but anger can be virtuous so long as "we are angry with the right people, at the right things, in the right way" (Aristotle, 1925/1998, p. 97).

In relation to its competitors in the media, *The Daily Show* strikes a virtuous balance in its expression of anger. The partisan punditry of Rush Limbaugh or Bill O'Reilly, by comparison, is effectively a trade in anger, while conventional news media seems spiritless as it passively conveys government spin and acts as a conduit for hypocrisy. On *The Daily Show*, anger at hypocrisy or other vices is of course primarily expressed through satire, and most overt expressions of anger are feigned and exaggerated for comic effect; nonetheless, the emotional core of the show might well be considered a restrained anger at injustice and hypocrisy that is expressed through humor as a form of catharsis and release. Indeed, Stewart has described himself as "a tiny, neurotic man, standing in the back of the room throwing tomatoes at the chalk board" ("Bill Moyers interview," 2003).

But on occasion Stewart will drop the intellectual detachment necessary for satire and simply express anger and disgust openly, as when after the former CEO of Tyco was acquitted he called the holdout juror a "cunt" to the audience's shocked surprise (McKain, 2005), or when he ranted against conservatives seeking to shift blame during Hurricane Katrina. Invariably, such eruptions by Stewart are in response to unusually blatant injustices, and as a form of emotional honesty they function rhetorically (though probably not in a calculated way) to generate credibility because they expose the essential decency of a human who is overwhelmed by cavalierly unjust or cruel behavior, and, moreover, because they fit with "the audience's desire"—and arguably, emotional *need*—for "this view be articulated and its belief that this view is ethical, or just, or valid" (McKain, 2005, p. 427).

Goodwill

We turn finally to consider *The Daily Show's* goodwill toward its audience. Of course, this trait is expressed implicitly, for example, in its use of good sense to expose hypocrisy, hold elites accountable, and deconstruct illusions fostered by other media, and through expressions of anger at injustices. In this section, however, we touch on how the show overtly indicates goodwill through the advocacy of deliberative democracy and commitment to the public interest on the part of politicians, media and common citizens.

Deliberative democracy, as Baym (2005) notes, is an ideal centered on open, free dialogue in which citizens engage with each other to find answers to common challenges together and it necessarily requires a strong commitment on the part of civic participants to each others' welfare and to norms of dialogue and debate not as competition or verbal combat but as a means of collective truth- and solution-seeking. Outside the confines of *The Daily Show*, Stewart frequently exhibits his commitment to this ideal as he did by chastising *Crossfire* hosts Tucker Carlson and Paul Begala for practicing political theater rather than debate and dialogue ("Stewart appearance," 2004), or when he expressed his frustration with the dominance of partisan punditry when interviewed by Bill Moyers:

> The whole idea that political discourse has degenerated into shows that have to be entitled *Crossfire* and *Hardball*, and you know, "I'm Gonna Beat Your Ass" or whatever . . . is mind-boggling . . . I don't understand how issues can be dissected from the left and from the right as though . . . even cartoon characters have more than left and right. ("Bill Moyers interview," 2003, n. p.)

But this ideal also permeates the show itself, especially during its interview segments. Beyond enhancing the show's apparent intelligence, as discussed above, they position the show as an integral part of a larger cultural dialogue, a Habermasian public sphere. The goal of the interview is not to score points on the guest or tear them down, nor even to make predictions that imply superior knowledge or insight (as with, e.g., *The McLaughlin Group*), but rather a genuine struggle on Stewart's part—both as an individual and as a delegate for the audience—to better understand the world, including national/global problems and possible courses of action (Baym, 2005).

When the guest is an author, Stewart often falls back on his trademark self-deprecating humor, implying the guest's superior knowledge, and to some degree playing the fool as he asks questions and makes quips to personalize the often erudite guests and make their work accessible to the general public without watering it down. It is, however, when his guests are politicians that Stewart's commitment to the public sphere and the demands of deliberative democracy become most evident. His interview style becomes more assertive as he uses both straight questions and jokes to cut through spin and demand answers.

For example, former U.K. Prime Minister Tony Blair appeared as his guest on September 14, 2010; Blair maintained his characteristic emphasis on the need to employ all possible means to combat terrorism while downplaying consideration of social and economic costs. Rather than contesting this position openly, Stewart employed insightful humor by making an analogy to cockroaches in New York City, noting that as a rich person he could certainly seal his apartment and bug-bomb it daily—but who wants to live that way? In this way, Stewart highlights the single-minded approach of "message control" and opens up the possibility for discussion outside the confines dictated by elites.

Conversely, however, politicians who have expressed desire for and commitment to reasonable and fair-minded discourse often become repeat guests and "friends" of the show. John McCain, for example, made many appearances, often agreeing with Stewart on the need for more reasonable dialogue in politics—though after adopting a more hard-line position in the 2010 Republican Senate primary in Arizona, and being ridiculed and chastised during *The Daily Show*'s news segments for his turnabout behavior, he has not returned.

And the show has recently made a further step in rekindling the public sphere. What began as a typical—for *The Daily Show*—satire of pundit Glenn Beck's "Restoring Honor" rally quickly snowballed into something much larger. The "Rally to Restore Sanity" (planned for the Washington Mall on October 30, 2010) is "Woodstock, but with the nudity and drugs replaced by respectful disagreement" ("Rally," 2010). In this most recent move, as throughout Stewart's tenure, *The Daily Show* continues to champion principles of ideological moderation, dialogue and civic participation.

Thus, the counterpoint to *The Daily Show*'s cynical and satirical dissection of spin, propaganda and illusory media norms is the show's elevation of reasoned discourse and its expectation that both politicians and citizens should abide by this standard, ideals that are arguably increasingly rare in contemporary media. In the show's vision of society, "dialogue . . . is the locus of democracy, the public process through which citizens determine their preferences and define the public will" (Baym, 2005, p. 273). In its implicit and explicit advocacy of this ideal, the show confirms its commitment to the well-being of its audience, the nation, and humanity at large.

CONCLUSION

Undoubtedly, there are many other aspects of *The Daily Show with Jon Stewart* that enhance its ethos. The show's inherent fair-mindedness, attacking absurdity regardless of the source, qualifies as an intellectual and moral virtue itself, although it permeates the show and is suggested in all the areas we discussed. Over the last decade it has evolved within the larger social milieu while maintaining constancy in terms of quality; its viewers have grown older with Stewart and seen correspondents come and go (including Stephen Colbert to his own wildly successful sibling parody show)—its simple longevity thus also serves to build credibility. And, as the show has become a cultural institution it is increasingly referenced by other media as a source, which further enhances its credibility and legitimacy (McKain, 2005).

Though there are many other aspects of the show which might be discussed in relation to its credibility, it should, however, be clear why *The Daily Show* has risen to hold such a significant status among many well-informed citizens: it exhibits all the traits of ethos—good sense and judgment, good moral character, and goodwill towards its audience. It exemplifies the classical ideal of *arete* (virtue and excellence) in the execution of its twin missions of satire and the advocacy of deliberative democracy and achieves a level of consistent quality rarely seen on contemporary television in either news or entertainment even as it creatively integrates the two realms.

And while it can be said to promote cynicism and disenchantment with politics and the media, it in fact seems to enhance people's sense of internal political efficacy, the feeling that one can understand politics, and engage in the political process to make a difference in the world (Baumgartner and Morris, 2006). Arguably this is because, as it dismantles the carefully constructed illusion of the superior—or for that matter, even tolerable—competence, knowledge and decency of elites in politics and the media, it helps return public affairs to the realm of non-elite citizens. It thus also furthers *eudaimonia*: the happiness, well-being and beautiful flourishing of individuals living in self-determined community with each other that for Aristotle and many other classical philosophers is the ultimate end-goal of human life.

Thus, while this essay has viewed the show through the framework of Aristotle's understanding of ethos, we close by drawing on Isocrates, whose conception of ethos maintained an integration of practical persuasive effects with the speaker's actual inner soul, and suggest that *The Daily Show* exemplifies these qualities as well:

> For Isocrates, ethos is both a legitimating source for and a praiseworthy effect of the ethical practice of the orator's art . . .[and] the orator is necessarily both a student and a teacher of the dynamics of civic responsibility. Heeding the call of *public* service as a person of "good repute," his presence and rhetorical competence are a "showing-forth" (*epi-deixis*) of an *ethos*, a principled self, that instructs the moral consciousness and actions of others and thereby serves as a *possible* catalyst for them to do the same for the good of their community. (Hyde, 2004, p. xv)

REFERENCES

Aristotle. (1998). *The Nichomachean Ethics*. (D. Ross, Trans.). New York: Oxford University Press, Inc. (Original work published 1925.)

———. (1984). *Rhetoric*. (W. R. Roberts, Trans.). In *The Rhetoric and Poetics of Aristotle*. New York: McGraw-Hill, Inc. (Original work published 1954.)

Awards for "The Daily Show with Jon Stewart." (n.d.). *The Internet Movie Database*. Retrieved from http://www.imdb.com/title/tt0115147/awards.

Baumgartner, J., and Morris, J. S. (2006). *The Daily Show* effect: candidate evaluations, efficacy, and American youth. *American Politics Research, 34*(3), 341–367.

Baumlin, J. S. (2006). Ethos. In T. O. Sloane (Ed.), *Encyclopedia of Rhetoric*. Oxford University Press (E-reference edition).

Baym, G. (2004). *The Daily Show* and the reinvention of political journalism. Paper presented at "Faith, Fun, and Futuramas," Third Annual Pre-APSA Conference on Political Communication Wednesday, September 1, 2004, Chicago, Illinois.

———. (2005). The Daily Show: discursive integration and the reinvention of political journalism. *Political Communication, 22*(3), 259–276.

Bill Moyers interviews Jon Stewart. (2003, July 11). *NOW with Bill Moyers*. (2003, July 11). [Television program transcript]. Retrieved from http://www.pbs.org/now/transcript/transcript_stewart.html.

Bormann, E. (1972). Fantasy and rhetorical vision: the rhetorical criticism of social reality. *Quarterly Journal of Speech, 58*, 396–407.

Coe, K., Tewksbury, D., Bond, B. J., Drogos, K. L., Porter, R. W., Yahn, A., and Zhang, Y. (2008). Hostile news: partisan use and perceptions of cable news programming. *Journal of Communication* 58, 201–219.

Colletta, L. (2009). "Political Satire and Postmodern Irony in the Age of Stephen Colbert and Jon Stewart."*Journal of Popular Culture* 42(5), 856–874.

Fox, J. R., Koloen, G., and Sahin, V. (2007). No joke: A comparison of substance in *The Daily Show with Jon Stewart* and broadcast network television coverage of the 2004 Presidential Election campaign. *Journal of Broadcasting and Electronic Media* 51(2), 213–227.

Holbert, R. L., Lambe, J. L., Dudo, A. D., and Carlton, K. A. (2007). Primacy effects of *The Daily Show* and national TV news viewing: young viewers, political gratifications, and internal political self-efficacy. *Journal of Broadcasting and Electronic Media* 51(1), 20–38.

Hyde, M. J. (2004). Introduction. In M. J. Hyde (Ed.), *The Ethos of Rhetoric* (pp. xiii–xxviii). Columbia, South Carolina: University of South Carolina Press.

Kraut, R. (2010, March 29). Aristotle's Ethics. In E. W. Zalta (Ed.), *The Stanford Encyclopedia of Philosophy (Summer 2010 Edition)*. Retrieved from http://plato.stanford.edu/entries/aristotle-ethics/.

Long, B. (2004, September 29). "'*Daily Show*' viewers ace political quiz." Retrieved from http://www.cnn.com/2004/SHOWBIZ/TV/09/28/comedy.politics/.

McKain, A. (2005). Not necessarily not the news: gatekeeping, remediation, and *The Daily Show*. *The Journal of American Culture, 28*(4), 415–430.

Morris, J. (2008). *The Daily Show with Jon Stewart* and audience attitude change during the 2004 party conventions. *Political Behavior* 31, 79–102.

Pew Research Center. (2008, May 8). *The Daily Show*: Journalism, satire, or just laughs? Retrieved from http://pewresearch.org/pubs/829/the-daily-show-journalism-satire-or-just-laughs.

Rally to Restore Sanity. (2010). Retrieved from http://www.rallytorestoresanity.com/.

Smith, C. R. (2004). *Ethos* dwells pervasively: A hermeneutic reading of Aristotle on credibility. In M. J. Hyde (Ed.), *The Ethos of Rhetoric* (pp. 1–19). Columbia, South Carolina: University of South Carolina Press.

Smolkin, R. (2007). What the mainstream media can learn from Jon Stewart: No, not to be funny and snarky, but to be bold and to do a better job of cutting through the fog. *American Journalism Review* 29(3), 18–25.

Stewart appearance on *Crossfire*.(2004, October 15). *Crossfire*. [Television program transcript]. Retrieved from http://politicalhumor.about.com/library/bljonstewartcrossfire.htm.

Trier, J. (2008). *The Daily Show* with Jon Stewart: Part 1. *Journal of Adolescent and Adult Literacy* 51(5), 424–427.

Chapter Two

Before and After *The Daily Show*: Freedom and Consequences in Political Satire

Robert N. Spicer

Satire is a slippery customer. It weaves in and out of reality and makes itself accessible enough for the (sometimes thoughtful) laugh in the moment, but it is just tricky enough to not be pinned down. For it is often we forget that the intention of the satirist is one thing; what the audience does with the satire is quite another. Satire opens doors to misinterpretation and, more importantly for the purposes of this chapter, misappropriation. The satirist leads a paradoxical existence, opening up opportunities to move outside of accepted discursive practices only to be folded back into established norms and political authority; questioning authority only to have the questions reinforce authority.

Shanti Elliot (1999) describes Bahktin's notions of "liberating relativity," the ambiguity of language that opens up creative spaces while at the same time creating misunderstanding within these ambiguous spaces. Elliot describes Bahktin's shift from carnival to dialogue, made up of the sender and receiver's "concrete identities" and the relationship between the two, the "contradictions within each person," "tone and context" in communication, all of which "shape an utterance more than the literal meaning of the words" (p. 135). In political satire the literal meaning of the utterance is a force that pulls the receiver out of the discursive moment, it can blind the receiver to the intent of the sender. In the case of political satire "liberating relativity" is a liberation allowing for communicative insecurity and uncertainty. While it liberates, satire also treads on dangerous ground at times.

So it is with *The Daily Show*, as with other sites of political satire, that the intentions of the satirist can be lost in the satire's subsequent use by others.[1]

19

The problem with Jon Stewart as an object of analysis is this ambiguous space he occupies, created by his use of "social commentary through comedy" allowing him to almost "have it both ways" so to speak; it allows him to be the jester and the political actor at the same time. He takes media figures like Jim Cramer to task over their coverage of the corruption on Wall Street, yet when he himself is taken to task for not doing the same to John Kerry his response is to say that "the show that leads into me is puppets making prank phone calls. What is wrong with you?" (Carlson, 2004). Yet, as Stewart himself has pointed out, this is the way it has been for political comedians, they engage in commentary on social issues through jokes (Stewart, 2010). So the satirist chooses the liberation of satire but is not forced to address consequences. In the political realm, can we have liberation with no consequences? Can there be freedom without responsibility?

The question is, *what is the satirist responsible for*? If, for example, viewers begin to see Jon Stewart as more credible than "real" news anchors, is he obligated to adhere to the ethical standards of the "real" journalist? Can Stewart continue to hide behind the claim that he is just a comedian? Given some of the acts of "real" journalism on *The Daily Show*, how should we locate it within the world of political media? Is it "just" comedy? Is it a political talk show? Can it be both? This chapter explores the ambiguity and "in-between-ness" of the space occupied by *The Daily Show*; it is an examination of *The Daily Show* as a site of political satire addressing its predecessors, its offspring and its present state. The "before and after" of the show refers to its place in both the history of political satire and in terms of its contemporaneous programming; what surrounds the show in both contexts is essential to this discussion. Thus, Stephen Colbert will also play a small part in this analysis as it only makes sense to mention Colbert as an extension of *The Daily Show*'s project of critiquing power in politics and media. The next section of this chapter works to define political satire and irony. This is followed by a discussion of what is termed the "play of political discourse" and its consequences. Both sections tie these discussions of theory into the content of *The Daily Show* in order to critique it and its place in political satire. Finally, the last section places *The Daily Show* in the context of contemporary news media, using examples from the program to discuss how news and political satire become intertwined in media flows.

The overarching theme that connects these sections is that of freedom and responsibility for the user of satire and the consequences of employing this form of questioning power. Satire can play the role of simple comedy, just there for the laugh at the expense of public figures and institutions, while questioning power and potentially increasing public cynicism. The viewer must ask, "if things are so bad, if the governing class is so corrupt, the public so lethargic, everything so beyond repair, why bother getting off the sofa?" Through his use of this satirical approach Jon Stewart has carved out a niche in media, a place where interviewees expect to come in for a laugh and to promote a book and sometimes end up getting a serious discussion about public issues. In the carnivalesque atmosphere of *The Daily Show*, these serious discussions are contiguous with the comically profane, where Stewart is not afraid to use language that, while not passing the censor's "bleep," is unambiguous to the television audience.

In his examination of popular culture Marcel Danesi (2008) asks why it is that "transgression [is] both so appealing and so appalling" (p. 58). According to Danesi, Bakhtin's explanation of the carnivalesque says that

> by releasing rebellion in a communal, theatrical way, the ritual transgression actually validates social norms. In effect, we come to understand the role of social norms in our life through mockery of them. Carnival theory explains why pop culture does not pose (and never has posed) any serious subversive political challenge to the moral and ethical status quo. Pop culture is not truly subversive; it just appears to be. (p. 59)

So, in carnival theory, through the lens of Danesi, we see that those who deride, antagonize and satirize social norms can undermine their own cause. This returns us to responsibility. What happens when comedy is mixed with politics? What responsibility does the comedian have at those times when they are mixed? Most importantly, one might ask why we need to depend on a comedian to shine a light on serious political concerns. In other words, does being a comedian give one the ability to ask questions that "real" journalists are, for whatever reasons, unable to ask? At that point, should there be any distinction between a comedian and a "real" journalist? These questions are examined in this chapter by looking at the role *The Daily Show* has played in politics and media in recent years.

DEFINING SATIRE: HAVING THE QUICKEST WAY WITH *THE DAILY SHOW*

Satire and irony have a long history in political commentary. However, this rhetorical strategy employed by Jon Stewart and Stephen Colbert, despite its rich history, is entangled in contemporary problems of theory and political philosophy. Chief among these problems is a question of postmodern thought in pop culture, media and politics. Here an extended quote from Claire Colebrook (2004) is useful specifically for conceptually connecting satire and irony.

> Despite its unwieldy complexity, irony has a frequent and common definition: saying what is contrary to what is meant (Quintilian 1995–98 [9.2.44], 401), a defini-

tion that is usually attributed to the first-century Roman orator Quintilian who was already looking back to Socrates and Ancient Greek literature. But this definition is so simple that it covers everything from simple figures of speech to entire historical epochs. Irony can mean as little as saying, 'Another day in paradise,' when the weather is appalling. It can also refer to the huge problems of postmodernity; our very historical context is ironic because today nothing really means what it says. We live in a world of quotation, pastiche, simulation and cynicism: a general and all-encompassing irony. Irony, then, by the very simplicity of its definition becomes curiously indefinable. (p. 1)

Irony, as Colebrook defines it, is the form Stewart's (and more so Colbert's) satirical comedy takes. As an extension of *The Daily Show*, Colbert plays a character on television; he is in a constant ironic state making it difficult to actually locate the text of his program. There is Stephen Colbert the actor and Stephen Colbert the fictional TV pundit emulating "Poppa Bear" Bill O'Reilly. Colbert even appears in interviews at times as his fictional alter ego, making it quite difficult to locate who the real Colbert is, when he is playing a part, or when he is making a joke.

Jon Stewart plays a similar role, but certainly not taken to the degree that Colbert has gone. Colbert's character is an act of "hyperreality"; he is in a way more "real" than Bill O'Reilly, who is one of the targets of the satirical performance. It somehow seems simultaneously appropriate and unsettling that the website for the National Public Radio program *Fresh Air* would refer to Colbert this way:

> Comic and journalist Stephen Colbert is the former senior correspondent on Comedy Central's *The Daily Show with Jon Stewart*. And true to the industry he parodies, Colbert's incisive work has landed him in the anchor's chair on a show of his own: *The Colbert Report*.[2] (Salit, 2005)

Colbert is apparently a "comic and journalist," two spaces that one might argue should not be occupied simultaneously; the paragraph even refers to news as "the industry he parodies." So is it the industry in which he works, or the one he skewers? Journalism is, at least in theory, a pursuit of facts; it should not employ a linguistic strategy of irony, of saying the opposite of what is meant, while attempting to present its audience with objective facts or what can be described as being as close as humanly possible to being objective facts. Colbert himself has raised concerns about the ambiguity of satire, the problems that can come along with interpretation of the art form.[3] The *Fresh Air* introduction above also refers to Colbert as a "former senior correspondent" which seems to ignore, or simply play along with, the fact that this is not a "real" title, but a satirical take on the news form, making light of the industry's attempt to bestow authority or the illusion of authority upon a network reporter.

While it would seem that Stewart is "playing" a role on *The Daily Show*, it is clear that he is not fabricating a personality in the way Stephen Colbert is. Colbert's character on *The Colbert Report* is clearly, as he admits himself in the *60 Minutes* quote cited in endnote 3, not a reflection of his real "self." Stewart's difference from his "real" self is subtler; he is acting, but not creating a separate personality that is built on a foundation of "trucked in" insincerity. Where the irony of *The Daily Show* becomes a problem for critical analysis is with the cavalcade of side characters that are featured on the program every night. This is a major reason that Colbert is essential to the analysis here; the segments with "senior correspondents" are the segments that gave birth to *The Colbert Report*; this is where Colbert got his start.

On most nights Jon Stewart plays a befuddled straight man to ironic dunces played by Samantha Bee, Wyatt Cenac and John Oliver, among others. As part of the play on the news form, appropriating the norms of the media format, each actor and actress playing a journalist takes on a title from a rotating list that is fabricated for the purposes of whatever story it is they are reporting on. For just a few examples, John Oliver was referred to as "*The Daily Show's* Senior British Person" when Stewart interviewed him about the transfer of power from former Prime Minister Gordon Brown to current Prime Minister David Cameron (Bodow and O'Neill, 2010d); in a story on Khalid Sheikh Mohammed being brought to New York to be put on trial for his involvement in 9/11, Samantha Bee was referred to as the "Senior Judicial Correspondent"[4] (Bodow and O'Neill, 2009b); and Jason Jones gave a "standup" on gay marriage in which he was given the title "referendumologist" (Javerbaum and O'Neill, 2006). In each of these instances, and all of the other segments featuring a "Senior Correspondent" of some kind, the title is generally preceded by Jon Stewart saying something along the lines of, "For more on this story we are joined by . . ." which keeps with the typical news genre style of "throwing the story to a correspondent," and again, satirizes the illusion of authority present in the news genre.

The "straight-man" act shifts for Stewart when his interviewees join him on the set. This is especially so for more serious guests. Stewart takes on a role that is shifting in its position vis-à-vis the guest, a role that can be unstable from the beginning to the end of the interview. At times Stewart does play very seriously with guests, asking them pointed or difficult questions, but also cracks jokes that are sometimes self-deprecating, other times poking fun at the guest and it is often used to punctuate the interview, transitioning the discussion into new territory or cutting tension created by a pointed question. This last device is part of the genius of Stewart's interviewing style, his ability to maintain the flow of a discussion. Jonathan Gray (2009) describes Stewart's interviews thusly:

Stewart's interviewing style can also prove remarkably disarming. He can at one moment be a charming, friendly comedian making silly faces and can then prove one of American television's most intelligent and well-informed interviewers, willing to pounce and requiring thoughtful answers. (p. 158)

Very often it is that Stewart is playing a bit of a clown to more serious guests, the opposite of his straight-man role to the rest of the cast of *The Daily Show*, but this comedy, one might argue, is what gives him the cover to ask those more difficult questions. His humor is disarming; thus his pointed questions do not have the same social consequences as they would were they to be asked by someone like Brian Williams.

This ironic strategy of "saying what is contrary to what is meant" that is employed by Colbert and the correspondents on *The Daily Show* dates back to Kierkegaard and beyond; to Quintilian as Colebrook says; to Defoe's *Shortest Way with the Dissenters*, a critique of "high churchmen" which he himself referred to in 1710 as an "ironical satyr." Maximilian Novak (1966) argues that, by "satire [Defoe] merely meant a didactic work containing a strong argument or attack; by irony, simply the idea that what he was saying was the opposite of what he meant" (p. 407). The preceding sentence could easily be rewritten with the name Colbert or Stewart replacing Defoe's and still retain its meaning. The difference is that in the eighteenth century Defoe defended his rhetorical strategy blaming "his audience for their lack of perception and excus[ing] himself for failing to label his irony" (p. 403). Instead of pointing out his audience's "lack of perception," Colbert chooses to enjoy the ride, while Stewart takes the rhetorical strategy of withdrawal and distancing from a position of importance, as demonstrated in his *Crossfire* interview or in his comment about the "news box" (Bodow and O'Neill, 2010d), which will be discussed later in the chapter.

This raises a question addressed by Agata Bielik-Robson (2002) who argues that freedom and responsibility ride in tandem. There is negative liberty and positive liberty, the freedom from imposition by the state and the freedom given or protected by the state. She argues that irony is "a natural attitude in the world which promotes individuality," thus going hand-in-hand with negative liberty, the dominant attitude rooted in a neoliberal and a postmodern politics of which Bielik-Robson is critical. She sees this postmodern, stage-crafted politics as unredeemable, problematic, as a political environment where the speaker takes no responsibility for what is said.

In the world where nothing appears necessary any longer, and everything seems equally contingent . . . irony rules: a softer, indeterminate attitude which naturally avoids all rigid identifications, contending itself with the shady sphere of "maybe." (para. 2)

Contrary to Bielik-Robson's argument, however, it is not the stagecraft that is problematic and there is not a total lack of responsibility. The stagecraft can be whimsical. If the audience is in on the joke the audience is more media literate, more aware of what is going on. The politician, the media figure, the activist and the audience all play their shared roles, we know that there is an element of comedy to it all and we share the experience and at times a laugh.

Another, though not perfect, characterization of satirical irony is as parasite. Irony, Bielik-Robson says, "has to rely on a well-established cultural substance which will not perish under its ironizing impact; it doesn't want to destroy its host, otherwise it would be self-destructive" (p. 2). So irony feeds off of that which it critiques, but it cannot destroy its object of criticism. If the object is destroyed it is no longer there to critique. So there is what Jack Bratich (2010) calls "snarkasm," a combination of sarcasm and snark, that "is a type of ironic consumption, but one particularly characterized by fascination, the vexing vacillation between attraction and repulsion" (p. 65).

The push and pull of this vacillation, the internalization of self-referentiality, the resulting cynicism and withdraw from the political is the true problem of satirical irony. This is the affective position to which the satirical figure must address itself. Satire and its resulting effects place the political satirist in a position of a constant cycle of plugging in and withdrawing from political discourse; Bielik-Robson frames it as a cycle in between the late-modernist perspective (Harold Bloom) and the postmodernist perspective (Richard Rorty). She argues that Rorty sees irony as forcing withdraw from the public, the rise of the individualist and privatized, whereas Bloom sees the opposite, that it forces a publicness, it forces the individual into cultural participation. In other words, the freedom of satire carries with it a need to take responsibility and cultivate out of satire useful moments of political creation where the satirist attempts to question authority, but is also proposing something politically productive.

James Klumpp (1997) proposes a rethinking of the political construction of freedom of speech that is useful to the present discussion. He argues for an ethics of speech that "begins with statements about the relationship between qualities in discursive practice and qualities in public life" (p. 123). He imagines this conception of speech as reflecting three important aspects or qualities: participation, richness and engagement. In this conception of speech "rhetoric is emergent in the continual transformational quality of interpretation" (p. 124). One can imagine satire, especially the satire of Jon Stewart as having a place in Klumpp's conception of discourse.

Through richly empowered and intertwined voices, discourse evolves into new forms. New complexes of vocabulary, metaphor, and argument permit new approaches to situations. The emergent creativity of this notion of invention is an essential strength of rich rhetorical discourse. (p. 124)

Klumpp voices concerns similar to those of Bielik-Robson's argument against the self-destructive ironizing impact. The intertwined voices cannot be allowed to spin out into infinity, there must be a web, an intertwining of voices, a meshwork, to use Ingold's (2009) wording.

Stewart moves along lines, creating a meshwork, "the paths along which life is lived. And it is the binding together of lines, not in the connecting of points, that the mesh is constituted" (Ingold, p. 38). In other words, Stewart and *The Daily Show* have a brand that is subversive, that critiques politics and media, but never becomes fully integrated within those systems; it is a position at which Stewart can step within the space of politics in order to swipe at it and then step back out to keep himself and his show at an arms length distance from it all. In other words, we can envision *The Daily Show* as being a line of flight from the media industry as a rhizomatic structure. Deleuze and Guattari (1983) write:

> There is a rupture in the rhizome whenever segmentary lines explode into a line of flight, but the line of flight is part of the rhizome. These lines always tie back to one another. That is why one can never posit a dualism or a dichotomy, even in the rudimentary form of the good and the bad. You may make a rupture, draw a line of flight, yet there is still a danger that you will reencounter organizations that restratify everything, formations that restore power to a signifier, attributions that reconstitute a subject. (p. 9)

The Daily Show represents just such a rupture and reencountering. This is the anti-political character of Jon Stewart that Hart and Hartelius (2007) describe. However, it is an anti-political character that is not necessarily Stewart's fault; it is more a characteristic of the media structure within which Stewart labors. He has no choice but to rupture and reencounter.

Satire as an art form, with the many examples that preceded Stewart and Colbert, critiques dominant belief systems creating these "lines of flight," or "lines of movement of desire away from hierarchical and socially imposed forms" (Best and Kellner 1991, p. 91). So, in a sense, Stewart and Colbert commit acts of "deterritorialization" where the "decoding of repressive social codes allows desires to move outside of restrictive psychic and spatial boundaries" (p. 88). These could be the "psychic and spatial boundaries" that protect a president from biting satirical criticism when he is sitting a few feet away from the satirist, or set expectations for how a guest should behave on a talk show on CNN; in both cases there is a setting of expectations for what is "polite" discursive activity in political media, and a subsequent breaking of those expectations. The problem is that even if we open lines of oppositional discourse, that discourse is often folded back into a mainstream discursive structure. Acts of excorporation have countering acts of incorporation; ruptures rejoin rhizomes; this is so even with biting satirical commentary.

This returns us to the initial definition of satire as parasitic. An improved conception of this relationship, instead of thinking of it as a simplex communicative form, would be a symbiotic, reciprocal feeding off of. In this sense these Deleuzian lines of flight, when satire is acting as a site of liberation, are also sites of repression or at least opening up opportunities for reinforcement of acts of repression. This reciprocity, as Lazzarato (2006) similarly argues in examining the logic of capital, in its forms of subjugation, "opens up antagonisms and contradictions" (p. 144). At the same time the antagonisms open up, there are possibilities for folding satire back into the dominant discursive forms in popular media. Stewart and Colbert present two key examples of reciprocity between satirical antagonism and re-appropriation by the target of that satire. Stewart and Colbert cultivate these sort of pop cultural bona fides, a "hipness" or credibility with a younger audience, by skewering political figures, by being ironic. These politicians then tap into the power of the hosts' connections with their audiences, connections that are based upon a collective mocking of the politicians, by coming on the show and being "good sports." So something that at first undermines that cultural capital of the politician becomes an opportunity for empowering the politician.

The cable news feud between Jon Stewart and CNBC commentator Jim Cramer perfectly exemplifies another aspect of this reciprocity or folding back. The very fact that it can accurately be described as a "cable news feud" makes this point. In the midst of the financial crisis in 2009 a video[5] of Cramer surfaced and began to circulate on political blogs. In an interview with TheStreet.com Cramer, author and host of the financial news program *Mad Money*, outlined the ways in which he and many others game the financial system. This video eventually migrated from mere blog chatter to be picked up by some media outlets including *The Daily Show*.

In an article on Poynter.org *The Daily Show* writer Elliot Kalan discussed the program as more than a critic of government, but also a "media critic" exposing "journalists' wrongdoings and shortcomings" (Tenore, 2009, para. 4) as the article describes it. In Kalan's own words, media critic is "a role we provide that we take very seriously"[6] (para. 5). The Cramer feud is one such moment of pointing out one media figure's wrongdoings and in so doing making a larger statement about the perceived corruption of the American economic system. Conversely, this is also a moment where satire is working in its reciprocal symbiotic relationship with the modes of power it is critiquing. As Stewart began to criticize Cramer, television news programs, particularly those on NBC stations owned by Cramer's employer General Electric, started to pick up on the story. They would play the clips of Stewart criticizing Cramer, then interview Cramer in response. Stewart would then play those clips and critique them; in a truly surreal media moment Stewart played a clip of *The Today Show* playing a clip of Stewart playing a clip of Jim Cramer.

The Daily Show focuses a great deal of energy on critiquing the media circus of cable news, as Stewart himself made a point of doing in his afore-mentioned appearance on *Crossfire*. However, in the case of his "feud" with Cramer, or as *The Daily Show* called it, the "Basic Cable Personality Clash Skirmish '09," the program did more to feed into this process that Stewart claimed was "hurting America" (Carlson, 2004) by giving it something to comment on. The more entertaining the disagreement became, the more it could be discussed by cable news. The opening sequence for *The Daily Show* the night Cramer appeared on the program said of the cable coverage that it amounted to little more than people talking about other people talking about it (Bodow and O'Neill, 2009a). This certainly satirizes how news media engage in infotainment but it also *feeds into* that infotainment. This is what Lazzarato (2006) describes as "antagonisms and contradictions"; relation-ships that are equally useful to power and those critiquing power. The open-ing segment of the Cramer episode of *The Daily Show* notes its use to corpo-rate media interests even as it satirizes those interests, referring to the ratings boost from the episode and the possible subsequent minor improvement in Comedy Central's revenue (Bodow and O'Neill, 2009a). It satirizes infotain-ment in cable news even as it participates in it.

This particular moment is highlighted in this chapter because it is emble-matic of the potential and the frustration embodied in *The Daily Show*. This interview between Jon Stewart and Jim Cramer symbolizes what *The Daily Show* could be, as a site of political subversion and radical critique of a political establishment especially in a time of economic crisis, and the ways in which the program falls short of that idealized role and becomes folded back into that establishment. In the aforementioned line about ad revenue from the opening segment, for example, the producers of the show draw attention to the problem of advertiser driven corporate media but in the process do nothing to create a politically productive discourse that could address the political/economic logic of that media system.

More than that, what is lost in the media hurly-burly, the infotainment of the coverage of the Stewart v. Cramer "grudge match," as one CNN reporter called it (Kraft, 2009), is the class critique that is present in what Stewart is saying. In criticizing the media coverage of the economic crisis and corrup-tion on Wall Street, Stewart was drawing attention to the serious problem of the lack of regulation of the financial sector, the risks that were being taken on Wall Street and the fact that the news media do not adequately inform the public about these problems. Stewart actually makes a serious point about the market, describing two classes of investors: one class that is putting their money into long term retirement savings and the other that is making risky investments in a rapidly transactional market. Herein lies a major missed opportunity in the larger media that is not the fault of *The Daily Show*. The news media picked up on this back and forth between Stewart and CNBC and made the story about Stewart v. Cramer when the real story, and Stewart's real critique, was with the financial media that are derelict in their duty to be watchdogs on the market, that are not fulfilling that idealized role, and the financial sector that put the American economy at risk through their own irresponsible behavior. So the press and class critiques are both lost in this media spectacle.

Stewart's class critique is not a worker against management critique; it is more a middle/working class against corporate/investor class critique. His audience basically includes that young, middle class, college-educated crowd that would have a pension or a 401(k). What is slightly problematic is that Stewart localizes the financial crisis to these two classes of people, as a 401(k) being threatened by reckless investors. In this interview Stewart refers to the 401(k) accounts of some abstract "we," but this does not really address those in the economy who are even lower on the scale, who do not have access to a 401(k). This is a moot point, however, as a class critique is outside of the realm of acceptable discourse in much of American politics. More to the point this class critique, this critique of capitalism not just as an economic system, but the mechanisms of its spectacle, the flows of semiocapital (Berardi, 2007) that Stewart is criticizing, these things are lost in the shuffle of the spectacle of media presentation of the "feud." Stewart even says at the beginning of the interview with Cramer that *The Daily Show* had directed their criticism at CNBC as a network and Cramer was only one part of a larger target. Yet, the media coverage of *The Daily Show* here reduced it to a personality feud between Cramer and Stewart.

An even more radical moment of political satire and its reciprocity with media power was Stephen Colbert's performance at the Washington Press Club dinner in 2006. The case of Stewart and Cramer is a mere matter of two media personalities volleying criticisms. Stephen Colbert was given the opportunity to satirize, and thus criticize, the President of the United States while standing only a few feet away from him in front of some of the most powerful people in politics and media. Not only that, while he was criticizing George W. Bush as a political figure, the rationale and handling of the Iraq War and U.S. foreign policy in general, he was also targeting the audience, harshly criticizing national reporters in attendance for not doing enough to question the administration and the war in Iraq.

After "roasting" President Bush, Colbert received a hero's welcome from the left blogosphere, but from much of the mainstream political media, he was a pariah. On the WNYC program *On the Media* Bob Garfield took a shot at Colbert by asking, "What is the sound of 2,700 people not applauding?"[7] (Rogers, 2006). Garfield discussed the media reaction to Colbert's performance during the program that day:

The Washington Post gossip column grumbled that Colbert, quote, "ignored the cardinal rule of Washington humor: make fun of yourself, not the other guy." Columnist Richard Cohen said Colbert was more than rude, he was a bully, and the first lady, it was reported, refused to shake Colbert's hand. Well, can you blame her? The Correspondents' Dinner is essentially a roast, the unwritten rules of which permit you to tweak the guest of honor without genuinely embarrassing or insulting him. What wife wants to squeeze a ball gown on just to witness her husband's public evisceration? So, yeah, the guest of honor got more than he bargained for, and so did the media hosts. Colbert was in his faux Bill O'Reilly mode when he said, "I have nothing but contempt for these people." But he wasn't necessarily joking. Again and again, he bashed the Washington press corps for five years of deference and docility, and again and again the crowd did not seem much amused. (Rogers, 2006)

This is just one of many examples of mainstream media outlets criticizing Colbert. While satire and irony can move outside political zones of comfort, they can also easily be reincorporated into and reinforce established and accepted discursive norms. In the case of Colbert, his performance made a policy statement, through satirical means, criticizing U.S. foreign policy, a statement that by and large was not given a voice in much of the news media at that point. The problem is that the critique is lost in the discussion of style and the audience is distracted from the substance of the argument being made.

Unfortunately for Colbert and by extension those who agreed with his perspective, his performance was used to create a contrast with the way one is "supposed" to engage in critical discourse in response to a president's policies. The reaction toward Colbert by much of the media was the equivalent of indignantly saying, "How rude!" By reacting in such a way establishment media take a critique and make it useful to fallaciously say to the audience, "don't listen to him, he insulted the president to his face!" There is a twofold strengthening of the norms being criticized here.

First, Colbert inadvertently reinforced established discursive norms in the same way *The Daily Show* does in Geoffrey Baym's (2009) description of their coverage of George W. Bush's announcement of George Tenet's retirement from the CIA in 2004. Baym juxtaposes clips from the evening news that featured clear, strong, concise soundbites of Bush referring to Tenet as "resolute" and praising him for his work. *The Daily Show* on the other hand featured an extended clip of Bush groping for words to describe Tenet, fumbling on his speech in the way many comedians portrayed the former president. Baym argues that both presentations "are 'accurate' in the strict sense of the word, but each achieves a markedly different textual effect" (p. 107).

What Baym does not say is that the juxtaposition of Stewart and the evening news reinforces for the audience what the news is "supposed" to be. In an attempt to remind the audience of Tenet's role in the handling of the run-up to the Iraq War (i.e. referring to the claim that Saddam Hussein had

WMD as a "slam dunk"[8]), *The Daily Show* reminds the audience that a news show is normally not so unabashed in their criticism of administration officials. To continue Baym's critique, what *The Daily Show* does through their satire is to reinforce the news form as a genre, a way of communicating ideas through certain story telling, editing and production techniques. This is true of most any news satire, including *The Colbert Report*, *The Onion*, the Weekend Update segment on *Saturday Night Live*; all of these sites of critique take on the form, use the form as it is and by doing so reinforce for the audience that this is a "normal" way of communicating through media. The reason *The Daily Show*'s use of the footage of Bush fumbling for words is funny is because the evening news would not show that footage. So the audience is amused by the *The Daily Show* clip *and* they are reminded that news media are supposed to show the footage of the president speaking clearly and concisely.

Second, Colbert, like *The Daily Show*, gives the media he critiques something to feed off of, in essence the energy that media require, *content*, especially controversial content. In so doing the most important way the satirical discourse in these two cases undermines their own missions is by *distracting the audience from the point of their satire*. In the case of Colbert's speech, the criticism of the Iraq War is lost in the shuffle of media discussion of his manners. In the case of Stewart the dishonesty of our economic system, the brazen way in which Cramer admitted to gaming the system, the way business media failed to critically cover corporate practices that resulted in a financial crisis, was lost in the coverage of the "feud" between two media personalities. The greatest tragedy in both cases is that Stewart and Colbert, in their satirical performances, make important points about economic and foreign policy, they give voice to alternative perspectives, but the important points they make are lost in the jokes and media spectacle.

The miscalculation made by Stewart and Colbert in otherwise brilliantly radical acts of political subversion is that satire, as Bielik-Robson argues, must be finite; it must be encircled "by a context of actuality, of something positive that already exists, which won't let irony proceed infinitely." She says irony too often "results in no creation at all, merely in subdued reproduction of already existing cultural forms—too much leads to equally fruitless subversion, an eternal clinamen, a petrified gesture of deviation" (p. 2–3). This is a problem for Colbert more generally—his satire and irony go into infinite existence; he never ceases to break from his ironic/satirical character. At the Press Club dinner the reaction of the audience is shock not just because they are the targets, but because he takes the moment right up to its greatest possible limit and never looks back until he is shaking the President's hand. The same is true for Stewart playing the straight-man on *The Daily Show* to the other members of the cast and then the jester to serious guests, never breaking from the comedic atmosphere, using, as Elliot argues, "laughter and excess [to] push aside the seriousness and the hierarchies of 'official' life" (p. 129).

Where this becomes problematic is in the interstices of politics, news, and entertainment, the increasingly small spaces between and thin lines that separate them. News is political infotainment; politics is more and more becoming the realm of Hollywood production values; entertainment takes political undertones while also informing the audience. This is the play of political discourse and the blurring of the lines between these realms; the existence in the interstices is the concern of the next section of this chapter.

THE PLAY OF POLITICAL DISCOURSE

The tales of blurred lines of political theater and political reality leave us with an important moral: take care with what you pretend to be. Satire has the potential for play in political discourse, but it also has the potential for negative ramifications. This is particularly evident in the concept of the "fake candidate" as described by Heather Osborne-Thompson (2009), who analyzes three moments in American politics. These are the 1968 presidential campaign, the ramifications of Ronald Reagan's image obsessed era of conservatism and the "post-network, brand-savvy, multi-platform media age in which we currently live" (p. 65). In her tracing of three "fake" presidential candidates Osborne-Thompson defines these moments in satire as oppositional and, referencing Nancy Fraser, locates this satire as coterminous with rising "subaltern publics" (*ibid*).

These publics, as Fraser says, are "discursive arenas where members of subordinated social groups invent and circulate counterdiscourses to formulate oppositional interpretations of their identities, interests and needs" (quoted in Osborne-Thompson, p. 65). For Osborne-Thompson, her three moments of political satire are moments when "marginalized perspectives . . . emerged as legitimate topics for political discussions . . . enacting or modeling the parameters for such conversations" (*ibid*). These moments, in other words, "respond to the increasingly alienating process of televisual politics by instructing viewers on how to talk back" (p. 64). The problem, again, is that while satire opens up oppositional discourses, these discourses can also be folded back into establishment political needs and the needs of commerce.

John Fiske (2003) makes this argument in his discussion of incorporation and containment, when establishment organizations (i.e. corporate or state interests) take oppositional moments and re-appropriate them into mainstream talk. This process "robs subordinate groups of any oppositional language" because it creates "a permitted and controlled gesture of dissent that acts as a safety valve and thus strengthens the dominant social order by demonstrating its ability to cope with dissenters" (p. 114). This process is evident in the *New York Times* account describing Colbert's aforementioned performance at the 2006 Press Club Dinner as a "heavily nuanced, [and] often ironic performance" with jokes that "sounded supportive of Mr. Bush but were quickly revealed to be anything but" (Steinberg 2006, para. 4). This is what makes this a moment of pure political radicalism while simultaneously confusing its own position. Colbert's character is irony brought to life, and sometimes the irony of the sender is lost on the receiver. In such instances the performance is folded back into that which it critiques. At the very least the *Times* account notes that satire requires a deeper analysis, rather than a surface reading, on the part of the viewer.

Equally important is that, when satire pretends, it creates expectations in pretend that it can't live up to in reality. The audience begins to follow the jester and what began as a joke evolves into something beyond the jester's control. Now polls find Jon Stewart to be "the most trusted man in news" (Kakutani 2008; Linkis 2009; "Now that Walter . . ." 2009) with viewers seeing him as a primary information source rather than a comedian satirizing news media. Once expectations have been built the jester must live up to them. These expectations are complicated by the fact that Stewart is on a comedy network rather than a news network.

Herein lies an intellectual dishonesty, described by Hart and Hartelius (2007) who argue that Stewart's attempt to avoid criticism via the rhetorical tactic of saying "I'm just a comedian" has allowed him to "evade critical interrogation, thereby making him a fundamentally anti-political creature" (p. 264) and presenting a stance that "makes cynicism attractive" (p. 263). Weaving this analysis back into concerns of commerce raised by Fiske, is the argument that Stewart's anti-politicism "urges [his audience] to steer clear of conventional politics and to do so while steering a Nissan" (*ibid*). This is what makes the potential of Stewart, in comparison to his reality, simultaneously frustrating and powerful. Stewart has the potential to be something "more" but if he took on a more explicitly political position he would somehow disempower himself.

Every week he is on the air, Jon Stewart is skewering political actors, and he is not only aiming at politicians. He puts the truth to journalists, economists, consultants and corporatists. In the midst of an economic meltdown he is the only media figure who dared to question CNBC and Jim Cramer; he told Lou Dobbs that his views on immigration were "abhorrent and wrong" (Bodow and O'Neill, 2009c); he pointed out to Alan Greenspan the contradiction of the very existence of the Federal Reserve and free market principles. Greenspan replied that Stewart was making an important point to which Stewart replied with a self-deprecating joke. Greenspan went on to explain the workings of human collective perception and its impact on how the market works, specifically the balance between a collective feeling of fear as opposed to euphoria relating to the performance of the market. Greenspan argued that if he could figure out the direction of those collective emotions (one is reminded here of Brennan, 2004, or Massumi, 2005) he could better predict the performance of the market. The problem, he told Stewart, is that human nature cannot be improved. Stewart replied to this with humorously profane depression (Bodow and O'Neill, 2007).

Could it be that Stewart's place as "just a comedian" gives him the political cover to do these things that "real" journalists might be afraid to do or are prevented from doing by their corporate media owners or the standards of journalism that would frame such statements as ignoring the norms of objectivity or fairness? Is this at least part of what makes Stewart so compelling as a media figure? Who else could elicit from Alan Greenspan a seven-minute discussion that is more interesting, informative and entertaining than much of anything else in popular culture and news today? What makes Jon Stewart what he is, is the fact that he is able to have a serious discussion with Alan Greenspan about the Fed and end it with an off-color remark that somehow feels entirely appropriate. He is able to punctuate a serious question about the Fed with a self-deprecating question, asking if he should leave the studio. Most importantly, he is able to pose the politically radical and important question, why do we have a Fed at all? This is a political question that is relegated to a small group of political figures like Ron Paul, a Republican congressman and former presidential candidate from Texas, and Bernie Sanders, an independent self-described democratic socialist senator from Vermont. Yet this radical question is given voice by the comedian Jon Stewart rather than an anchor on the "real" news.

What Stewart and Colbert do when they are able to obtain interviews with important political figures is to truly blur the lines of reality, to make an infiltration of the real as Osborne-Thompson says (p. 79–81). One might think of Colbert's appearance on *Meet the Press* or *The O'Reilly Factor*. In thinking of these images we are confronted with the reality of fantasy, that the "walls that formerly separated political insiders and outsiders, cable and network, pundits and parodists is now quite permeable" (Osborne-Thompson, p. 80). The argument can be made that the reason these media figures, supposedly serious newsmen like Tim Russert or Bill O'Reilly, would subject themselves to the jokes of Stephen Colbert is because it allows them to tap into Colbert and Stewart's audiences in the same way that politicians do. This is just good business. We must not forget that this is what media, even news media, are: businesses.

The "infiltration of the real" brings us full circle to where we began; satire is a slippery customer. It is often that the satirized take on the signs of satirization and wear them with pride. Those signs become so embedded in the meanings of the satirized that the public begins to forget that the signs were intended to be derisive. Most prominent among these instances is the Democratic Party's logo, the donkey. Originally intended to imply that Democrats were "asses," the donkey has become a logo that the party includes on its campaign literature, websites and yard signs. Nicholas Backlund (1994) points out that the first time Democrats were linked to the donkey was in "a lithograph of unknown authorship" featuring the image of "Andrew Jackson astride a donkey, whipping it furiously with a stick that represents his veto" (p. 195). Although Thomas Nast, the originator of the Republican elephant, did not create the Democratic donkey, he also used it to satirize the Democrats and "perhaps figuring that it's easier to join them than to fight them, the Democratic Party itself finally appropriated the donkey as its national symbol" (*ibid*).

Thus satire is faced with a warning; take care with what you say and what you pretend to be. The production process does not end at the point of consumption; the audience is able to re-appropriate content for their own use. The corporation is able to re-appropriate. The politician is able to re-appropriate. Media figures and institutions are able to re-appropriate. This is especially so in the new media age of use and re-use of content. These are the questions with which this chapter concludes. What is the potential of satire? What is the potential downside of satire? Is satire a truly radical, subversive form of communication or merely a small swipe at power that is easily folded back into the interests of that power?

CONCLUSION

What this chapter has discussed is the peculiar middle-space, the in-between, that is occupied by Jon Stewart and satirists in a general sense. One might think of George Carlin, Lenny Bruce, Kurt Vonnegut; these social commentators who employed at times vulgarity in order to engage in that act of social commentary. These are figures who attempted to occupy the precarious space between their individual ethical positions, the media institutions that carried their messages and the immanent and inescapable political institutions and processes at which they aimed their critique. Attempting to make our way through the vulgarity to get to the kernel of political criticism one is reminded of the last paragraph of Foucault's preface to *Anti-Oedipus*:

> The traps of *Anti-Oedipus* are those of humor: so many invitations to let oneself be put out, to take one's leave of the text and slam the door shut. The book often leads one to believe it is all fun and games, when something essential is taking place, something of extreme seriousness. (Deleuze and Guattari, 1983, p. xiv)

There are a variety of doors slammed on *The Daily Show* as Foucault fears happening with *Anti-Oedipus*. There is the door of Hart and Hartelius who decry Stewart's attempt to "evade critical interrogation" by hiding behind his position on a comedy network (a critique that the argument in this chapter finds partially compelling). There is the door of Bernie Goldberg who made a similar critique on *The O'Reilly Factor*, saying "to" Jon Stewart via the forum of that cable news interview,

> If you just wanna be a funny man, who talks to an audience that will laugh at anything you say; that's okay with me, no problem. But, if clearly you wanna be a social commentator, more than just a comedian, and if you wanna be a good one, you better find some guts. (Tabacoff, 2010)

To this Goldberg added that in order to be truly "edgy" Stewart would need to start criticizing liberals more often. This, of course, echoes Tucker Carlson's criticism that Stewart was too easy on John Kerry during the 2004 campaign. Stewart telling various commentators from Fox News Channel, that he featured in a montage of clips, to go "bleep" themselves (Bodow and O'Neill, 2010b) prompted Goldberg's statement. In response to Goldberg's response Stewart made the statement that he, like so many comedians before him, uses jokes as social commentary. This was followed by Stewart dancing in front of a quintet of gospel singers in robes singing "go 'bleep' yourself" to Bernie Goldberg (Bodow and O'Neill, 2010c). As juvenile as it may seem, it would appear that given the lack of response from Fox News to the singing that Stewart won the "debate."[9]

All of this, however, misses an important point about *The Daily Show* and its place within the flows and streams of media. It would be useful here to engage Henri Lefebvre's (2004) concepts of rhythms and the conceptual conflict between the present and presence, the need to "take images for what they are, simulacra, *copies conforming to a standard*, parodies of presence" (p. 23). There is a give and take between how we perceive traditional news media and what they actually are; the before and after invoked in the title of this chapter is how the news parody of *The Daily Show* forces "real" news into a position of being a "copy conforming to a standard" so to speak. *The Daily Show* is a present that creates the illusion of the presence of the history of American journalism and its watchdog function.

The question becomes, though, is Jon Stewart moving closer to the "news box" or is the "news box" moving closer to him, as he claims? There is a challenge to locating Stewart in the political/mediascape. What is the place he inhabits? Where does he exist? The best answer may be that he does not fully and discretely occupy any particular political space and not some other but instead exists between those things that come before and after him. Jon Stewart's media life, to appropriate Tim Ingold's concepts, is "led not inside places but through, around, to and from them, from and to places elsewhere" (p. 33). Ingold uses the concept of wayfaring to describe actual physical movement through and to spaces. Here it is used metaphorically to describe political spaces and paths along which Stewart and satirists in general move.

These are multiple streams that, to continue to intersect Ingold with Lefebvre, are not lines with connectors but instead a meshwork that is constituted in the "binding together of lines, not in the connecting of points" (p. 38). This binding together of lines/streams is happening in news media when Stephen Colbert is invited on *Meet the Press*, or Jon Stewart goes on *Crossfire*. More than that, this meshwork of infotainment is more pronounced in the absence of Stewart and Colbert. We begin to see how the question that must be addressed is not just, why do polls show *The Daily Show* to be a trusted news source, but rather, why do the "real" news sources take on so many of the characteristics of entertainment? Infotainment is not a new concern in news media, but it has become of much greater concern with the rise of cable news, the twenty-four-hour news cycle and the growing popularity of *The Daily Show*.

For example, in one story on *The Daily Show* Stewart mocked the hyperbole of news blogs that continually feature headlines saying that he "destroyed" or "eviscerated" or "disembowled" various media outlets and figures (Bodow and O'Neill, 2010a). In a comical reaction to the segment the news blog *The Huffington Post* featured the headline, "Disemboweler Jon Stewart Eviscerates Blogosphere" (Huffington Post, 2010). What is supposed to be a political news site in this instance engages in the ironic play in a sort of self-deprecating fashion, which is especially self-deprecating since some of the headlines featured in the *The Daily Show* segment were from the *Huffington Post*.

The comedic aesthetic infiltrates the "real" news on television as well. For example, the ABC Sunday talk show *This Week* has a regular segment called the Sunday Funnies that features amusing clips from talk shows with jokes about politics and current affairs. A LexisNexis search of transcripts from CNN, MSNBC, and Fox News shows that the terms Jon Stewart or *The Daily Show* have been mentioned on the three cable news networks a total of 228 times in the last six months[10] (92, 57, and 79 times, respectively). Some of these are passing mentions; others are more integral to the programming. In one episode of *Countdown with Keith Olbermann* a clip from *The Daily Show* is seamlessly integrated into a report as though it were actual news reporting.

Keith Olbermann, Host of Countdown: Democratic Senator Mary Landrieu, who represents thousands of Louisiana fishermen whose fishing season came to an abrupt end at 6:00 p.m. prevailing local time tonight is unmoved by the implications of this spill, budging not at all in her demand for new drilling, even after Jon Stewart pointed out on *The Daily Show* that her position on the safety of that drilling has budged quite a bit from the days when she lined up squarely to defend it, along with the long line of Republicans. (Olbermann, 2010)

This comment from Olbermann is followed by a clip from *The Daily Show* in the same way that the genre of cable news talk shows incorporates interview clips from other news programs. In this instance, the distinction between a "fake" news show and a "real" news show becomes completely meaningless, is totally ignored, for the sake of both rhetorical affect and entertainment value for which Olbermann's producers are aiming. As they aim, they continue to tighten the knots of the meshwork of these different media lines or flows of media.

As with the satirists who preceded him, Jon Stewart is faced with the unintended consequences of his actions. Whether he wants to be seen as a credible news source is a moot point; he is now seen by some as more credible than "real" news anchors (Riggio, 2009). A recurrent theme in this chapter has been unintended consequences; the unintended reinforcement of the targets of satire; and the unintended trust bestowed upon a media outlet. Intended or not, media figures like Jon Stewart must live with freedom and responsibility. Stewart cultivated that trust, intentionally or not, by making the public laugh, but also fulfilling the often-unfulfilled promises of "real" journalists, informing the public. Perhaps we should simply stop pretending there is such a thing as a "fake" journalist and just start referring to Stewart as a journalist. No "real," no "fake," just journalists. Either way, we should heed the words of Foucault and pay attention, look past the jokes and see that "something essential is taking place, something of extreme seriousness."

NOTES

1. One key point here is that the audience can sometimes misinterpret the meaning of satire. For example, there are studies that have shown conservative viewers interpret Stephen Colbert as being conservative rather than satirizing conservatism (Baumgartner and Morris, 2008; LaMarre, et al., 2009). A study done in the 1970s found similar results in viewers of *All in the Family* (Vidmar, 1974). It showed that the Archie Bunker's bigotry worked to reinforce the beliefs of viewers who shared the character's beliefs rather than making them see *All in the Family* as being satirical.

2. This is from the 7 December 2005 episode of National Public Radio's *Fresh Air*, which can be found at http://www.npr.org/templates/story/story.php?storyId=5040948andps=rs.

3. On one hand, when asked about studies that showed that conservatives interpret Colbert's politics as also being conservative he replied,

I'm thrilled by it! From the very beginning, I wanted to jump back and forth over the line of meaning what I say, and the truth of the matter is I'm not on anyone's side, I'm on my side. . . . The important thing is that the audience laughs. (Ascher-Walsh 2009, para. 2)

On the other hand, Colbert has said he does not like to let his own children watch *The Colbert Report* because, referring to his performances he said, "I truck in insincerity. With a very straight face, I say things I don't believe" (Schorn, 2006, p. 4). "Kids can't understand irony or sarcasm, and I don't want them to perceive me as insincere," he went on to say (*ibid*). It would appear, however, that there might also be some adults who can't understand irony or sarcasm.

4. Equally humorous in this episode is Stewart referring to Former New York Mayor Rudy Giuliani as a "9/11-ologist." This is a reference to Giuliani's frequent use of 9/11 as a rhetorical tool in his campaign speeches. During the Democratic presidential primary then Sen. Joe Biden said of Giuliani, "there's only three things he mentions in a sentence: a noun and a verb and 9/11" (Cooper, 2007).

5. A post on this interview appeared on *The Huffington Post* in 2009 but The Street.com has since had the video of the interview removed from YouTube for copyright reasons. http://www.huffingtonpost.com/2009/03/11/jim-cramer-shorting-stock_n_173824.html.

6. Kalan's comment also reinforces *The Daily Show's* attempt to have it both ways. On one hand Jon Stewart has on multiple occasions said that he is a comedian, in particular that moment from CNN's *Crossfire*. On the other hand, a writer from the show also says they take the role of media critic "very seriously." These two moments would seem to be in conflict with one another. Either you are just a comedy program or you take your role as media critic very seriously, even if that role is a satirical criticism.

7. This episode of National Public Radio's *On the Media*, can be found at the following URL: http://www.onthemedia.org/transcripts/2006/05/05/09.

8. This is one moment from Bob Woodward's (2004) book *Plan of Attack* that received some media coverage. Woodward recounts an Oval Office meeting between President George W. Bush, and various members of the Bush Administration, in which George Tenet, the Director of Central Intelligence, described the claim that Saddam Hussein possessed weapons of mass destruction as a "slam dunk" (p. 249).

9. It should also be noted that the Stewart v. Goldberg feud was the number one story on MSNBC's *Countdown with Keith Olbermann* on 21 April 2010, which might strengthen Stewart's argument that the "news box" is moving closer to him rather than the other way around.

10. These numbers reflect a search done on 2 August 2010.

REFERENCES

Ascher-Walsh, R. (2009). Stephen Colbert, 'arch conservative.' Retrieved 23 November 2009 from http://articles.latimes.com/2009/jun/01/news/en-colbert1.

Backlund, N. (1994). Red, white and bland. In M. Bierut, et al. (Eds.), *Looking closer: Critical writings on graphic design.* (p.193–198). New York: Allworth Press.

Baumgartner, J. and Morris, J. (2008). One 'nation,' under Stephen? The effects of *The Colbert Report* on American youth. *Journal of Broadcasting and Electronic Media*, 52(4), p. 622–643.

Baym, G. (2009). *From Cronkite to Colbert: The Evolution of Broadcast News.* New York: Paradigm Publishers.

Berardi, F. (Bifo). (2007). Schizo-economy. *SubStance*, 36(1), p. 76–85.

Best, S. and Kellner, D. (1991). *Postmodern theory: Critical interrogations.* Boulder, CO: Guilford Press.

Bielik-Robson, A. (2002). Limits of Irony: Freedom and Responsibility in Culture. Unpublished paper presented at the conference *Freiheit und Verantwortung*, organised by University in Poznań.

Bodow, S. (Head Writer) and O'Neill, C. (Director). (2007, September 18). [Television series episode]. In J. Stewart (Executive producer), *The Daily Show with Jon Stewart.* New York: Viacom.

———. (2009a, March 12). [Television series episode]. In J. Stewart (Executive producer), *The Daily Show with Jon Stewart.* New York: Viacom.

————. (2009b, November 16). [Television series episode]. In J. Stewart (Executive producer), *The Daily Show with Jon Stewart*. New York: Viacom.

————. (2009c, November 18). [Television series episode]. In J. Stewart (Executive producer), *The Daily Show with Jon Stewart*. New York: Viacom.

————. (2010a, February 4). [Television series episode]. In J. Stewart (Executive producer), *The Daily Show with Jon Stewart*. New York: Viacom.

————. (2010b, April 15). [Television series episode]. In J. Stewart (Executive producer), *The Daily Show with Jon Stewart*. New York: Viacom.

————. (2010c, April 20). [Television series episode]. In J. Stewart (Executive producer), *The Daily Show with Jon Stewart*. New York: Viacom.

————. (2010d, May 12). [Television series episode]. In J. Stewart (Executive producer), *The Daily Show with Jon Stewart*. New York: Viacom.

Bratich, J. (2010). Affective Convergence in Reality Television: A Case Study in Divergence Culture. In Kackman, M., Binfield, M., Payne, M., Perlman, A., and Sebok, B. (Eds.), *Flow TV: Television in the Age of Media Convergence*. (p. 55–74). New York: Routledge.

Brennan, T. (2004). *The transmission of affect*. Ithaca, NY: Cornell University Press.

Carlson, T. (host). (15 October 2004) *Crossfire*. [Television broadcast]. Washington D.C.: CNN.

Colebrook, C. (2004). *Irony (The New Critical Idiom)*. New York: Routledge.

Cooper, M. (2007). Biden-Giuliani Smackdown Enlivens Campaign Trail. Retrieved 1 November 2007 from http://www.nytimes.com/2007/11/01/us/politics/01biden.html.

Danesi, M. (2008). *Popular culture: Introductory perspectives*. Lanham, MD: Rowan and Littlefield Publishers.

Deleuze, G. and Guattari, F. (1983). *Anti-Oedipus*. Minneapolis: University of Minnesota Press.

Elliot, S. (1999). "Carnival and Dialogue in Bakhtin's Poetics of Folklore." *Folklore Forum*, 30 (1/2), p. 129–139.

Fiske, J. (2003). Understanding popular culture. In W. Brooker and D. Jermyn (Eds.), The audience studies reader (pp. 112–116). New York: Routledge.

Gray, J. (2009). Throwing Out the Welcome Mat: Public Figures as Guests and Victims in TV Satire. In J. Gray, J. Jones and E. Thompson (Eds.), *Satire TV: Politics and Comedy in the Post-network Era*, p. 147–166. New York: NYU Press.

Hart, R. and Hartelius, J. (2007). The political sins of John Stewart. *Critical Studies in Media Communication*, 24(3), p. 263–272.

Huffington Post. (2010). Disemboweler Jon Stewart Eviscerates Blogosphere. Retrieved 21 May 2010 from http://www.huffingtonpost.com/2010/02/05/disemboweler-jon-stewart_n_450715.html.

Ingold, T. (2009). Against Space: Place Movement and Knowledge. In Kirby, P. (ed.), *Boundless Worlds: An Anthropological Approach to Movement* (p. 29–44). Oxford: Berghahn Books.

Javerbaum, D. (Head Writer) and O'Neill, C. (Director). (2006, November 13). [Television series episode]. In J. Stewart (Executive producer), *The Daily Show with Jon Stewart*. New York: Viacom.

Kakutani, M. (2008). Is Jon Stewart the Most Trusted Man in America? Retrieved on 21 October 2009 from http://www.nytimes.com/2008/08/17/arts/television/17kaku.html.

Klumpp, J. (1997). Freedom and Responsibility in Constructing Public Life: Toward a Revised Ethic of Discourse. *Argumentation*, 11, p. 113–130.

Kraft, J. (Senior Broadcast Producer). (2009, March 12). *American Morning* [Television broadcast]. New York: CNN.

LaMarre, H; Landreville, K. and Beam, M. (2009). The irony of satire: political ideology and the motivation to see what you want to see in *The Colbert Report. International Journal of Press/Politics*, 14(2), p. 212–231.

Lazzarato, M. (2006). Immaterial labor. In *Radical thought in Italy*, Virno, Paolo, Buckley, S. and Hardt, M. (Eds.). Minneapolis: University of Minnesota Press.

Lefebvre, H. (2004). *Rhythmanalysis: Space, Time and Everyday Life*. London: Continuum.

Linkis, J. (2009). Online Poll: John Stewart is America's Most Trusted Newsman. Retrieved on 21 October 2009 from http://www.huffingtonpost.com/2009/07/22/time-magazine-poll-jonst_n_242933.html.

Massumi, B. (2005). Fear (The spectrum said). *Positions*, 13(1), p. 31–48.

Novak, M. (1966). Defoe's shortest way with the dissenters: hoax, parody, paradox, fiction, irony, and satire, *Modern Language Quarterly* 27, p.402–417.

"Now that Walter Cronkite has passed on, who is America's most trusted newscaster?" *Time.* (2009). Retrieved from http://www.timepolls.com/hppolls/archive/poll_results_417.html.

Olbermann, K. (host). (2010, May 4). *Countdown with Keith Olbermann* [Television broadcast]. New York: MSNBC.

Osborne-Thompson, H. (2009). Tracing the fake candidate in American television comedy. In J. Gray, J. Jones and E. Thompson (Eds.), *Satire TV: Politics and Comedy in the Postnetwork Era*, p. 64–82. New York: NYU Press.

Rigggio, R. (2009). Why Jon Stewart is the most trusted man in America. Retrieved 26 October 2009 from http://www.psychologytoday.com/node/31268.

Rogers, K. (Senior Producer). (2006, May 5). *On the Media* [Radio broadcast]. New York: WNYC.

Salit, A. (Producer). (2005, December 7). *Fresh Air* [Radio Broadcast]. Philadelphia: WHYY.

Schorn, D. (2006). The Colbert Report: Morley Safer Profiles Comedy Central's 'Fake' Newsman. Retrieved from: http://www.cbsnews.com/stories/2006/04/27/60minutes/main1553506.shtml?tag=contentMain;contentBody.

Steinberg, J. (2006). After Press Dinner, the Blogosphere Is Alive With the Sound of Colbert Chatter. Retrieved on 21 October 2009 from http://www.nytimes.com/2006/05/03/arts/03colb.html?_r=1andex=1146801600anden=b953727404f0926dandei=5087 percent0A.

Tabacoff, D. (Executive Producer). (2010, April 19). *The O'Reilly Factor* [Television broadcast]. New York: Fox News Channel.

Tenore, M.J. (2009). 'Daily Show' producers, writers say they're serious about media criticism. Retrieved 17 November 2009 from http://www.poynter.org/column.asp?id=101andaid=173534.

Vidmar, N. (1974). Archie Bunker's bigotry: A study in selective perception and exposure. *Journal of Communication*, 24(1), p. 36–47.

Woodward, B. (2004). *Plan of Attack*. New York: Simon and Schuster.

Chapter Three

Cramer vs. (Jon Stewart's Characterization of) Cramer: Image Repair Rhetoric, Late Night Political Humor, and *The Daily Show*

Josh Compton

A battle of words between Jon Stewart of Comedy Central's *The Daily Show* and Jim Cramer of CNBC's *Mad Money* culminated in a face-to-face encounter on *The Daily Show* in March 2009. Stewart initially criticized CNBC's coverage of financial issues in the context of the economic crisis, and after Cramer seemed to take personal offense, Stewart directed his attacks toward Cramer. After days of back and forth rhetorical volleys, the two men met for a face-to-face exchange watched by 2.3 million people (Frankel, 2009a). The interview was a substantive, sometimes humorous, exchange. One journalist concluded that the interview "felt like a Senate subcommittee hearing" (Stanley, 2009, p. C1), while another described it as "at once hilarious, scarily intense and illuminating about the failure of financial journalism in the lead-up to the credit crisis" (Foley, 2009, p. 26). Many observers crowned Stewart the winner, and implications of their sparring reverberated, drawing reactions from journalists, politicians, business people, and even the White House Press Secretary, Robert Gibbs. During the rhetorical bashing Cramer received before and during his *Daily Show* appearance, Cramer attempted image repair.

To better understand image repair in the context of late night comedy, and specifically, *The Daily Show*, this chapter traces Jim Cramer's image repair strategies using a typology of image repair developed by William Benoit (1995, 2000). Taking a closer look at Stewart's attacks and Cramer's image repair attempts with the aid of Benoit's typology reveals a unique merging of politics, entertainment, and financial reporting. The dynamics of the often-humorous exchange between two television personalities, coupled with the seriousness of the financial issues, make for a rich illustration of image repair rhetoric.

An ever-growing body of scholarship of late night television humor reveals unique effects of late night comedy television (see Compton, 2008, for a review). This chapter turns from what late night television is doing to viewers toward a story of one person's attempt at image repair through the venue of late night television comedy. At the same time, this is a story of that venue—how one show and its host served as the channel of attacks and the channel of attempted image repair, with humor confounding expectations of what works and what doesn't during image repair.

IMAGE REPAIR

Benoit's (1995, 2000) typology of image repair strategies provides a useful analytical framework for analyzing Stewart's and Cramer's rhetoric. Benoit's typology summarizes decades of research in image, *apologia*, and accounts(e.g., Ware and Linkugel, 1973; Scott and Lyman, 1968), to offer five rhetorical strategies (some with subdivisions, or tactics): *denial, evasion of responsibility, reducing offensiveness, corrective action*, and *mortification*. These approaches are options for image repair when one faces criticism of responsibility for an offensive act or acts (Benoit, 1995). *Denial* occurs when the accused claims that an offensive act did not occur or that the accused did not do the offensive act, whether through *simple denial* or *shifting the blame* to another target. *Evading responsibility* occurs when someone attempts to avoid accountability for the offensive act. Four tactics of evading responsibility include *provocation* (claiming that an act was a justified response to another act), *defeasibility* (claiming that an act was unavoidable or outside of the accused person's control), *accident* (rejecting intent to do the offensive act), and *good intentions* (claiming that the person accused meant well). *Reducing offensiveness* turns attention toward the act itself. Six tactics of reducing offensiveness include *bolstering* (drawing attention to positive attributes of the accused), *minimization* (downplaying the severity of the act), *differentiation* (comparing the act to worse acts), *transcendence* (considering the act in a context of higher ideals or considerations), *attacking the accuser* (derogating the credibility of the critic), and *compensation* (some form of reimbursement for those harmed). *Corrective action* outlines a way for the accused to repair any damage and/or to prevent the act from occurring again. Finally, *mortification* is an expression of regret for the act, often an apology

(see Benoit, 1995, 2000, for a thorough treatment of these strategies and tactics.)

Benoit's typology has been used to study a number of image repair situations, including politics (e.g., Benoit, 2006), public relations crises (e.g., Benoit, 1997b), sports (e.g., Brazeal, 2008), religious rhetoric (e.g., Miller, 2002), and entertainment (e.g., Benoit and Anderson, 1996). Image repair scholars have also considered late night television comedy programs as venues for image repair attempts—the actor Hugh Grant's appearance on *The Tonight Show* with Jay Leno after Grant had been arrested for "lewd behavior" with a prostitute (Benoit, 1997a). The Cramer/Stewart late night comedy exchange is unique in that Stewart, the one launching the attacks on Cramer's image, was also the host of the show on which Cramer appeared as a guest. Of course, the basis of the image attack is also notably different from the exchange between Leno and Grant.

Early Attacks and Responses

Jim Cramer was not the initial target of Jon Stewart's criticisms of CNBC's economic reporting (see Bodow and O'Neil, 2009a). Instead, Stewart mocked CNBC's Rick Santelli. Santelli had criticized some homeowners, calling them "losers" for making bad financial decisions, and later, cancelled his scheduled appearance on *The Daily Show*. In response, on March 4, 2009, *The Daily Show* broadcast several clips from CNBC, highlighting Santelli's rant specifically and CNBC's reporting in general, using a technique called "quick-cut editing" (Kurtz, 2009, p. A1). Cramer was among the reporters and analysts featured in the clips.

Cramer published a response in a column on the financial website, Main-Street.com, on March 10, 2009. Cramer (2009) asserted that he was taking criticism from the "'liberal' media (from serious columnist Frank Rich to entertainer Jon Stewart) while being defended by Rush Limbaugh, the standard-bearer for the Republicans" (para. 1). He continued:

> [Rich and Stewart] seize on the urban legend that I recommended Bear Stearns the week before it collapsed, even though I was saying that I thought it could be worthless as soon as the following week. . . . The absurdity astounds me. . . . The fact that I was right rankles me even more. (Cramer, 2009, para. 14)

Cramer used a few image repair strategies in his first rebuttal. He attacked Stewart by dismissing him as an "entertainer" (contrasted with a "serious columnist") and then engaged in simple denial, claiming that he did not do what Stewart had implied (i.e., recommending Bear Stearns stock in the days before its collapse.) Finally, Cramer used bolstering, asserting that he was right, and he tried to dismiss the criticisms as "absurdity." He would repeat similar strategies during television appearances—on his own MSNBC show,

Mad Money, and also on morning talk shows on cable and network television. Two of these appearances—on *Today* and *The Martha Stewart Show*—are particularly notable in how they either supported or detracted from Cramer's strategy of dismissing Stewart as a comedian. During his *Today* appearance, he continued to brand Stewart an "entertainer," to dismiss Stewart as "a comedian" (see "Controversy . . . ," 2009). Later, in his last chance during the interview to engage in successful image repair strategies, Cramer instead denied responsibility, shifted the blame to the CEO of Wachovia, and employed defeasibility, claiming that he was at the mercy of the market. In his final statements, he returned to attacking his accuser, dismissing Stewart as a comedian ("Controversy . . . ," 2009).

But Cramer changed his strategy during his appearance on *The Martha Stewart Show* (see Shea, 2009). During this appearance, Cramer claimed to have modeled his show, *Mad Money*, after Stewart's *The Daily Show*, and at one point, Cramer called Stewart his "idol" (cited in Shea, 2009). With these comments, Cramer turned from a fairly consistent strategy of attacking his accuser and, instead, complimented Stewart.

While Cramer attempted image repair, Stewart continued to mock Cramer with stinging jokes and creative video clips (see Bodow and O'Neil, 2009b, 2009c). The war of words (and clips and television appearances) culminated with Cramer's appearance on *The Daily Show*.

Face-to-Face Attacks and Responses—*The Daily Show* interview

Cramer appeared as a guest on Stewart's *The Daily Show* on March 12, 2009 (see Bodow and O'Neil, 2009d). Stewart began the interview pointing out that his criticisms were not initially aimed at Cramer, but instead, at CNBC's financial reporting in general. Cramer replied that many people should share the blame, and Cramer also argued that the financial crisis was an extraordinary occurrence. With this approach, Cramer's defense was that no one could have predicted the crisis—the economic situation was beyond anyone's control (defeasibility). Also notable during these opening remarks was Stewart's attempt to focus—and arguably, redefine—his attacks. Stewart characterized the issue as something larger than Cramer. With this broadened scope, even if Cramer were to successfully repair his own image, this would not refute Stewart's overall critique. From the beginning of the interview, Cramer found himself in a challenging image repair situation.

After Cramer emphasized that he was one of many people who should share blame—which fed Stewart's argument that this issue is bigger than Cramer—Stewart asked Cramer why he seemed to take the criticism personally. Cramer denied that he was angry at *The Daily Show*—or that he was angry at any criticism, for that matter—and turned to bolstering to reduce the offensiveness of the charge, noting the size of CNBC and its reputation as a leader in financial reporting. Cramer then moved toward more bolstering and also defeasibility, noting that mistakes are understandable when broadcasting live commentary and reporting for many hours each day. In response, Stewart suggested that CNBC could broadcast fewer hours each day, eliciting laughter from the audience.

After this general overview, Stewart spelled out his attack with more precision, pointing to specific criticism of CNBC's coverage—that it is misleadingly framed as thoughtful, informed financial reporting. Stewart also introduced a video clip of a CNBC promotion with the tagline, "In Cramer We Trust." After showing the clip, Stewart made a comparison between *The Daily Show* and Cramer's show, *Mad Money*, noting that while there may be similarities between what Cramer does and what Stewart does on their respective programs, *The Daily Show* doesn't tout itself as more than an entertainment program. With this clip and the following exchange, Stewart returned to his specific attack—that CNBC mischaracterizes what they do. By equating some of Stewart's and Cramer's approaches on *The Daily Show* and *Mad Money*, Stewart preempted attempts by Cramer to attack the accuser.

Cramer's response was that all financial experts make mistakes, and that honest financial analysts admit their mistakes. Cramer added that he makes great efforts to offer helpful financial commentary. Two of these tactics fall under the strategy of evading responsibility: defeasibility and good intentions. In making the defeasibility appeal, Cramer returned to an earlier argument that it is impossible to avoid making mistakes, that mistakes are an inevitable part of financial reporting. He also claimed good intentions, framing himself as someone who tried to offer good advice and analysis. One tactic attempted to reduce offensiveness, comparing his approach to financial reporting with those who falsely claim to never make mistakes. In response to Cramer's attempt to reduce offensiveness, Stewart rejected Cramer's dichotomous frame and refocused on issues of accuracy.

Stewart then showed a video clip from a 2006 interview for the website, TheStreet.com, featuring Cramer describing a "short selling" hedge fund strategy. After the clip, Stewart asked for an explanation. Cramer used denial, claiming that he was explaining but not admitting to advocating the strategy, and Cramer attempted to shift the blame to others who did these things.

Before Cramer could finish, Stewart cut him off to point out that in the clip, Cramer seemed to be admitting to something Cramer did. Cramer responded with minimization—that while Cramer might have been unclear on the clip, he was not engaged in the activities that he described. He also claimed good intentions and a shared goal with *The Daily Show*—to draw attention to irresponsible financial activities. This was a notable exchange, as Cramer turned from differentiating what he does (a financial analyst) with what Stewart does (a comedian) to equating their approaches. Cramer tried the same strategy as Stewart, creating a situation where criticisms of Cramer were also criticisms of Stewart. But in the process, Cramer's strategy weakened Cramer's most consistent strategy of image repair—to attack Stewart by dismissing him as a comedian.

Stewart's response to Cramer's defense was to show another segment of the video clip of Cramer explaining that what he was describing was legal and boasting that he was one of the few who would acknowledge this financial strategy. After showing the video segment, Stewart contrasted the way that Cramer presented himself on the clip with the way Stewart wanted Cramer to conduct himself on CNBC—that is, contrasting Cramer talking about seemingly suspect financial behavior with Cramer offering responsible financial analysis. With this approach, Stewart pitted Cramer against himself: Cramer versus Jon Stewart's characterization of Cramer, further cutting off Cramer's strategy of attacking the accuser. In effect, Stewart turned Cramer into his own critic, making the attacking the accuser strategy even more problematic for Cramer.

Next, Cramer attempted to differentiate the approach of his financial reporting with how Stewart characterized his reporting. Cramer explained that his goal was to expose irresponsible financial activities and bring them to the attention of financial regulators. In a lengthy analysis, Stewart argued that CNBC could and should draw attention to this but didn't do this as well as it should.

To this attack, Cramer offered his first semi-apology and commitment to attempt corrective action. Cramer admitted that CNBC could improve its financial reporting and that he personally should improve. Notably, Cramer stopped short of offering an apology for his mistakes, nor did he outline specific corrective action steps. But next, Cramer returned to his strongest attempt to bolster and argue good intentions, noting that he had been attempting to explain risky financial practices and to work with Congress for reform.

Stewart countered Cramer's claims of bolstering and good intentions with a reference to the video, once again reframing the attack and pitting Cramer against Cramer. Stewart contrasted one version of Cramer as a thoughtful analyst and the other as someone doing silly things while offering unhelpful advice. Cramer's response to Stewart's comparison was an offer of generic corrective action—to try to improve.

One might expect Cramer's response to resolve the debate. He offered his most complete statement of responsibility, and he also committed to trying harder. Mortification and corrective action are often effective in image repair (Benoit and Drew, 1997), and especially when combined (Brinson and Benoit, 1996). However, in response to Cramer's remarks, Stewart returned to where he started the interview, pointing out that the problem transcended Cramer and involved the financial news industry, an industry too close to the people it should be investigating. Cramer responded to this charge with denial and then attacked his accuser with a mild rebuke, claiming that this charge was unfair. Stewart interrupted Cramer's interruption to acknowledge that some CNBC analysts do their job well, and Stewart and Cramer had an exchange about responsible financial reporting, with Cramer turning again to defeasibility by accusing CEOs of lying to him. Stewart called him out on this tactic, claiming that Cramer was acting as if he were guilt-free, and then Stewart played two clips from 2006 of Cramer talking about controversial financial practices, including fomenting and rumor-spreading. (Cramer contends throughout the interview that he is describing but not advocating such practices during these video clips.)

Cramer began to respond, but Stewart interjected with some of the most emotional statements of the interview, expressing heated reaction to the clips. Also during this response, Stewart attempted to connect what Cramer described on the video clips to the larger economic crisis. This cut off Cramer's strategies of defeasibility and shifting blame. Cramer responded by claiming that he was exposing irresponsible financial strategies, but Stewart interrupted, returning to criticism of CNBC's reporting, then arguing that financial analysts such as Cramer can't claim to have been taken completely by surprise by the economic crisis (i.e., Stewart attacked the strategy of defeasibility).

With these remarks, Stewart rebutted Cramer's attempt at defeasibility, and launched another image attack on the strategy. Cramer's response was to shift the blame and offer another claim of defeasibility, recounting the story of a CEO who Cramer claimed was dishonest with him. Stewart responded with mock surprise that a CEO of a company would lie, Cramer acknowledged the mocking with his own feigned surprise, and Stewart pointed out that the goal of financial reporting is to uncover such dishonest claims.

Cramer shifted blame again, including criticism of the Justice Department for failing to indict those who may be responsible. Stewart offered a lengthy response, and at one point, asked Cramer about CNBC's advocacy—whether they were trying to help those doing the dangerous financial actions or those hurt by these actions. Cramer answered with attempts at bolstering, pointing out his practice of drawing attention to apparent wrongdoings by using entertaining methods like throwing banana cream pies.

At this point, Stewart made a surprising rhetorical move. Instead of refuting Cramer's attempts to bolster—which Stewart did earlier in the interview—Stewart returned to his original frame of the situation, broadening the scope from Cramer to the financial news industry. Cramer's response to this redirect meandered among multiple image repair tactics: bolstering (claiming that some CNBC reporters take great efforts to offer sound advice and analysis) defeasibility (noting that some of their guests are not always forthright), and shifting the blame (redirecting blame to those who aren't honest).

Stewart returned to generalizations about how CNBC reports financial practices, comparing CNBC reporting to an infomercial—an often-ridiculed form of television advertising that is usually in the guise of a television program. Cramer tried to emphasize his desire to draw attention to risky financial practices, to explain to viewers that investing and financial decision-making are difficult. Stewart cut this strategy off by pointing out that one of CNBC's programs is named *Fast Money*. Cramer began to respond, but following audience laughter, turned to a new variation of a strategy that he used earlier: shifting the blame. But there was one notable difference: Cramer shifted blame to viewers, telling Stewart that he and CNBC were simply meeting the demands of what people wanted. Stewart shifted the blame back to the financial news industry. In a retort, Stewart pointed out that some market demands shouldn't be met—such as for illegal activities or drugs. Then Stewart questioned Cramer about the priorities of the financial news industry.

As Stewart tried to broaden the scope to financial reporting on CNBC in general, Cramer shifted blame to some people who had appeared on CNBC shows, once again trying to shift the blame to some guests who had appeared on their programs and admitting that CNBC should have done a better job exposing inaccuracies. Besides shifting the blame, Cramer also expressed mild mortification in this response—regret that he and his colleagues had not done more to uncover dangerous financial practices.

Cramer then turned the discussion to a success story (i.e., bolstering), noting times that he was critical of people such as former Treasury Secretary Ben Bernanke. But then, Cramer shifted strategies, pointing out that he is an analyst and entertainer, and in this role, he can't control whether other people are honest. It was a remarkable turn. Cramer used a previous attack against Stewart—that Stewart was simply a comedian—to serve as Cramer's own defense strategy.

To this shift in image repair tactics, Stewart responded that financial reporters should investigate claims made by others, offering a standard for good financial reporting. But next, Stewart gave Cramer a space to save face by pointing out that the problem was larger than Cramer and that Cramer should not be the only target of criticism. Accepting this opportunity, Cramer responded with mortification once again, expressing regret that he hadn't better anticipated the financial collapse and then, once it happened, that he took too long to point out the problems.

In the concluding remarks, Stewart offered a general means of corrective action, albeit one buffered with humor. He encouraged CNBC to market Cramer's program more accurately, to aim for more responsible financial reporting, and in return, Stewart said that he would return to silly humor. Cramer agreed, and they ended the interview with a handshake.

DISCUSSION

From March 4, 2009 (the date that Stewart identified Cramer as an example of the financial reporting that he criticized) to March 12, 2009 (the date that Cramer appeared on Stewart's show), Cramer used at least twelve image repair tactics: attacking the accuser, simple denial, bolstering, shifting blame, defeasibility, defensibility, good intentions, minimization, mortification, provocation, corrective action, and differentiating. Of these strategies, Cramer seemed to focus on attacking the accuser, defeasibility, and bolstering by dismissing Stewart as a comedian, by noting inherent challenges of financial analysis, and by highlighting moments when he had offered good advice.

By many measures, Cramer's attempts to repair his image before and during the interview with Stewart failed. A nationwide survey (n=448) conducted by IICD Research indicated that 74 percent of those polled believed that Stewart benefited most from the interview, and that Cramer's perceived likeability, believability, and sincerity fell after people watched the interview (Stewart vs. Cramer, 2009). Commentators were also critical of Cramer's attempts. Daniel Frankel of *Daily Variety* concluded: "Cramer largely delivered mea culpas and offered little, if any, effective defense of his show or his channel" (2009a, p. 1), while an editorial in *Grand Rapids Press* compared Cramer to "a misbehaving kid who had been called into the principal's office" (Mad comic vs. 'Mad Money,' 2009, p. A13). Reviews posted online concurred (Etheridge, 2009). Indeed, Cramer's image repair rhetoric was so thoroughly panned that his image repair attempts may have not only failed but even backfired, derogating Cramer—and CNBC's—image (Bianco, 2009). Some thought that Cramer should have pushed back more against the video clips that Stewart showed during the interview by pointing out how the clips were edited or by providing additional context for his comments (Kurtz, 2009). Future investigations should consider long-term impacts of Cramer's attempts at image repair, but an evaluation of the image repair attempts before and during his appearance on *The Daily Show* suggests that he did not have much success.

This review of Cramer's attempts at image repair also tells us a lot about his critic during these exchanges, Jon Stewart, and *The Daily Show*. Of Cramer's dozen rhetorical tactics to repair his image, perhaps none failed more than attempts to attack his accuser. Cramer repeatedly tried to lessen Stewart's criticisms by calling Stewart, for example, "a comedian [who] runs a variety show" ("Controversy," 2009). But Stewart was immune. He could not be dismissed this way. As Robert Bianco of *USA Today* put it: "Stewart may be a comic, but he's an incredibly smart and increasingly influential one—a media darling whose comments get amplified by print, TV and the Internet" (2009, p. 3D). Stewart also has a record of well-publicized criticisms of media, including his appearance on CNN's *Crossfire* a few months before it was cancelled (Bianco, 2009; Stelter, 2010). Attacking one's accuser is a risky image repair strategy (Benoit and Anderson, 1996), and although humor is one way to enhance the strategy (Benoit and Anderson, 1996), the accuser in this instance was already using humor much more effectively to attack.

Furthermore, Stewart used Cramer's attempts at image repair as grounds for even more attacks. After Cramer's first attempt to respond to Stewart's criticism, Stewart used Cramer's words to set up another reel of video clips during an episode of *The Daily Show*—a reel that was "even funnier, nastier" (Bianco 2009, p. 3D) than those used in the original criticism of CNBC.

Stewart often preempted Cramer's image repair options. For example, Cramer found himself in a situation where attacking his accuser meant attacking himself after Stewart equated some of their approaches (see Bodow and O'Neil, 2009d). Cramer's attempts at bolstering were met with video clips of Cramer offering seemingly suspect advice. When Cramer tried to reinforce a consistent line of defense (e.g., bolstering by pointing out the good calls that he had made), Stewart changed the line of attack (e.g., broadening his criticism to an indictment of the financial news industry in general). Stewart's mastery of humor helped him to seamlessly move from one attack to the next. Furthermore, as Benoit and Hirson (2001) observed about Garry Trudeau's comic strip, *Doonesbury*, and Trudeau's attacks on the tobacco industry: A comic strip "will not be held to the same standards of evidence and proof as an industry response (however, as a comic strip, it is possible that some of its attacks could be dismissed for the same reason)" (p. 285). Of course, a comic strip is not the same as a comedy television program (in general, or *The Daily Show* in particular). Nevertheless, in this case, it appears that Stewart's criticism was taken seriously, and that humor offered him some leeway as he debated Cramer.

Cramer attempted corrective action—a strategy we do not often find in celebrity attempts to repair image, including Hugh Grant after his arrest (Benoit and Anderson, 1996) or NFL player Terrell Owens after he was let go by the Philadelphia Eagles (Brazeal, 2008). Corrective action is often an effective strategy for image repair (Benoit and Drew, 1997). However, Cramer's offer of corrective action was generic—that he would make an effort to do a better job with his financial reporting (see Bodow and O'Neil, 2009d). Perhaps Cramer would have had more success had he offered a more defined plan for corrective action. But then again, it might not have mattered. If the audience accepted Stewart's frame that his criticisms were of the entire financial news industry, Cramer's personal plan of corrective action—regardless of its level of specificity—would not have deflected the attack.

It wasn't just that Cramer lost. Stewart won. When Cramer appeared on *The Daily Show*, the episode saw its second-largest audience to that point in

2009 (Frankel, 2009a). *The Daily Show* website had an increase of 65 percent unique users for the week of March 9, 2009 (Frankel, 2009b). According HCD Research, viewers found Stewart more believable and sincere after they watched the interview when compared to their pre-interview perceptions (Stewart vs. Cramer, 2009). While Stewart didn't completely escape criticism from commentators (e.g., Cohen, 2009), the CEO of NBC Universal (see Stelter, 2009), or CNBC (see Stetler, 2009), Stewart received more praise than disapproval following the interview.

Stewart's attack on the financial news industry in general and of Cramer in particular is consistent with the tenor of *The Daily Show* (see Brewer and Marquardt, 2007, for a quantitative analysis of *The Daily Show*'s metacoverage of news media, and Baym, 2005, for a qualitative analysis). So it's not surprising that *The Daily Show* launched these criticisms. Perhaps it's more surprising that Cramer responded—very publicly, and often. Some critics concluded that Cramer would have been better off ignoring Stewart (e.g., Bianco, 2009). That Cramer didn't is notable (see Benoit and Hirson, 2001). His response gives credence to *The Daily Show*'s and Jon Stewart's credibility. It also suggests that Cramer concluded that perceptions of his responsibility and offensiveness of the acts (in this case, his advice) warranted his response. With image repair, perceptions of responsibility and offensiveness are critical, as perceived responsibility and offensiveness determine the need for image repair (Benoit, 1995, 1997a, 2000).

As for the offensiveness of the act, one journalist concluded that Stewart "wasn't lambasting CNBC for being wrong; he was after them for being arrogant. And there's a big difference" (Arrogant know-it-alls are easy targets, 2009, p. D5). As for Cramer's responsibility, we find a mixed message. Stewart repeatedly emphasized that his criticisms were not about Cramer specifically but instead, financial television reporting in general. But not all observers were convinced that Cramer wasn't the focus of Stewart's criticisms (e.g., Bookman, 2009).

CONCLUSION

Humor both confounds and assists image repair rhetoric, particularly when image repair attempts are later used as the basis for continuing humorous attacks, as Stewart did with Cramer. To date, a handful of studies have looked at humor in image repair, concentrating mainly on humor as a strategy of image repair and not of attack (e.g., Benoit, 1997a; Benoit and Anderson, 1996; Liu, 2007, 2008; but see Benoit and Hirson, 2001). Expectations of humor may have confounded Cramer's efforts to use his appearance on *The Daily Show* as image repair. As Stanley (2009) noted, Cramer "might have been expecting a more jocular give-and-take" (p. C1), and Cramer told some of his colleagues "he felt blindsided" (Kurtz, 2009, p. A1). Indeed, the face-to-face—although on a comedy program—was not considered particularly funny. "There were laughs," wrote David Lieberman in *USA Today*, "but in the larger sense there was nothing funny about" the interview (2009, p. 1B). Another journalist noted: "Stewart didn't mock Cramer. He eviscerated him" (Littwin, 2009, p. A2). Of course, late night comedy television can be a successful forum for image repair (e.g., Benoit, 1997a). But the serious nature of the exchange between Stewart and Cramer—in tone and in topic—may have countered any benefits Cramer expected by appearing on a comedy program. Additionally, in this instance, the host of the comedy show was also the one launching the attacks. Humor's interaction with image repair attempts needs continued exploration (Benoit and Hirson, 2001; Liu, 2007).

Roles are not always clear-cut when analyzing image repair in an entertainment context. We find this with Benoit and Anderson's (1996) analysis of the feud between Murphy Brown (a fictional sitcom character) and Vice President Dan Quayle, for example, as the lines became murky as to who was attacking whom. Much of the rhetoric surrounding the Cramer/Stewart confrontation focused on defining and redefining one another. Cramer struggled with Stewart's role—at first dismissing Stewart as "a comedian [who] runs a variety show" ("Controversy . . . " 2009) to later elevating Stewart to his "idol" (cited in Shea, 2009). Stewart criticized the role of the financial news industry generally and Cramer's work specifically. At one point, Stewart even pitted Cramer against himself, characterizing two Cramers (see Bodow and O'Neil, 2009d).

Not long after Cramer appeared on *The Daily Show*, the exchange was used as the standard for late night comedy appearances. Writing about President Obama's appearance on *The Tonight Show* with Jay Leno, one critic wrote: "Because Leno is no Jon Stewart and Jim Cramer is not the president of the United States, [the] affable interview was never going to produce the kind of watershed catharsis that Stewart's grilling of the CNBC crazy man gave us last week" (Peterson, 2009, p. E7). Wickham (2009), writing for *USA Today*, used the Cramer/Stewart interview as a benchmark for good print journalism.

With changing tactics, multiple forums, and a context of humor, the back-and-forth between Jim Cramer and Jon Stewart serves as a unique look into image repair rhetoric, late night political humor, and *The Daily Show*. Cramer's image repair strategies may have, indeed, boosted an image—just not the image that Cramer had in mind.

REFERENCES

Arrogant know-it-alls are easy targets. (2009, March 16). *Chattanooga Times Free-Press* (Tennessee). Retrieved from LEXIS-NEXIS Academic database.

Baym, G. (2005). *The Daily Show*: Discursive integration and the reinvention of political journalism. *Political Communication, 22*(3), 259–276.

Benoit, W. L. (1995). *Accounts, excuses, apologies: A theory of image restoration strategies.* Albany: State University of New York Press.

———. (1997a). Hugh Grant's image restoration discourse: An actor apologizes. *Communication Quarterly, 45*(3), 251–267.

———. (1997b). Image repair discourse and crisis communication. *Public Relations Review, 23*(2), 177-186.

———. (2000). Another visit to the theory of image restoration strategies. *Communication Quarterly, 48*, 40–44.

———. (2006). President Bush's image repair effort on *Meet the Press*: The complexities of defeasibility. *Journal of Applied Communication Research, 34*(3), 285–306.

Benoit, W. L., and Anderson, K. K. (1996). Blending politics and entertainment: Dan Quayle versus Murphy Brown. *Southern Communication Journal, 62*(1), 73–85.

Benoit, W. L., and Drew, S. (1997). Appropriateness and effectiveness of image repair strategies. *Communication Reports, 10*(2), 153–163.

Benoit, W. L., and Hirson, D. (2001). *Doonesbury* versus the Tobacco Institute: the smoke starters' coupon. *Communication Quarterly, 49*(3), 279–294.

Bianco, R. (2009, March 16). Memo to Jim Cramer: Three rules to consider; 'Mad Money' host could have avoided appearing clueless. *USA Today*, Life section, p. 3D. Retrieved from LEXIS-NEXIS Academic database.

Bodow, S. (Head Writer), and O'Neil, C. (Director). (2009a, March 4). [Television series episode]. In J. Stewart (Executive producer), *The Daily Show with Jon Stewart*. New York: Viacom.

———. (2009b, March 9). [Television series episode]. In J. Stewart (Executive producer), *The Daily Show with Jon Stewart*. New York: Viacom.

———. (2009c, March 10). [Television series episode]. In J. Stewart (Executive producer), *The Daily Show with Jon Stewart*. New York: Viacom.

———. (2009d, March 12). [Television series episode]. In J. Stewart (Executive producer), *The Daily Show with Jon Stewart*. New York: Viacom.

Bookman, J. (2009, March 19). More on the Jon Stewart/Jim Cramer ruckus. *The Atlanta Journal-Constitution*, Online Edition. Retrieved from LEXIS-NEXIS Academic database.

Brazeal, L. M. (2008). "The image repair strategies of Terrell Owens." *Public Relations Review, 34*, 145–150.

Brewer, P. R., and Marquardt, E. (2007). Mock news and democracy: Analyzing *The Daily Show*. *Atlantic Journal of Communication, 15*(4), 249–267.

Brinson, S. L., and Benoit, W. L. (1996). Dow Corning's image repair strategies in the breast implant crisis. *Communication Quarterly, 44*(1), 29–38.

Cohen, R. (2009, March 17). Don't blame Jim Cramer. *Washington Post*, Editorial Copy Section, p. A15. Retrieved from LEXIS-NEXIS Academic database.

Compton, J. (2008). More than laughing? Survey of political humor effects research. In J. C. Baumgartner and J. S. Morris (Eds.), *Laughing matters: Humor and American politics in the media age* (pp. 39–63). New York: Routledge.

Controversy over whether President Obama is taking on too many issues at the expense of the economy; Jim Cramer and Erin Burnett discuss. (2009, March 10). NBC News Transcripts. *Today*. Retrieved from LEXIS-NEXIS Academic database.

Cramer, J. (2009, March 10). Cramer takes on the White House, Frank Rich, and Jon Stewart. MainStreet.com. Retrieved from http://www.mainstreet.com/article/moneyinvesting/news/cramer-takes-white-house-frank-rich-and-jon-stewart?page=1.

Etheridge, E. (2009, March 13). Fight night: Cramer vs. Stewart. *Opinionater*. Available: http://opinionator.blogs.nytimes.com/2009/03/13/fight-night-cramer-vs-stewart/.

Foley, S. (2009, March 14). Satirist Stewart wins with a knockout in U.S. TV's 'Battle of Brawl Street.'*The Independent* (London), World Section, p. 26. Retrieved from LEXIS-NEXIS Academic database.

Frankel, D. (2009a, March 16). *Daily Show* Stock Soars. *Daily Variety*, News Section, p. 1. Retrieved from LEXIS-NEXIS Academic database.

———. (2009b, March 12). Host With a Left Hook. *Daily Variety*, News Section, p. 1. Retrieved from LEXIS-NEXIS Academic database.

Kurtz, H. (2009, March 14). Stewart's time to channel our anger; satirist accuses CNBC of failing its audience. *Washington Post*, A-Section, p. A1. Retrieved from LEXIS-NEXIS Academic database.

Lieberman, D. (2009, March 13). Jim Cramer takes his lumps on *The Daily Show*. *USA Today*, Money Section, p. 1B. Retrieved from LEXIS-NEXIS Academic database.

Littwin, M. (2009, March 15). Cramer vs. anti-Cramer: Justice in fake journalism. *Denver Post*, A Section, p. A2. Retrieved from LEXIS-NEXIS Academic database.

Liu, B. F. (2007). President Bush's major post-Katrina speeches: Enhancing image repair discourse theory applied to the public sector. *Public Relations Review, 33*(1), 40–48.

———. (2008). From aspiring presidential candidate to accidental racist? An analysis of Senator George Allen's image repair during his 2006 reelection campaign. *Public Relations Review, 34*, 331–336.

Mad comic vs. 'Mad Money.' (2009, March 18). *Grand Rapids Press* (Michigan), Editorial, p. A13. Retrieved from LEXIS-NEXIS Academic database.

Miller, B. A. (2002). *Divine apology: The discourse of religious image restoration*. Westport, CT: Praeger.

Peterson, K. (2009, March 21). Obama's *Tonight Show* appearance continues celebritized politics. *San Diego Union-Tribune*, Lifestyle Section, p. E7. Retrieved from LEXIS-NEXIS Academic database.

Scott, M. H., and Lyman, S. M. (1968). Accounts. *American Sociological Review, 33*, 46–62.

Shea, D. (2009, March 12). Jim Cramer: I'm "nervous" for "Daily Show," Jon Stewart is my "idol." Posted to Huffington Post, http://www.huffingtonpost.com/2009/03/12/jim-cramer-im-nervous-for_n_174312.html.

Stanley, A. (2009, March 14). High noon on the set: Cramer vs. Stewart. *New York Times*, Section C, p. C1. Retrieved from LEXIS-NEXIS Academic database.

Stelter, B. (2009, March 23). Yes, Stewart, CNBC still trusts Cramer. *New York Times*, Section B, p. B6. Retrieved from LEXIS-NEXIS Academic database.

———. (2010, February 6). In visit to FOX News, Jon Stewart faults FOX News. *New York Times*, Section C, p. C4. Retrieved from LEXIS-NEXIS Academic database.

Stewart vs. Cramer. (2009, March 16). *PR Newswire*. Retrieved May 4, 2010, from LEXIS-NEXIS Academic database.

Ware, B. L., and Linkugel, W. A. (1973). They spoke in defense of themselves: on the generic criticism of *Apologia. Quarterly Journal of Speech, 59*, 273–283.

Wickham, D. (2009, March 17). Funny men making news a bad sign for newspapers. *USA Today*, Editorial Section, p. 10A. Retrieved from LEXIS-NEXIS Academic database.

II

Arguments

Chapter Four

The (not-so) Laughable Political Argument: A Close-Textual Analysis of *The Daily Show with Jon Stewart*

John W. Self

During the summer of 2008, there was uproar over a political cartoon on the July 21 cover of *The New Yorker* magazine.[1] The cartoon portrayed then-presidential candidate Barack Obama in the Oval Office dressed in tradition-al Arab/Muslim garb with a turban on his head and sandals on his feet. Michelle Obama was portrayed as a militant black nationalist with a giant afro, camouflage pants and a bandolier of bullets across her shoulder. In the background, an American flag burns in the fireplace with a portrait of what appears to be Osama bin Laden above it. The cartoon made Obama look like a Muslim extremist. The cover, as it was designed to, set off a frenzy in the press. Since this political cartoon dominated the news for a couple of days, *The Daily Show with Jon Stewart* decided to comment on the cartoon and the coverage of it. On July 15, 2008, Stewart pointed out that earlier in the day Bill Burton, the Communication Director for the Obama Campaign, said "*The New Yorker* may think, as one of their staff explained to us, that their cover is a satirical lampoon of the caricature Sen. Obama's right-wing critics have tried to create. But most readers will see it as tasteless and offensive. And we agree" (Malcolm, 2008, para. 4). Stewart rejected the spin coming from the Obama campaign. Stewart even advocated for a different statement from the Obama campaign. A statement that pointed out that it is only Muslim extremists that get upset about political cartoons and Obama is not a Muslim extremist. Stewart concluded: "It's just a fucking cartoon!" (Bodow and O'Neill, 2008).[2]

Also that night, Larry King asked Barack Obama himself about the cartoon on his show *Larry King Live*. In response, Obama said:

Well, I know it was the "New Yorker's" attempt at satire. I don't think they were entirely successful with it. But you know what, it's a cartoon, Larry, and that's why we've got the First Amendment. And I think the American people are probably spending a little more time worrying about what's happening with the banking system and the housing market, and what's happening in Iraq and Afghanistan, than a cartoon. So I haven't spent a lot of time thinking about it. ("Interview with," 2008, para. 11)

Stewart attacked the Obama campaign for their response to the cartoon and attacked the media for the way that they covered the story. While this was not unexpected for a satirical news program, or even interesting for that matter, what political communication scholars were concerned about was whether or not it had an effect on the political rhetoric of others.

As the aforementioned example illustrates, the Obama campaign's message changed slightly as the day progressed. One doubts that the Obama campaign saw what Stewart said earlier in the day. *The Daily Show* taped its show at 5pm Eastern (aired it at 11pm Eastern) and *Larry King Live* taped its show at 9pm Eastern. It isn't likely that the campaign saw or heard about Stewart's jokes, but that doesn't mean they didn't think about what the jokes might have been. This is the difficulty of researching political comedy and its effects. We know that political comedy plays a role in our understanding of politics, but we don't know how much of a role it plays or how it works. There is much to be learned about humor used in a political environment. Since 2000, there have been a plethora of studies on political humor. While the theories that explain why something is funny have stood the test of time (relief theory, superiority theory, and incongruity theory), there have not been many studies on how humor is used as rhetoric (Critchley, 2002; Meyer, 2000). This book attempts to fill that gap.

To be sure, Jon Stewart is an entertainer first. But it is also clear that Stewart is engaging in more than entertainment. He is carrying out an argument as well. This chapter considers how Stewart uses comedy as a form of argument. Relying on the theoretical work of Meyer (2000) and Booth (1974), close-textual analysis was employed to examine the comedy of *The Daily Show with Jon Stewart* and explain how Stewart's jokes become potent rhetorical arguments. The study resulted in four distinct benefits of satire as political arguments.

BACKGROUND, THEORY, AND METHOD

Political comedy is an atypical form of political communication. Usually, we get our political information from televised news, newspapers, family, friends, as well as the more traditionally studied forms of political communication such as advertising, debates, speeches, and websites. Neuman, Just and Crigler (1992) suggested that all the information we gather from these sources is dropped into a "pool" that we draw on when making political decisions or arguments called a political cognition. With that said, it is not just the usual sources of information, mentioned above, that feed our political cognition. Information from soft or entertainment media falls into that "pool" of knowledge as well. Thus, it is important to closely examine the rhetoric of shows such as *The Daily Show* in order to see how they function rhetorically. The best way to do that is through close textual analysis.

Close textual analysis "seeks to study the relationship between the inner workings of public discourse and its historical context in order to discover what makes a particular text function persuasively" (Burgchardt, 2000, p. 545). This calls for the audience to look at Stewart's show as something more than entertainment. Leff (1986) noted that close textual analysis focuses on the rhetorical action within a text, what the words *do*. What Stewart's words *do* is argue. Baym (2005) maintained that "*The Daily Show* can be understood as an experiment in the journalistic, one that . . . has as much to teach us about the possibilities of political journalism" (p. 261). *The Daily Show* is not fake news; it is alternative news. Stewart's rhetoric offers this alternative by reinterpreting the news he is "reporting." However, before an analysis of *The Daily Show* as argument can be complete, an accounting of how humor works rhetorically must be done.

Meyer (2000) noted that the three main theories of humor origin (superiority theory, relief theory and incongruity theory) only explain why something is funny and do not help rhetorical critics when they try to understand what a humorist is trying to do persuasively with his or her humor. Meyer (2000) contended that each theory of humor origin seems "especially fitted to specific situations" (p. 316). This observation led Meyer to view these theories of humor origin in rhetorical contexts. He extrapolated from those "specific situations" to four unique rhetorical functions of humor: identification, clarification, enforcement and differentiation (Meyer, 2000).

Using humor to demonstrate how the speaker and the audience are alike is the identification function of humor (Meyer, 2000). We might do this when we joke about how we are stupid because we mistakenly said one thing when we meant another. We make the joke because we are relieving the embarrassment of the moment, but it is also something that everyone has done at some point in their life, so the audience can identify with the embarrassment. The clarification function of humor works slightly differently. Here, the humorist uses the joke to sum up his or her points or to simplify and shed light on the speaker's views (Meyer, 2000). A quote widely attributed to Mark Twain demonstrates this rhetorical function of humor:

> When I was a boy of fourteen, my father was so ignorant I could hardly stand to have the old man around. But when I got to be twenty-one, I was astonished at how much the old man had learned in seven years (Schmidt, 1997).

While also being funny, the Twain quote clarified the point that we don't appreciate the wisdom of our fathers until we are older.

The clarification and identification functions work to rhetorically unify the audience. That is, when we use humor in these ways, we are seeking to bring the audience together as a whole by either making sure that everyone understands what is being said or to show how the speaker and everyone in the audience are alike.

The enforcement and differentiation functions of humor work in the opposite manner. Enforcement works by using humor to gently level criticism at an individual to impose social norms (Meyer, 2000). An example of this might be a professor who says "Thank you for joining us today," to a student who walks in late to class. The sarcastic comment is funny to the rest of the class, but not so much for the student who walked in late. Also, there is no doubt in anyone's mind that the professor is sending a message to the late student (and every other student, for that matter) not to be late again. The differentiation function goes further. Here, the rhetor uses humor to contrast his or her views with that of his or her opponent or an out-group (Meyer, 2000). Racist or sexist jokes can perform this rhetorical function. They rhetorically (and sometimes literally) cast out the out-group by ridiculing them.

The differentiation and enforcement functions work rhetorically to divide the audience. They use humor to separate the butt of the joke from the speaker and his or her audience (at least a portion of the audience). These four functions fall along a continuum, seen in figure 4.1.

Those jokes which function rhetorically as identification and clarification (the unifying end of the spectrum) focus on the normality of the situation. Jokes that use the enforcement and differentiation functions of humor focus on the incongruity of the situation.

CAN HUMOR BE AN ARGUMENT?

Looking at the humor of Jon Stewart on *The Daily Show*, humor is rarely used to unify the audience. More often than not, the humor of *The Daily*

Figure 4.1.

Show is divisive. Take, for example, Stewart's outlook on the "outrage" of members of Congress on both sides of the aisle conjured up during the Eric Massa scandal. Rep. Eric Massa (D-NY) had been accused of groping male staffers and using sexually suggestive language, which would constitute sexual harassment. In fact, Massa stated in "interviews on CNN and the Fox News Channel [that] he groped a staffer and 'tickled him until he couldn't breathe' as part of his fiftieth birthday celebration, then recanted in the next interview and said he never groped anyone" (Leonnig, 2010, p. A2). As one can imagine, House Republicans called for an investigation, Massa's resignation and more. This led Stewart to show a clip of House Minority John Boehner who stated in an interview: "There are a lot of people, including some of the leaders on the Democrat side, who were, in fact, informed of this. . . . Then they should suffer the consequences" (Bodow and O'Neill, 2010b). The camera then came back to Stewart, who mentioned that "Boehner's ethical stand would carry slightly more weight" if he had not contradicted his own position in the Mark Foley sexting scandal in which the Democrats were accusing then Speaker Denny Hastert (R–IL) of ignoring the problem for political reasons. Stewart then showed a clip of Boehner to expose his hypocrisy:

> [Video of Boehner from October 17, 2006] The Speaker is a wonderful guy . . . Denny Hastert and I have been friends for 16 years. He has done a marvelous job leading House Republicans. . . . It is pretty clear to me that the Speaker had no knowledge of these instant messages (Bodow and O'Neill, 2010b).

Stewart then explained that Hastert did, in fact, know about Rep. Mark Foley's (R-FL) exceedingly sexual texts to male congressional pages. Stewart also noted how this angered Nancy Pelosi (Bodow and O'Neill, 2010b). The Democrats were "outraged" in the same way that Republicans were during the Massa scandal. They also called for investigations, resignations, etc. The show then cut to a clip of Pelosi from October 3, 2006 when she said:

> They just don't get it. . . . They are so out of touch with the American people that they didn't know it was wrong to ignore the repulsive behavior of one of their members; a member of Congress who should be held to a higher ethical standard.

Stewart then went on to skewer Pelosi using the same language he had when taking Boehner to task: "Of course, Pelosi's ethical stand would carry slightly more ethical weight" if she had not later gone on to make politically motivated excuses for "Congressman Grabass J. Ticklington [Eric Massa]" a member or her own party.

[Cut to video of Nancy Pelosi being interviewed on March 4, 2010] There had been a rumor, uhh, but just that. No formal notification to our office . . . They did not report to me, because, you know what, this is rumor city (Bodow and O'Neill, 2010b).

In this clip, Stewart had no intention of unifying his audience with John Boehner or Nancy Pelosi. He was most definitely being divisive. Stewart went past enforcement and engaged in differentiation. When Stewart pointed out that both Pelosi's and Boehner's "ethical stand would carry slightly more weight," he was punishing and trying to ostracize them for their hypocrisy presented in the form of manufactured outrage and lack of action (Bodow and O'Neill, 2010b). Stewart argued that both Boehner's and Pelosi's ethical positions were bankrupt. Of course, this is the nature of satire and *The Daily Show* is a satirical news show. Thus, an understanding of satire, and of Stewart by extension, requires an understanding of irony.

HOW DOES THE HUMOROUS ARGUMENT WORK RHETORICALLY?

We need to begin the examination of the rhetorical use of humorous argument by understanding the nature of satire. "I would suggest that true satire demands a high degree of both commitment to, and involvement with, the painful problems world, and simultaneously a high degree of abstraction from the world" (Hodgart, 1969, p. 11). Feinberg (1967) is in agreement:

> It is generally assumed that satire appeals primarily to the intellect. But the mechanism of satire is not that simple. The intellect seeks order. But the basic technique of satire is distortion, usually in the form of exaggeration, understatement and pretense; and distortion implies disorder (p. 4).

This disorder is due largely to irony. "[T]he 'chief device' of satire is irony" argued Morner and Rausch (cited in Gring-Pemble and Watson, 2003, p. 137). Booth (1974) wrote the seminal piece on irony and laid out the foundation of how irony works and how the audience participates in irony. First, the audience must reject the literal meaning of the ironist's discourse. After the audience has done this, the second step is to try out alternate explanations, all of which will be incongruent with the literal meaning. Once the audience has developed alternative explanations, the audience must decide about the author's knowledge or beliefs. This is the third, and most critical, step. The audience cannot determine if the author's statement is ironic unless they determine that the author wanted them to reject the face value of the statement. Only then can a statement be recognized as irony. Once a statement is recognized as irony, new meaning can be constructed by the audience (the fourth step) based on the alternate explanations developed in the second step.

Tindale and Gough (1987) went further than Booth (1974) and discussed the audience as a whole rather than just the individual's reading of satire. They built on Kaufer's (1977) ideas on how irony bifurcates the audience into two groups: confederates and victims. The confederates are those who go through the four steps Booth described. Victims are those who cannot, or will not, reject the literal meaning of the statement as explained in step one of Booth's process.

The confederates understand the irony because of the tone of the humorous argument. Here, tone does not just mean the timbre of Stewart's voice, but also the tenor of the content. Tone foregrounds the incongruity which makes the statement funny. There has to be a relationship between the satirist and the confederates of the audience. Good satirists, like Stewart, are keenly aware of their audiences. They rely on the tone of their argument and "certain accepted norms and we [the confederate audience] recognize the irony by assessing his statements against these norms within the context of the argument" (Tindale and Gough, 1987, p. 9). The confederates that make up the target audience are a self-selecting group. They actively listen or watch the show paying careful attention to the context and reading the satiric rhetoric for clues. They have to. The jokes aren't nearly as funny without careful attention to the details of the context. Stewart relies on the context to make the jokes more entertaining. Because the arguments are enthymematic, they require more from the audience. A basic knowledge of current events and the political landscape are a necessity in order to fully appreciate the jokes. The audience cannot half-heartedly watch satire and fully comprehend the message. The confederate members of the audience are focused and actively participating in the argument.

Take, for example, *The Daily Show's* coverage of the blizzard of February 2010 (Bodow and O'Neill, 2010a). Booth's (1974) first step in understanding irony is that the audience needs to appreciate that what the rhetor says is not meant literally. During the segment, Stewart quite subtly noted "while cable news takes their weather coverage very seriously, perhaps more seriously than anything else they cover, it's easy to forget that these snow storms bring joy to two types of people; children and global warming deniers" (Bodow and O'Neill, 2010a). This statement was followed by four FOX News video clips which asserted, based on the cold and snowy weather, that any talk about global warming is ridiculous. Stewart quickly took a jab at cable news in general by noting how seriously they take their weather coverage. Stewart implied that weather, a daily event that is relatively benign on most days, gets a lot of resources dedicated to it, whereas actual news events get slighted. This was the first clue that Stewart gave to let the audience know that what was about to follow should not be taken seriously. Stewart then sets up the bit with a quick and subtle joke, mocking global warming deniers. This portion of the humor was understated in comparison to what would follow. At this point, the audience has been divided into confederates and victims. Granted, if they are watching the show, most were likely to be confederates, those that "get it." At this point, most of the audience has recognized that they cannot take what Stewart and company are saying at face value.

Just in case there were some victims still watching, Stewart then turns to his correspondents and furthers the satire by referring to them as "the best fucking weather team on the planet" (Bodow and O'Neill, 2010a). This was a jab at CNN, which consistently referred to its staff of reporters as the best political team on TV. Booth's first step calls on the audience to view the rhetoric with some suspicion, recognizing that it shouldn't be taken at face value. At this point, after dropping the phrase "the best fucking weather team on the planet," there may be some who still have not recognized the irony. Stewart continued by throwing it to Aasif Mandvi, the Senior Meteorologist (for the purposes of this segment), who was standing outside the studio in the falling snow. Mandvi then noted that there has been much press about global warming and the horrible effects that will follow as a result, including rising ocean levels. Mandvi then looked up, and in a calm voice "refuted" global warming claims by stating, "Well, today, that lie stands exposed with evidence that any child can understand. I give you frozen water, falling from the sky" (Bodow and O'Neill, 2010a). Mandvi's analysis began to set up the *reductio ad absurdum* (the reduction of the opposing argument to its most absurd point) of the bit. Stewart asked if Mandvi is perhaps premature in his conclusion from such a small amount of data. Mandvi then replied that he had data and presented a graph showing that the average New York City temperature over the previous seven months. The graph, in fact, showed a cooling trend in the average temperature from August of 2009 to February of 2010, something anyone who understands the change of seasons would expect.

Soon after, another Senior Meteorologist, Samantha Bee interrupted. She was supposedly reporting from a beach in Byron Bay, Australia. She disagreed with Mandvi and argued "Global warming is real because I am hot. . . . It hit 90 degrees today, in February" (Bodow and O'Neill, 2010a). Stewart pointed out that it is summer in Australia, to which Bee noted that the temperature for the next few days was expected to rise one or two degrees each day. This led her to conclude that the temperature would reach a staggering 120 degrees by the end of the week. Then, the back and forth between Stewart and his correspondents eventually devolved into a shouting match between Mandvi and Bee.

Finally, the third Senior Meteorologist, Jason Jones interrupted the shouting of Bee and Mandvi by screaming. Stewart quickly turned to him and asked if he was okay. Jones stated that the sun had disappeared and a "not-as-bright sun" (the moon) had come up in its place. For Jones, this was proof of "global darkening" (Bodow and O'Neill, 2010a). Mandvi then screamed, in a panicked voice, that it is dark where he is too. Bee then, engaging in a non-sequitur, screamed a line from the movie *A Cry in the Dark*: "A dingo took my baby! That means that dingoes will take every baby" (Bodow and O'Neill, 2010a). The segment ended with all three correspondents shrieking in panic.

The ridiculousness of these reports caused us to look for an alternative interpretation, Booth's (1974) second step. While there may be a few interpretations, including one that would take what Stewart and company said at face value, the most obvious is that Stewart and the correspondents are engaging in *reductio ad absurdum*, or reducing FOX's argument about global warming to its most absurd point. Stewart, Mandvi, Bee and Jones together performed an argument which stated that FOX News had committed a hasty generalization fallacy. Mandvi, Bee and Jones played the part of the reactionary and hysterical correspondents, which satirizes, in this case, FOX News. Stewart played the role of the voice of reason, which the correspondents ignored.

The Daily Show sets up their rebuttal by giving evidence that FOX News argued that global warming must not be occurring or real because the East Coast was experiencing a massive snow storm at the time. Mandvi, the first correspondent to "report," echoed the conclusion FOX made by standing outside in the snow and stating "today that lie [global warming] stands exposed with evidence that any child can understand. I give you frozen water, falling from the sky" (Bodow and O'Neill, 2010a). This made the fallacious FOX argument look even simpler (and less convincing). Bee entered the conversation and "reported" that in Australia (where she was) it was getting warmer every day, something one would expect during the summer, so global warming must be true. Finally, Jones "reports" that it just got dark where he is, so "global darkening" must be occurring. As the performance moved from correspondent to correspondent, the hasty generalization fallacy becomes more and more apparent in each of the reporter's reasoning. The story ended with the most ridiculous hasty generalization from Bee when she stated "A dingo took my baby! That means that dingoes will take every baby" (Bodow and O'Neill, 2010a). Rather than point out the fallacy and make a serious counter-argument, *The Daily Show* chose to mock FOX News' position by using its own logic against it and making FOX News look absurd.

Booth's (1974) third step occurred when the audience recognizes that Stewart and his correspondents are not really making arguments about global warming, global cooling or global darkening. Booth's fourth step, the construction of a new meaning, was built after the audience recognized that *The*

Daily Show was reducing FOX's position to the absurd and seeing Stewart as really taking the opposite position.

Looking at the categories Meyer (2000) laid out, we can see how Stewart's humor functioned. With the clear knowledge that this was satire and irony, we know that Stewart's position was the opposite of what he actually said. Primarily, Stewart relied on the superiority theory of humor, demonstrating how his position was better by ridiculing the opposing side. Rhetorically, then, Stewart's humor fulfilled an enforcement function according to Meyer's (2000) typology. The social norms that Stewart and his correspondents were trying to get FOX News to adhere to are those where we expect people to argue with a certain level of intellectual honesty. Stewart and his correspondents were leveling criticism by pointing out the ridiculousness of FOX's assertions that the big snow storm of 2010 is evidence that global warming is a hoax.

Remarks such as this should also be read as differentiation. Stewart did this enthymematically, since his position is never stated, yet clearly understood. While he ridiculed FOX's position on global warming, he also separated himself from that position by enacting FOX's logic on a simpler level. Stewart differentiated himself (and the audience that is with him) from the FOX News Channel. Fundamentally, then, what Stewart did was use humor divisively: to separate himself, and those who think like he does (the confederates in the audience), by mocking the opposition and claiming a superior position. This is congregation by segregation and is how the humorous argument works rhetorically.

WHAT MAKES THE HUMOROUS ARGUMENT POTENT?

With an explanation of how the irony and satire of Stewart basically function, an examination of how irony and satire work with a particular audience is in order. Perelman (1982) contended that the goal of argumentation is to get the audience to accept the conclusion in the same way that they accept the premises that lead to the conclusion. Perelman (1982) continued by saying "the speaker should depart from his premises only when he knows that they are adequately accepted; if they are not, the speaker's first concern should be to reinforce them with all the means at his disposal" (p. 21). For Stewart, irony and satire are the means at his disposal.

Perelman argued that all argument begins with agreement, or what he called communion. Perelman (1982) then stated it was important to "distinguish between those [points of communion] which bear upon *reality*. . . from those that bear on the *preferable*" (p. 23). Arguments that start with points of communion which bear on reality seek to establish an "ontological certainty," an objectivity, from which to launch the argument. This cannot be the case with satire. Satire does not demand, nor does it seek, objectivity. "Satire jars us out of complacence into a pleasantly shocked realization that many of the values we unquestioningly accept are false" (Feinberg, 1967, p. 15–16). The idea of finding a point of communion that bears on the preferable is not to find an "ontological certainty" from which to launch an argument, but rather a rallying point, a value, for a particular audience. Values "break with indifference or with the equality of things, wherever one thing must be put before or above another, wherever a thing is judged superior and its merit is to be preferred" (Perelman, 1982, p. 26). This is where satirists begin. Cuddon (1998) maintained:

> The satirist is thus a kind of self-appointed guardian of standards, ideals and truth; of moral as well as aesthetic values. He is a man (women satirists are *very* rare) [sic] who takes it upon himself to correct, censure and ridicule the follies and vices of society and thus to bring contempt and derision upon aberrations from a desirable and civilized norm (cited in Gring-Pemble and Watson, 2003, p. 131).

Also relying on Perelman as a theoretical base, Crosswhite (1989) pointed out that discourse that aims at a particular audience seeks persuasion (not conviction), seeks effectiveness (not validity), and seeks adherence to a value (not a fact). Thus, those who participate in the argument are a self-selecting group. While people may tune in to watch *The Daily Show* for entertainment purposes, they are also exposing themselves to argument. When they hear a joke or satiric line embracing a value they hold, the rallying point (the point of communion) from which Stewart launches his argument, they then join the particular audience that Stewart aims at four nights a week, an audience primarily made up of confederates. This occurred, for example, when Stewart impersonated Glenn Beck in a couple of shows.[3] Clearly Stewart was not worried about validity or fact while he impersonated Beck, but the impersonation upheld the values of the audience while simultaneously mocking the opposing side. This created a crack through which persuasion may enter. What makes the humorous argument potent is its reliance on common values between the arguer and the audience. This makes the argument potent only to those audiences with values similar to Stewart's. This study, however, is not concerned with whether or not persuasion occurred, but rather with how great the appeal was. There are those who would argue that satire is a weak form of argument.

WHAT ARE THE STRENGTHS OF HUMOR
AS AN ARGUMENT?

Gring-Pemble and Watson (2003) noted that there are three main weaknesses of irony and satire as argument. First, satire and irony are "inherently and inescapably polyvalent," thus potentially leading viewers to alternate readings outside of Stewart's (p. 146). Second, because viewers may have alternate readings, this eliminates any prescriptive element the argument may have. Finally, satire and irony have "a tendency toward *reductio ad absurdum*, which may encourage some readers to accept moderate forms" of what is being ridiculed (p. 147). None of these statements are disagreeable; after all, Brockriede (1975) maintained "[h]uman activity does not usefully constitute an argument until some person perceives what is happening as an argument" (p. 179). However, Gring-Pemble and Watson (2003) have limited humor unnecessarily.

Humor in general, and satire in particular, have four definite strengths as a form of argument. First, satire gives an argument presence. Presence is "the displaying of certain elements on which the speaker wishes to center attention in order that they may occupy the foreground of the hearer's consciousness" (Perelman and Olbrechts-Tyteca, 1969, p. 142). Satire presents the familiar in a new form. "Presence acts directly upon our sensibility" (Perelman and Olbrechts-Tyteca, 1969, p. 35). When it does that, it gives us a fresh outlook, thus pushing the issue, and the particular argument, to the forefront of our minds. Take, for example, Stewart's coverage/criticism of CNN on the night of October 12, 2009 (Bodow and O'Neill, 2009). After poking at CNN for fact checking a *Saturday Night Live* sketch, Stewart acknowledged that fact checking is one of the services news program are supposed to provide. Stewart then noted:

> Arizona Republican Senator Jon Kyl tried to sneak a whopper past John King. Watch:
>
> [Video of Jon Kyl on CNN, Kyl talking] "Almost everyone agrees that we could save between 100 billion and 200 billion dollars if we had effective medical malpractice reform."
>
> [Stewart talking again] Holy one to two hundred billion dollars just for malpractice reform? That is an impressively high, citation free, completely made up number! (Bodow and O'Neill, 2009)

Stewart took the video out of the smaller context in which it was originally seen (on CNN) and placed it in a broader context for us to view it and pointed out the obvious error by Kyl in much the same way a public speaking professor would chastise a student who had forgotten to cite his or her sources. This made the "slip" by Kyl stand at the forefront of our minds, thus boosting Stewart's overall claim about the lack of accountability of politicians and the press.

The second strength of satire as argument is catharsis for the audience member. A straightforward argument against the establishment can build anger and tension in an audience that subscribes to the same value system, developing a sense of being wronged. An ironic and satirical argument, if presented adeptly, can stir the audience. It can stoke the fire of anger, but at the same time, it can release the pressure. As for satire:

> The chief effect of satire is pleasure. That pleasure may consist of relief from dullness. . . . Or, in Freud's view, it may be relief from authority. Satire offers the consolation of superiority, which is useful even if it is ephemeral; for many people even a momentary feeling of superiority is rare. Satire may also provide a fresh perspective, detachment, or balance. But essentially it offers aesthetic pleasure (Feinberg, 1967, p. 261).

Satire gives the audience a sense of satisfaction, a release. For the confederate audience member there is a sense of relief that someone in public life "gets" their frustration with the status quo, with the current state of affairs. Continuing with the example of Senator Jon Kyl on CNN, Stewart played several clips of Kyl rattling off numbers without any citations. *The Daily Show* then played a clip from the end of the interview: [John King in studio]"We will talk more about this as it reaches the floor, I assure you. We are out of time on this day . . . " (Bodow and O'Neill, 2009). Stewart responded by yelling and cursing at John King. He then calmed down and thought out loud that perhaps King wanted the Congressional Budget Office (CBO) report before he accused Kyl of lying or, at the very least, ill informed. Stewart pointed out that the CBO report said that:

> malpractice savings would only amount to 11 billion dollars, even over a ten year period it's still only 54 billion off the deficit . . . I'm sure after the report came out they had a huge fact-check segment on the [pause by Stewart, puts finger to ear as if someone in the control room is talking to him] . . . I'm being told they did not (Bodow and O'Neill, 2009).

While making his point, Stewart yelled at Kyl and King after the video of them played, thus expressing our anger (as well as his) as a part of the confederate audience. Stewart did this particularly well later in that segment after another anchor refused to check another guest's numbers. The anchor ended the segment by stating "Let's leave it there" (Bodow and O'Neill, 2009). Stewart responded by yelling into the camera, begging the anchors to do their job as members of the fourth estate. *The Daily Show* then showed nine clips of various CNN anchors saying "Let's leave it there" in quick succession. "Aaaaaauuuughhhhh!" Stewart screamed and tore apart his notes, "You have twenty-four hours in a day! How much more time do you need!?" (Bodow and O'Neill, 2009). As Stewart vented his anger, he effectively vented our anger as well. Since we "get it," it was a relief for the confederates to know that we are not the only ones who have noticed that the emperor is not wearing any clothes.

The third advantage, the potency of the arguments, develops out of this notion of catharsis. For the self-selecting audience that tunes in to *The Daily Show*, these arguments are very powerful. They ring true with the audience. These arguments fit into the audience's belief and value systems. In this particular case, the audience starts from the same place, the same values, that Stewart did. Winick (1976) argued:

> [J]okes are told by a teller to an audience that is perceived as being equal to the teller. They reflect special appeals of socioeconomic status, age, gender, ethnicity, and other subgroup differentiators. The nuances of speech and intonation, which are so important in jokes are very in-group related (p. 126).

As Stewart scolded King and Kyl (in this particular case) and differentiated his position from their behavior satirically, he simultaneously identified with his audience of confederates. The way that Stewart has presented the issue, he would have you believe that the confederate audience are among, if not the intellectually elite, at least the intellectually honest.

Lastly, this form of argument does have a persuasive effect beyond the confederates. When we hear a good joke, we usually want to tell someone else about it. Thus, the self-selecting audience has the potential to grow. Young (2008) noted that the "audience for satirical sketches and stand-up, rehashed incessantly via YouTube, parallels Rush Limbaugh and Sean Hannity radio listenership put together" (para. 2). That is to say the audience could grow to those who do not regularly watch *The Daily Show*. The confederates of the regularly watching audience are "evangelizing" to other potential confederates. Young (2008), however, goes further:

> But when you have the technology to shoot it repeatedly throughout the cybersphere and into every office and home over and over just in case you missed it the first time, you find not only that the king has no clothes, but also that the obscene-yet-hilarious image is imbedded in your mind forever (para. 4).

So, the audience has great potential to grow beyond those who self-select and watch the show during its first airing. Moreover, assuming that people forward video clips from Stewart to other like-minded people who have similar latitudes of acceptance and non-committal, social judgment theory further explains the persuasiveness of the satire (Sherif, Sherif and Nebergall, 1965).

In sum, humorous arguments have several strengths. First, and foremost, is the unique presence a humorous argument creates in the mind of the audience. Second, a humorous argument helps the particular audience with an emotional release (catharsis), giving them the opportunity to vent their frustration. Third, these arguments are based on the common values between the arguer and audience, which allow the catharsis to occur. Finally, the nature of humor creates a desire to share what we find funny with others. That means that the potential audience can grow beyond the self-selecting group that tunes into the show thanks to modern technology.

WHAT ARE THE POTENTIAL EFFECTS OF HUMOROUS ARGUMENTS?

Given that most Americans' ego-involvement in politics isn't very high (with the exception of those people on the extreme right- and left-wing of American politics), then social judgment theory would contend that these people would have decent sized latitudes of non-commitment and latitudes of acceptance due to their low levels of ego-involvement with politics (Sherif, Sherif and Nebergall, 1965). If that is the case, a humorous argument would likely fall into the latitude of acceptance (or maybe into the latitude of non-commitment) of the audience member. The audience member would perceive the argument to be closer to his or her anchor position than it really is, thus allowing assimilation to occur. Plus, there are some audience members who will come back and watch other bits or have those bits sent to them via e-mail. While persuasion wouldn't occur with just one bit or sketch, the forwarding of clips from friends, the appearance of clips on blogs and other news shows will place the humorous argument into the political cognition of these more passive viewers. Because the clip (the argument) is humorous, it will be remembered and at the forefront of people's minds. The fact that it is funny is what gives it what Perelman (1982) called presence. It is a more subtle method of persuasion than traditional argument, to be sure, but it is persuasion nonetheless. This means that a person's opinion could be slowly changed over time with a well-directed campaign of incremental position change. Watched on a daily basis, as Stewart often is, this could lead to some real effects. During the presidential campaign, Young (2008) elaborated:

> Think the state of the economy has helped Obama? Try Tina Fey. Attempt to find one person who hasn't caught a glimpse of the Sarah Palin look-alike's weekly hilarious and spot-on parody of the Republican vice presidential nominee. Viral? It's become a fatal epidemic for the McCain campaign that's all but infected any possibility of credibility that might have been harvested from Palin's selection. Impact?

Try election-changing— why do you think Palin showed up on *SNL*? (para. 5, 6 and 7)

This attitude is precisely why rhetoricians and scholars of political communication are fascinated with satirical shows like *The Daily Show*.

CONCLUSION

2008 may have been the first election in which we have seen the full potential of satire in effect, though it is difficult to say. Neuman, Just and Crigler (1992) maintained that we each develop a political cognition and we draw on that information when making arguments and decisions. The sleeper effect frequently occurs. We separate the content of the information and the source of the information in our mind. So we may inadvertently draw on humor when making a political argument or decision. Thus, the potential for satire to affect our political behavior is real.

What is evident from the exploration of the current research on satire and Jon Stewart is that satire is argumentative. It is an enthymematic form of argument which requires audience participation. Satire's rhetorical functions include enforcement and differentiation, making satire a divisive form of argument.

The effects of political humor are no joke and they are something that we should take seriously. The audience of *The Daily Show* is required to deconstruct the statement and then reconstruct (see Booth, 1974) its meaning. The members of the audience are confederates; they feel like they are "in the club." They get it. They are superior to those who do not get it. Thus, Gring-Pemble and Watson (2003) are right in that irony and satire are difficult methods of argument to use when arguing and appealing to the masses. Assuming that his audience holds similar values to Stewart (or close enough), social judgment theory maintains that incremental persuasion (assimilation) can occur. This would gently move people, making humor a persuasive force in our political process. However, those that convert because of the satirical argument must have a similar mindset or value system to Stewart's and the rest of *The Daily Show* team. Certainly, the show engages in indirect forms of argument. Even though the arguments are indirect, they have what Perelman called "presence," and that makes them enlightening. Thus, *The Daily Show with Jon Stewart* is full of moments of Zen.

NOTES

1. The cartoon can be seen at http://www.newyorker.com/online/covers/slideshow_blittcovers#slide=1.
2. The word "fucking" was bleeped out of the episode. Subsequent uses of the term quoted in this essay were also bleeped.
3. A couple of clips can be found at http://www.thedailyshow.com/watch/thu-november-5-2009/the-11-3-project and at http://www.thedailyshow.com/watch/thu-march-18-2010/conservative-libertarian.

REFERENCES

Baym, G. (2005). The Daily Show: Discursive integration and the reinvention of political journalism. *Political Communication, 22,* 259–276.

Bodow, S. (Head Writer), and O'Neill, C. (Director). (2008, July 15). [Television series episode]. In J. Stewart (Executive producer), *The Daily Show with Jon Stewart.* New York: Comedy Central.

———. (2009, October 12). [Television series episode]. In J. Stewart (Executive producer), *The Daily Show with Jon Stewart.* New York: Comedy Central.

———. (2010a, February 10). [Television series episode]. In J. Stewart (Executive producer), *The Daily Show with Jon Stewart.* New York: Comedy Central.

———. (2010b, March 15). [Television series episode]. In J. Stewart (Executive producer), *The Daily Show with Jon Stewart.* New York: Comedy Central.

Booth, W.C. (1974). *A rhetoric of irony.* Chicago, IL: The University of Chicago Press.

Brockriede, W. (1975). Where is argument? *Journal of the American Forensic Association, 9,* 179–182.

Burgchardt, C.R., (Ed.). (2000). *Readings in rhetorical criticism* (2nd ed.). State College, PA: Strata Publishing.

Critchley, S. (2002). *On humour.* London, England: Routledge.

Crosswhite, J. (1989). Universality in rhetoric: Perelman's universal audience. *Philosophy and Rhetoric, 22,* 157–173.

Feinberg, L. (1967). *Introduction to satire.* Ames, IA: The Iowa State University Press.

Gring-Pemble, L., and Watson, M.S. (2003). The rhetorical limits of satire: An analysis of James Finn Garner's Politically Correct Bedtime Stories *Quarterly Journal of Speech, 89,* 132–153.

Hodgart, M. (1969). *Satire.* New York, NY: McGraw-Hill Book Company.

"Interview with Sen. Barack Obama" (2008, 15 July). Transcript, *Larry King Live.* Retrieved 11 August 2008 from http://transcripts.cnn.com/TRANSCRIPTS/0807/15/lkl.01.html.

Kaufer, D. (1977). Irony and rhetorical strategy. *Philosophy and Rhetoric, 10,* 90–110.

Leff, M. (1986). Textual criticism: The legacy of G.P. Mohrmann. *Quarterly Journal of Speech, 72,* 377–389.

Leonnig, C.M. (2010, 11 March). Pelosi's office was told of concerns about Massa; Ex-congressman's chief of staff relayed his worries in October. [Electronic version]*Washington Post.* Found online on Lexis-Nexis.

Malcolm, A. (2008, 16 July). Barack Obama tries to repair a PR blunder, but 2 days too late. Retrieved from http://latimesblogs.latimes.com/washington/2008/07/obama-muslim-1.html.

Meyer, J.C. (2000). Humor as a double-edged sword: Four functions of humor in communication. *Communication Theory, 10,* 310–331.

Neuman, W.R., Just, M.R., and Crigler, A.N. (1992). *Common knowledge: News and the construction of political meaning.* Chicago, IL: The University of Chicago Press.

Perelman, C. (1982). *The realm of rhetoric* (W. Kluback, Trans.). Notre Dame, IN: University of Notre Dame Press. (Original work published in 1977.)

John W. Self

Perelman, C. and Olbrechts-Tyteca, L. (1969). *The new rhetoric: A treatise on argumentation* (J. Wilkinson and P. Weaver, Trans.). Notre Dame, IN: University of Notre Dame Press.

Schmidt, B. (1997). Mark Twain quotations, newspaper collections, and related resources. Retrieved from http://www.twainquotes.com/Father.html.

Sherif, C.W., Sherif, M. and Nebergall, R.E. (1965). *Attitude and attitude change: The social judgment-involvement approach.* Westport, CT: Greenwood Press, Publishers.

Tindale, C.W., and Gough, J. (1987). The use of irony in argumentation. *Philosophy and Rhetoric, 20*, 1–17.

Winick, C. (1976). The social contexts of humor. *Journal of Communication, 26*, 124–128.

Young, S. (2008, October 26). The farce is with them. [Electronic version]*The Philadelphia Inquirer.* Retrieved from http://www.philly.com/philly/opinion/20081026_the_farce_is_ with_them.html.

Chapter Five

Models of Democratic Deliberation: Pharmacodynamic Agonism in *The Daily Show*

Kelly Wilz

In September of 2009 amidst the stormy health care reform debate, the U.S. secret service was busy investigating an online survey that asked whether people thought President Barack Obama should be assassinated. The poll, posted on Facebook, asked respondents, "Should Obama be killed?" The choices were: "No, Maybe, Yes, and Yes if he cuts my health care" (The Guardian, 2009). During that same month, John L. Perry wrote in Newsmax "There is a remote, although gaining, possibility America's military will intervene as a last resort to resolve the 'Obama problem.' Don't dismiss it as unrealistic" (Krepel, 2009). In December of 2009, Senator Tom Coburn told seniors that if health care passed they would "die sooner." Congressman Alan Grayson referred to the Republican solution to health care as "Don't get sick. If you get sick, die quickly" (Krepel, 2009). Divisive, angry, and hyperbolic rhetoric exuded from elected officials on both sides of the aisle, from political commentators, talk show hosts, and from everyday citizens. Debates focused not on issues of policy, but on fear, who would come out safe politically, who would win, and who would lose.

Days after the health care bill was passed, at least ten Democrats reported vandalism or death threats from constituents (Bendavid and Johnson, 2010). Someone left a coffin on the lawn of Representative Russ Carnahan's home in Missouri. Glass doors and windows were broken at the district offices of Representatives Louise Slaughter of New York and Gabrielle Giffords of Arizona. Vandals damaged Democratic Party offices in Wichita, Cincinnati and Rochester, N.Y., and Representative Bart Stupak of Michigan, whose last-minute compromise on abortion funding guaranteed final passage of the bill, received a flood of abusive phone calls at his office and at his home. One voice mail was left by a woman who wanted Stupak to know that "there are millions of people across the country who wish you ill" (Robinson, 2010). A fax with the title "Defecating on Stupak" depicted an image of a gallows with "Bart (SS) Stupak" on it and a noose attached. The fax was captioned, "All Baby Killers come to unseemly ends, Either by the hand of man or by the hand of God" (Abrams, 2010). Democrats were quick to blame the rhetoric of GOP leaders for such acts, pointing to Jon Boehner who called the health care bill "Armageddon," and to Sarah Palin who posted a map with gun sights over twenty districts with Democratic House members she would like to defeat and who tweeted "Don't Retreat, Instead— RELOAD" (Abrams, 2010).

Heated political debate is nothing new, but what seems to be lacking now more than ever are models of healthy, respectful, democratic debate. While much scholarship has revealed the relationship between dehumanization and discourses of division, very few critics explore the rhetorical and symbolic process by which enemies become allies, or the day-to-day communicative processes which serve to model healthy democratic debate. I wish to analyze rehumanizing discourses and the processes by which these come into being as a way of challenging the dominant dehumanizing discourses, narratives, myths, and attitudes that have contributed to such discourses of division. Although, as theorist Kenneth Burk notes, humans are continuously at odds with one another, rarely do models of discourse deal with how to work within this division to create identification between people. First, I will look to Friedrich Nietzsche's discussion of metaphor and tropes of similitude, or what he deems the process of "taming opposites" through an agonistic aesthetic to explore how these dominant narratives and conventions can become initially challenged through new metaphors. Then, I will look at Kenneth Burke's metaphor of courtship to illuminate how the process of rehumanization and healthy democratic debate can occur within specific case studies, and how this entire process occurs within the visual model presented in Comedy Central's *The Daily Show*. Through a close textual analysis of an interview between Tony Snow and Jon Stewart and between William Kristol and Jon Stewart, this essay will analyze a communicative process that can serve as a model for engaged, productive, and healthy democratic debate and discussion where enemies and allies might be able to find more similarity than difference in the midst of opposing worldviews.

TAMING OPPOSITES/RESISTING THE MYTH

Friedrich Nietzsche argues that to reveal the "true narrations of our world," we must overcome the lies or myths which are conventionalized by our everyday discourse. Nietzsche is trying to articulate a response or corrective to that condition of "naturalized conventions" which guide our everyday thought processes. Nietzsche argues that if convention acts as a repressor, we need to look to dramatic moments to alter those conventions, and that to wage war against these myths or conventions is to negate the older ideal to the point of presenting it as the antithesis of all ideals.

To do this, Nietzsche looks to rhetoric. Thomas (1999) argues that Nietzsche's critique of Platonism corresponds to a revised conception of rhetoric which features "two competing views of the world: the philosophical, Platonic view, which treats the world as the reflection or appearance of abstract essences, in which language plays a secondary role; and the rhetorical view, which treats language as primary, understanding the world as that which is negotiated by and through language" (p. 1). Here, Thomas argues that within Nietzsche's texts, "rhetoric questions representation and in so doing questions the fundamental grounding of the field of problems in which philosophy appears. In this space, rhetoric threatens philosophy; it becomes philosophy's dangerous other, both tied to philosophy and a threat to it" (p. 52).

Mootz (2006) argues that "Nietzsche's rhetorical conception of critique comes through most clearly when we recognize that his writings exemplify the theoretical activity to which he refers, when we recognize that he 'rethinks philosophy *through rhetoric*'" (p. 96) Whitson and Poulokos (1993) argue that "For Nietzsche, rhetoric is not an epistemological undertaking but rather part of a greater artistic act—the act of ordering the chaos of life. This act produces signs that will function *not* as truth but as beautiful veils masking the chaos in which people live" (p. 136). To "order the chaos of life," Nietzsche's discussion of aesthetics offers a partial answer to the problem of transforming society's calcified attitudes. Ultimately the power to challenge convention comes from the rhetorically aesthetic ability to "tame opposites," or articulate similarities where there seem to be none. Within the myth that humans' state of division will necessarily make it so that any discourse of contestation will ultimately result in enemy construction, Friedrich Nietzsche's conception of an agonistic aesthetic as it has been appropriated by democratic theorists is a useful model that looks to conceptualize the healthy pluralism that resists reducing antagonists to enemies, and looks to articulate similarities and points of contact and convergence.

Theorists like Mouffe argue that permanence of conflict and antagonism is a central feature of radical and plural democracy and that pluralism is necessary for democracy and dissensus—conflict and contestation "diversity and disagreement—is a necessary condition of pluralism" (Schrift, 2000, p. 194). Similarly, Schaap (2006) argues that "an agonistic theory of democracy provides a critical perspective from which to discern what is at stake in the politics of reconciliation" (p. 255–77). Schrift (2000) notes that "Nietzsche acknowledges that to preserve freedom from dominance one must be committed to maintain the institution of the agon as a shared public space for open competition. It was, according to Nietzsche, through their healthy respect for competition that the Homeric Greeks were able to "escape 'that pre-Homeric abyss of a gruesome savagery of hatred and pleasure in destruction' . . . and without a healthy and respectful competition, Greek culture could only deteriorate, as evidenced by the declines of Athens and Sparta following their respective rises to unrivaled cultural hegemony" (p. 193). Here, it is evident that Nietzsche was not critical of "democracy" in and of itself. Rather, his criticism lay in our/Western culture's perversion of democracy, and he would make agonism central to democratic practice seeing that the problems with democracy and democratic institutions lie not in these institutions but in *us*. Shrift claims, "There is in fact nothing more thoroughly harmful to freedom than liberal institutions" because, as Schrift claims, in their drive to make everything equal, they [liberal institutions] undermine the will to power that is necessary for freedom to exert itself in the overcoming of resistances. Political action, therefore, requires a condition of plurality in which people with differing backgrounds, perspectives, and abilities come together: "being seen and heard by others derive their significance from the fact that everybody sees and hears from a different position. This is the meaning of public life" (Arendt, 1958, p.57).

These theorists argue that in Nietzsche, we can find arguments that promote democracy as agonistic—a democracy which embraces a contestation of experiences. Schrift argues of Nietzsche that "the virtues of a democratic subject—the virtues of 'public spirit, benevolence, consideration, industriousness, moderation, modesty, indulgence and pity'—stand in direct opposition to the virtues manifest in the masters' agonal striving. Indeed, these latter virtues (and the passions that underlie them) are seen as the greatest threat to the democratic community" (p. 229). In this sense, "a genuinely agonistic ethos presumes not merely pluralism but plurality in Arendt's sense: a diversity of (distanced) views on the same object or issue . . . action is at the heart of politics (p. 242). This type of agonistic democracy or discourse attempts to locate "Anything that serves to loosen or question norms, inspire 'resistance,' empower historically oppressed groups, or build 'more slack into the system'"(p. 242). Schrift, in analyzing Hannah Arendt's discussion on agonism, argues that "Arendt's agonism . . . focuses on public spiritedness, independent judgment, and self-distance in addition to initiatory action . . . Arendt wants to maintain a distinction between *homme* and *citoyen*. . . For it is only when differences are mediated politically, through shared institutions and shared citizenship, that they can be . . . the 'cause of liberty'" (p. 243).

Nietzsche argues that in order to understand human relations and how they function in this agonistic realm, we must realize that human relations aren't reducible to words on paper—that human relations should be viewed as symbolic reactions, and that we should engage one another through interpretive practices separating deed from doer, and by looking at our identities and political action as a constant process. Husting (2006) argues that "the enemy of political action is closure or 'constatation,' the ways that identities and aspects of the world become understood as given or unassailable" (p. 164–65). If we separate the argument from the actor and look at political action as a continual process, we avoid agonism reducing to enemy relations, which assumes condition of division and contestation, but allows for strategies to create connectivity enough to tolerate and deal with the differences. This can be understood further through Burke's metaphor of courtship.

COURTSHIP, IDENTIFICATION, AND PHARMACODYNAMIC AGONISM

Kenneth Burke proposes theories and principles for understanding symbol systems and shows how humans are inseparable from using those symbols. Burke (1989) believes that the ability to use symbols enables human beings to imagine, select, create, and define the situations to which they respond (p. 8). He then applies those same principles in criticism to explain and analyze rhetorical discourse, and shows how rhetorical analysis can illuminate both literary texts and human relations in general. He has understood rhetoric as "persuasion"; the nature of rhetoric as "addressed" to an audience for a particular purpose, rhetoric as the art of "proving opposites", rhetoric as an "appeal to prejudices"; rhetoric as "agonistic"; rhetoric as an art of gaining "advantage"; rhetoric as "demonstration"; rhetoric as the verbal counterpart of dialectic; rhetoric as opposed to dialectic; and rhetoric in a Marxist sense of persuasion as "grounded in dialectic" (Hochmuth Nichols, 1993, p. 4). But a key function of rhetoric for Burke is identification. He claims that in the simplest case of persuasion, "you persuade a man only insofar as you can talk his language by speech, gesture, tonality, order, image, attitude, idea, *identifying* your ways with his" (Burke, 1969, p. 55). He claims that "in identification lies the source of dedications and enslavements, in fact of cooperation" and that "we might well keep it in mind that a speaker persuades an audience by the use of stylistic identifications; his act of persuasion may be for the purpose of causing the audience to identify itself with the speaker's interests; and the speaker draws on identification of interests to establish rapport between himself and his audience. So there is no chance of our keeping apart the meanings of persuasion, identification ("consubstantiality"), and communication (the nature of rhetoric as "addressed") (p. 46).

Identification is the primary term for Burke because of man's state of division and the fact that humans are continuously at odds with one another. Identification, therefore, is compensatory to division. He claims, "If men were not apart from one another, there would be no need for the rhetorician to proclaim their unity. If men were wholly and truly of one substance, absolute communication would be of man's very essence" (p. 22). His solution, however, is not to strive for perfect or "pure identification;" rather he acknowledges that in (hu)man's current state, "opponents can join battle only through a mediatory ground that makes their communication possible thus providing the first condition necessary for their interchange of blows. But put identification and division ambiguously together . . . and you have the characteristic invitation to rhetoric. Here is a major reason why rhetoric, according to Aristotle, 'proves opposites'" (p. 25).

Burke discusses the productive model of the metaphor of courtship which moves us from the realm of emphasizing a discourse of "rattling the system" to one of specifically reaching (or identifying with) an audience. Here in his theory of symbolic action is a theory of human and social relations. Specifically, Burke is trying to figure out how we can construct human relations so they don't default to warring relations and offers what he deems "comic correctives" as a rhetorical response to victimization which occurs through oversimplification. Here, a "perspective by incongruity" expressed as a comic corrective takes aim at a sort of monistic thinking that fails to reveal the limits of a single form of thought to understand and experience reality (p. 23). He claims, "a new taxonomy, a new vocabulary produces an additional angle to see reality. The comic enables us to increase the use of incongruity and in this a fashion to produce new ways of seeing, to overcome the particular blindness of our accustomed usages" (p. 26). He looks at reconstructing the narratives surrounding demonizing and claims that we need to turn the source of "enemy" and "problem" into a form that can be corrected, rather than that which is deemed evil or in some other way vilified. This rhetorical transformation of evil into error is key. Courtship for Burke is a matter of trying not to default to prejudice or scapegoating, but to bring people to a higher level of consciousness.

Also, the idea of consubstantiation is key. For Burke, consubstantiation is developed as theoretical heuristic for coping with division inherent within our everyday human relations. Burke (1969) claims that "by the principle of courtship in rhetoric we mean the use of suasive devices for the transcending of social estrangement" (p. 208). The major idea for Burke is that courtship involves a sort of reciprocity, or the vulnerability of being open to being persuaded. Through this process or this model of engagement, each actor engages one another through strategies and tactics, but always the goal is a "transcending of social estrangement." Here conflict and contestation is celebrated and the actors' goal is to separate deed from doer; separate the argument from the actor to create connectivity enough to tolerate and deal with the differences. What we must do as critics, then, is uncover models of "courtship" to further explore how connectivity can be created as to reduce the tendency of discourse to reduce to enemy relations, and how constructive rhetoric can be crafted through civil discourse, which is present in Jon Stewart's interviews in *The Daily Show*.

Specifically, the cultural encounters one witnesses on *The Daily Show* model Hawhee's conception of agon as an "encounter" rather than a division between two sides or as a contest. She suggests that agon as encounter "constitutes the more pervasive agonal dynamic, a dynamic that also figures prominently in the development of rhetoric as an agonistic force . . . which produces rhetoric as a gathering of forces—cultural, bodily, and discursive, thus problematizing the easy portrayal of rhetoric as telos-driven persuasion or as a means to reach consensus" (Hawhee, 2002, p. 186) Within Hawhee's conception of the agon, it is not as though there is *no* struggle or contest whatsoever. On the contrary—Hawhee argues that in ancient Greece, athletics "made available an agonistic model for early rhetors to follow as they developed their art" (p. 187). As Mouffe (2000) argues, contestation lies at the heart of democratic deliberation: "instead of trying to erase the traces of power and exclusion, democratic politics requires us to bring them to the fore, to make them visible so that they can enter the terrain of contestation" (pp. 34–35). However, Hawhee argues that "it must be noted from the outset that the agon is more than the one-on-one sparring that is emphasized in most treatments of the topic. That is, agonism is not merely a synonym for competition" (Hawhee, 2002, p. 185). This conception of the agon also looks at how arête, or a kind of virtuosity drove agonistic encounters "as Greeks sought after the esteem of others through competitive engagement and display of their abilities, be they skill at javelin throwing or delivery of an encomium" (p. 187). She notes that in pharmacodynamic language today, the term agonism "designates the bonding of a drug chemical with what is termed a receptor . . . the agonistic bonding then triggers a change in cellular activity" (p. 194).

This metaphor is useful because it shows how agonism denotes an encounter, the production of a response, and a subsequent *change* in *both* substances. This pharmacodynamic use of agonism runs counter to the assumed and traditional conception of agonism as sparring or battle where one side "wins." As Hawhee notes,

> The productive quality of agonism delineated by Hesiod, while overshadowed in contemporary uses of the term by the destructive, "takeover" force, nevertheless still

inheres in contemporary pharmocological research, where agonism is a key concept in drug-cell relations. This relatively recent instantiation of the word is instructive, for its metaphorics actually help illustrate more precisely what I take to be Hesiod's distinctions. In pharmacodynamic language, the term agonism designates the bonding of a drug chemical with what is termed a receptor, a special area on the outer surface of the cell membrane. The agonistic bonding then triggers a change in cellular activity. In other words, agonism denotes an encounter, the production of a response, and a subsequent change in both substances (p. 194).

In this instance, the encounter encourages responses from both parties, and *both* substances are changed. There is no "winner" or "loser"; rather both are equally affected. Here, too, within this model, there are no enemies and heroes, only equal adversaries. As Mouffe (2000) argues:

> politics is always concerned with the constitution of a 'we' and this 'we' is always articulated in contrast to a 'them.' What is distinctive about democratic politics is not that it seeks to resolve this inevitable conflict between competing identities. Rather it aims to mediate the conflict in such a way that the other is perceived not as an 'enemy to be destroyed' (or excluded from the political community?) but as an 'adversary,' i.e. one with whom we disagree vehemently but whose right to contest the terms of our political association we respect (p.101).

Ivie (2002) notes that "an important question to address, then, is how to communicate politically without an exclusionary aim for consensus and unity or a reduction of difference to total otherness. That is, how can the citizens of a pluralistic polity speak from and across their differences productively in the divisive environment of agonistic politics?" (p. 278).

This structure provides a useful model for examining *The Daily Show*. Whereas shows like *Crossfire* or *Hannity and Colmes* relied on one side "beating" the other and each side remaining firm in their beliefs (thus no "substance" ever changes), Stewart, within his interactions with a variety of guests encourages responses, enters the engagement with a level of humility, and is willing to be "changed" in terms of his views. Shows like *Hannity and Colmes* and *Crossfire* represent Ivie's argument that rhetorical advocacy turns "dark and cynical only when competing perspectives and interests are ignored and suppressed rather than engaged and bridged sufficiently to muddle through the moment."*The Daily Show*, then, offers a comic corrective to these "diseases of cooperation" which can only be treated through comic values of tolerance and contemplation "by exploring how people in political communities might transcend themselves enough to observe their foibles even while acting strategically toward one another . . . with maximum consciousness by rounding out their overly narrow perspectives through verbal sparring with political adversaries" (p. 279). This is apparent within many of Stewart's interactions with guests, as he has had political figures from all ends of the spectrum on his show. In 2007 alone, Jon Stewart had interviewed such guests as: John McCain, Barack Obama, John Bolton, Mike Huckabee, Andy Card, Lynne Cheney, Joe Biden, Bill Kristol, Bill Clinton, Tony Snow, and many others in the political arena. In every interview, the debate may become heated, and Stewart is clear as to where his political beliefs lie, but he never disrespects his guests or their opinions, and sincerely listens to their arguments. Even within Stewart's seemingly liberal position, he critiques all political actors in their inability to bring this country together and attempts to speak to a broad audience, rather than just pandering to the immediate audience who attend the live show. In every encounter, Stewart embodies the sort of vulnerability and humility Burke speaks of while offering a clear model of agonistic democracy in action.

JON STEWART AS ADVOCATE FOR AGONISTIC DEMOCRACY

On October 15, 2004, Jon Stewart, the late-night host of Comedy Central's *The Daily Show*, appeared on CNN's *Crossfire* to promote *America (The Book): A Citizen's Guide to Democracy Inaction*. During the interview, Stewart criticized the state of television journalism and pleaded with the show's hosts to "stop hurting America," referring to both Tucker Carlson and co-host Paul Begala as "partisan hacks." From the beginning of the interview, Stewart challenged their need to fight with one another:

Carlson: Thank you for joining us.

Stewart: Thank you very much. That was very kind of you to say. Can I say something very quickly? Why do we have to fight?

(Laughter)

Stewart: The two of you? Can't we just—say something nice about John Kerry right now.

Carlson: I like John. I care about John Kerry.

Stewart: And something about President Bush.

Begala: He'll be unemployed soon?

(Laughter)

Begala: I failed the test. I'm sorry.

Carlson: See, I made the effort anyway.

Begala: No, actually, I knew Bush in Texas a little bit. And the truth is, he's actually a great guy. He's not a very good president. But he's actually a very good person. I don't think you should have to hate to oppose somebody, but it makes it easier.

(Laughter)

Stewart: Why do you argue, the two of you?

(Laughter)

Stewart: I hate to see it.

Carlson: We enjoy it. (CNN, 2004).

Stewart asserted that *Crossfire* had failed in its responsibility to inform and educate viewers about politics as a serious topic. He claimed, "And I made a special effort to come on the show today, because I have privately, amongst my friends and also in occasional newspapers and television shows, mentioned this show as being bad. . . . And I wanted to—I felt that that wasn't fair and I should come here and tell you that I don't—it's not so much that it's bad, as it's hurting America" (CNN, 2004). Stewart complained that the show engaged in partisan hackery instead of honest debate, and said that the hosts' assertion that *Crossfire* is a debate show is like "saying pro wrestling is a show about athletic competition" (2004). This exchange became one of the most widely viewed internet videos at that time and a topic of much media discussion (Kurtz, 2005).

In January 2005, CNN announced that it was canceling *Crossfire*. When asked about the cancellations, CNN's incoming president, Jonathan Klein, said about Stewart's appearance on the show, "I think he made a good point about the noise level of these types of shows, which does nothing to illuminate the issues of the day" (Kurtz, 2005). Launched in 1982 by Pat Buchanan and Tom Braden, *Crossfire* had a series of high-profile hosts, from liberals Michael Kinsley, Bill Press, and Geraldine Ferraro to conservatives Mary Matalin and John Sununu. Like *Crossfire*, other conservative vs. liberal debates spread across the cable spectrum, from *Hardball* to *Hannity and Colmes*, and while these shows claimed to be modeling civic democratic debate, honorably giving their viewer "both sides of the story," these shows constructed a level of discourse that most resembled a screaming match at best.

The Daily Show, on the other hand, emulates a model of democratic interaction that falls in line with Nietzsche's, Burke's, and Hawhee's conception of agonistic debate. Many cultural critics have analyzed various aspects of *The Daily Show* and its relation to communication and rhetorical studies. Studies have ranged from an analysis of the ways in which Stewart and his writers rework the rules of news and celebrity (Baym, 2007), to a discussion of how the show constructs its unique brand of masculinity (Brooten, 2007), to how Jon Stewart "jams" the transmission of dominant brand messages by parodying the news media's dissemination of the dominant brand (Warner, 2007). Many have also argued that *The Daily Show* provides critical lessons on media literacy. Trier (2008), for example, explains that *The Daily Show* uses intelligence and humor to critique mainstream media and specifically political news on mainstream media, referring to interviews in which Stewart discusses media bias, the relationship between the media and the presidential administration, and his personal role as a public figure (Trier, 2008). Michael A. Xenos and Amy B. Becker (2009) argue that programs like *The Daily Show* "facilitate the acquisition of political information from hard news sources, particularly among less politically sophisticated comedy viewers, thus serving as a gateway to political attention and knowledge" (Xenos and Becker, 2009). Smolkin and Groves (2007) even go so far as to argue that Stewart and his team often seem to steer closer to the truth than traditional journalists.

There is no doubt that Stewart has made a name for himself as cultural critic prompting Howard Kurtz (2007) to argue that news journalists are faced with graying, shrinking audiences as younger viewers flock to Stewart, "whose influence on the real newscasts is palpable" (Kurtz, 2007). But none have analyzed how specific interviews and interactions between Jon Stewart and his guests can serve as a useful model of democratic deliberation and interaction. Many of these interviews, specifically those between Jon Stewart and those with whom his views conflict (Lynne Cheney, Tony Snow, William Kristol, and others) offer an example of Burke's model of courtship and Friedrich Nietzsche and Debra Hawhee's conception of an agonistic aesthetic. Two particular agonistic encounters are of interest in this case study: an interview between Stewart and former White House Press Secretary Tony Snow in 2007 and an interview between Stewart and William Kristol in 2009.

A PHARMACODYNAMIC ENCOUNTER

On October 15, 2007, Tony Snow visited *The Daily Show* for a second time.[1] From the outset, Stewart is warm, welcoming, and one of the first things he does is compliment Snow on how great he looks, how healthy he looks, and asks how Snow is feeling (referring to Snow's battle with cancer.) Stewart actually spends a fair amount of time asking Snow about his life, his health, and his job as the White House press secretary. Visually, Snow and Stewart are always presented as on the same level. They are both shot in high key lighting, their chairs are placed the same distance from the ground, and much of the interview occurs within the frame of a long shot where both are presented together in the same view. Throughout the interview, it's a comfortable back and forth, reinforced by shot-reverse-shots which give each man equal time while explaining his position. But for the most part, the audience is presented with long shots of the two engaging each other on equal ground. Stewart then moves on to discuss Snow's departure as press secretary, noting that the pressure of the job must be incredible. Snow and Stewart then joke at the fact that Snow only left this job because he wanted more money, and Stewart thanks Snow for his candidness and honesty. Stewart then compliments Snow on his ability to do his job very well. This jovial banter is a far cry from other talk shows where people with differing opinions seem to lack any sense of commonality or humanness at all. The conversation then turns to how Snow has handled reporters in the past and the conversation turns more serious. Stewart discusses the fact that it must be difficult for the Bush administration to deal with reporters and vice versa because the administration is so "irrational." Snow smiles, sips his coffee and slyly asks, "How so?"

From here, we get a civilized debate about how the Bush administration seems to be hypocritical in the way in which they denounce partisanship, yet politicize the administration in an unusual way. Snow responds by asking Stewart to find a time when Bush was the actual one throwing mud. This is the first time we see Snow disagree with Stewart. Their debate continues, but again, it never evolves into a screaming match, and the times where they most seem to disagree, (specifically about Bush and his administration), they are able to remain civil. They even end up agreeing toward the end of the debate that there should be a plan when going to war. By the end of the debate, Stewart reaches out and enthusiastically shakes Snow's hand, remarking how fun the debate was and how much he appreciates Snow coming on. Lastly, we see Stewart commenting on how much he respects Snow as a person and how much he appreciates what Snow brings to the conversation. Overall, we are able to see two very different perspectives regarding political life and the Bush administration in a way that does not evolve into personal attacks or other dehumanizing processes.

This process of agon as encounter is repeated specifically in other interviews like those with John McCain and Lynne Cheney, where he again acknowledges respect for them and what they do, for their opinions, and the interviews never regress into verbal assaults on each other's character. This pharmacodynamic form is present in the fact that both parties encounter one another, both interact and debate, and both come out of the interaction *changed*. There are many times when Stewart *and* his opponents say, "I never thought of it that way," or "I can see your point there." Each party, with the help of Stewart's lightheartedness and wit, vulnerability and humility, is able to come into the encounter in an attempt to truly gain insight into the other party's perspective.

A more recent example of this type of encounter occurred in July of 2009 amidst the health care debate. Stewart's guest, William Kristol, discussed, amongst other things, his take on health care reform. Like the Snow interview, Kristol and Stewart are also presented on the same level, they are also both shot in high key lighting, their chairs are placed the same distance from the ground, and the majority of the interview occurs from the view of a long shot where both are presented together in the same frame. And, like the Snow interview, the audience again witnesses a comfortable back and forth, reinforced by shot-reverse-shots giving each participant equal time to explain his position.

During the first part of the interview, Stewart commends Kristol for correctly predicting that Sarah Palin would end up on the ticket with McCain. There is a jovial back and forth as Kristol, referring to Palin, explains how she has a couple years to make her case and educate herself more on national and international issues. Kristol also promises to get Palin booked on *The Daily Show*. Smiling, he jokes, that he has no clout, but says he will email her and say "do Jon Stewart." From there, Stewart tosses around some sexual innuendos, and both laugh heartily.[2]

In the most serious part of the discussion, Stewart and Kristol discuss their disagreements regarding health care reform. Kristol explains why he didn't support a public health option, arguing in essence that the existence of Medicare and Medicaid provide health coverage to those most in need. They disagree, but through the course of their debate, Kristol admits government-run health care for soldiers is superior to private health plans. Even in the most heated part of the debate, both men remain amicable—Stewart even joking with Kristol. By the end of the interview, they actually acknowledge the places in which they agree, Kristol claiming that he actually isn't opposed to spending more money on health care; rather he is merely opposed to the administration's current policy. At the conclusion of the interview both men share kind words: Stewart commenting on how much he enjoys their conversations and Kristol agreeing. Despite their disagreements, like the Snow interview, there is no name-calling, disparaging remarks—just calm, civilized debate with both parties acknowledging their respect for one another.

During the Snow interview and the Kristol interview, there are no winners or losers. As stated previously, this discourse of courtship involves a sort of reciprocity, or the vulnerability to being open to being persuaded. Through this process or this model of engagement, each actor engaged one another through strategies and tactics, acted with "maximum consciousness, and "transcended social estrangement." Just as Arendt argues that political action requires a condition of plurality in which people with differing backgrounds, perspectives, and abilities come together, here we see how Snow and Stewart and later Kristol and Stewart, as adversaries, not enemies, perform a model of democracy where people may disagree vehemently but respect each other enough to allow the other to speak his or her mind.

CONCLUSION

For thirty minutes, four times every week, Jon Stewart and *The Daily Show* offer a clear model of robust and engaged democratic debate in a way that does not merely pit one opinion against another. Using these theories of cultural production allow us to understand how *The Daily Show* provides a model which can help us to better understand human relations through the rhetorical processes of language, and how to communicate with people who have too narrow of reference on a subject to bring in other values that are taken into conflict. Part of this process involves creating new myths and metaphors, as suggested by Nietzsche, to describe human interaction and understanding that the myths we currently live by are not natural, given, or unchangeable. Knowing this, we are then able to craft the rhetoric (via Burke) needed to identify with one another. *The Daily Show* reminds us that just as we construct ideas that differences will result in warring relations, this model provides a corrective to that position. This model suggests that just as we create certain myths, we also have the ability to create new myths, ways of interacting and being in the world with one another.

In our current nation's democratic deficit where the absence of dissenting voices illuminate our weakened democracy, where dissent is still equated with anti-Americanism, nightly debates between Stewart and the most influential political figures in our country are needed now more than ever. As Ivie says, "Democracy would be better served by the rowdy rhetorical spirit of Coyote . . . as a comic corrective to tragic inclinations than by a strictly rational model of deliberation that masks elite privilege and power" (Ivie, 2002, p. 283–284). If (hu)man's natural state really is one of division as

Burke argues, we need models of democratic debate which show how human beings can and should debate one another civilly and humanely "here and now" under, as Ivie states, "actual conditions of agonistic politics rather than forestalling it endlessly until the masses are miraculously formed into elites and diversities of culture, interest, and perspective are somehow reduced to a homogenous consistency of purpose and understanding" (p.284).

NOTES

1. For a transcript of this episode, see http://lincmad.blogspot.com/2007/10/jon-stewart-spars-with-tony-snow.html.
2. For a transcript of this conversation, see http://www.huffingtonpost.com/2009/07/28/bill-kristol-admits-publi_n_246145.html.

REFERENCES

Abrams, J. (2010, March 25). Pelosi condemns threats against Congress members. *The Associated Press*. Retrieved from http://www.washingtonpost.com/wp-dyn/content/article/2010/03/25/AR2010032500277.html.

Arendt, H. (1958). *The Human Condition*. Chicago: University of Chicago Press.

Baym, G. (2007). Crafting new communicative models in the televisual sphere: Political interviews on The Daily Show. *Communication Review, 10* (2), 93–115.

Behler, E. (1995). Nietzsche's study of Greek rhetoric. *Research in Phenomenology, 25*, 3.

Bendavid N. and F. Johnson. (2010, March 26). Parties exchange barbs over threat reports. *The Wall Street Journal*. Retrieved from http://online.wsj.com/article/SB20001424052748704094104575143782325623718.html.

Brooten, L. (2007). Masculinity, media militarization, and *The Daily Show*. *Conference Papers— International Communication Association*, 1.

Brummett, B. (1993). *Landmark essays on Kenneth Burke*. Davis, CA: Hermagoras Press.

Burke, K. (1935). *Permanence and change; an anatomy of purpose*. New York: New Republic inc

———. (1969). *A rhetoric of motives*. Berkeley: University of California Press.

Burke, K., and Gusfield, J. R. (1989). *On symbols and society*. Chicago: University of Chicago Press.

CNN.com. (2004). Jon Stewart, Transcripts: CNN Crossfire: Jon Stewart's America, *Crossfire*. CNN. http://transcripts.cnn.com/TRANSCRIPTS/0410/15/cf.01.html.

Girard, R. (1986). *The scapegoat*. Baltimore: Johns Hopkins University Press.

Guardian. (2009, September 28.) U.S. Secret Service investigates Facebook poll on Barack Obama assassination: Survey reportedly asked whether users thought the U.S. president should be assassinated. *The Guardian*. Retrieved from http://www.guardian.co.uk/world/2009/sep/28/facebook-poll-obama-assassination.

Hawhee, D. (1999). Burke and Nietzsche. *Quarterly Journal of Speech, 85* (2), 129.

———. (2002). Agonism and arete. *Philosophy and Rhetoric, 35* (3), 185–207.

Hochmuth Nichols, M. (1993). Kenneth Burke and the "new rhetoric," in Brummett, B. *Landmark Essays on Kenneth Burke*. Davis, CA: Hermagoras Press.)

Husting, G. (2006). Neutralizing protest: The construction of war, chaos, and national identity through U.S. television news on abortion-related protest, 1991. *Communication and Critical/Cultural Studies, 3* (2), 162–180.

Ivie, R. L. (2002). Rhetorical deliberation and democratic politics in the here and now. *Rhetoric and Public Affairs* 5, 277–85.

———. (2005). Democratic dissent and the trick of rhetorical critique. *Cultural Studies/Critical Methodologies,* 5 (3), 276–293.

Jordan, M. (2007). "Truthiness" and consequence: *The Daily Show, The Colbert Report,* and truth as satire. *Conference Papers—International Communication Association,* 1.

Krepel, T. (2009, September 29). Newsmax columnist: Military coup "to resolve the 'Obama problem'" is not "unrealistic."*Media Matters.* Retrieved, from http://mediamatters.org/blog/200909290042.

Kurtz, H. (2005, January 6). Carlson and *Crossfire,* exit stage left and right at CNN, a defection and a deletion. *Washington Post.*

———. (2007). *Reality show.* New York: Free Press.

Mali, J. (1992). *The rehabilitation of myth: Vico's New science.* Cambridge; New York: Cambridge University Press.

Mootz, F. (2006). Nietzsche and radical rhetorical critique, in *Rhetorical Knowledge in Legal Practice and Critical Legal Theory.* Tuscaloosa: University of Alabama Press.

Mouffe, C. (2000). *The democratic paradox.* London ; New York: Verso.

Nietzsche, F. W., Kaufmann, W. A., and Hollingdale, R. J. (1968). *The will to power* (Vintage Books ed.). New York,: Vintage Books.

Roberts-Miller, P. (2005). Robert Montgomery Bird and the rhetoric of the improbable cause. *RSQ: Rhetoric Society Quarterly, 35* (1), 73–90.

———. (2006). Agonism, Wrangling, and John Quincy Adams. *Rhetoric Review, 25* (2), 141–161.

Robinson, E. (2010, March 26). Stopping the health-care madness. *The Washington Post.* Retrieved from http://www.washingtonpost.com/wp-dyn/content/article/2010/03/25/AR2010032502413.html.

Schaap, A. (2006). Agonism in divided societies. *Philosophy and Social Criticism, 32* (2), 255–277.

Schaeffer, J. D. (1996). Vico and Kenneth Burke. *RSQ: Rhetoric Society Quarterly, 26* (2), 7–17.

Schrift, A. D. (1990). *Nietzsche and the question of interpretation : between hermeneutics and deconstruction.* New York: Routledge.

———. (2000). *Why Nietzsche still?: Reflections on drama, culture, and politics.* Berkeley: University of California Press.

Smolkin, R. and Groves, E. (2007). What the mainstream media can learn from Jon Stewart. *American Journalism Review,* 29 (3), 18–25.

Steinhart, E. (2000). *On Nietzsche.* Australia; Belmont, CA: Wadsworth Thompson Learning.

Thomas, D. (1999). *Reading Nietzsche rhetorically.* New York: Guilford Press.

Trier, J. (2008). The DailyShow with Jon Stewart: Part 1. *Journal of Adolescent and Adult Literacy,* 51 (5), 424–427.

Vico, J., and Marsh, D. (1999). *New science: principles of the new science concerning the common nature of nations: Third edition, thoroughly corrected, revised, and expanded by the author.* London ; New York: Penguin.

Warner, J. (2007). Political culture jamming: the dissident humor of *The Daily Show with Jon Stewart. Popular Communication,* 5 (1), 17–36.

Whitson, S. and Poulokos, J. (1993). Nietzsche and the aesthetics of rhetoric. *Quarterly Journal of Speech,* 79 (2), 131–45.

Xenos, M. and Becker Amy B. (2009). Moments of Zen: Effects of *The Daily Show* on information seeking and political learning. *Political Communication,* 26 (3), 317–332.

Chapter Six

Purifying Laughter: Carnivalesque Self-Parody as Argument Scheme in *The Daily Show with Jon Stewart*

Aaron Hess

That *The Daily Show with Jon Stewart* has had a profound impact on journalism is not news. Not even fake news. Time and time again, *The Daily Show* has been recognized through awards, popular press, and academic research (Baym, 2005, 2007). Immensely popular among the eighteen to thirty crowd, *The Daily Show* continues to draw audiences and build a lasting reputation. But beyond its influence as comedic news satire, the program and especially its host Jon Stewart have been noted for its vicious critique of the modern news industry. Certainly, as many others in this volume discuss, the structure, form, and style of *The Daily Show* target the news industry and its claims to "fair and balanced" reporting. However, the essence of *The Daily Show* is an argument, an argument that targets elements of the modern journalism era of infotainment and punditry through personality. Indeed, there are moments of the program when Stewart targets particular aspects of the news, whether it is false narrative of Fox News and its cadre of pundits, or the financial networks' dropping the ball in the popping of the stock market bubble of 2007–2008, or the missed opportunity of true debate and discussion on CNN's *Crossfire*. In these moments, the "fakeness" of *The Daily Show* becomes quite real. In popular media, these pointed critiques have led *The Daily Show* and Jon Stewart to be noted as "holy grail" and a "game-changer" in the news (Weisman, 2008). The reach of *The Daily Show*'s satire has extended into the mainstream media to challenge established norms and ethics of journalism.

This essay examines those moments when *The Daily Show* extends beyond the ironic reporting of the news to making specific arguments against the people and programs of the twenty-four-hour news networks. On a number of occasions, *The Daily Show* and its host will target very particular aspects of the mainstream news media. While the examples of this act are numerous, four particular moments will be under consideration in this essay. Each of these moments displays how *The Daily Show* reaches outward and has affected other programming. Indeed, in these cases, *The Daily Show* becomes a topic of news. Through a rhetorical analysis of argument, I argue that through laughter and the carnivalesque, *The Daily Show* engages in radical critique of the news industry. Operating from a premise of comedy and carnivalesque, the show frequently argues that the news media is not holding up to its responsibility to the American public with informed deliberation about real social issues. While this argument can be recognized frequently in its nightly "broadcast," the moments when Jon Stewart tackles pundits and networks head on, and especially when they try to respond to the criticism, display how the argument of the program cannot be answered with standards of journalism. In other words, *The Daily Show* enjoys a dual role of being comedy and being a critique of the news industry. When targets of the critique attempt to argue back at the program based upon the latter, Jon Stewart rests upon the former as the central premise of the show. Examining *The Daily Show* through its rhetorical maneuvering of argumentative premises or argument schemes (Warnick and Kline, 1992) provides evidence for its unique positioning of radical critique through self-parody and the carnivalesque.

FOUR TARGETS OF RADICAL CRITIQUE[1]

First, Jon Stewart appeared in 2004 on CNN's now-defunct *Crossfire* with conservative Tucker Carlson and liberal Paul Begala. *Crossfire* was a well-known debate program. Structured into left versus right discussion, the program sought to ask hard-hitting questions of guests from across the political spectrum. On *The Daily Show*, *Crossfire* was a frequent victim of satire, especially during the segment "Even Stevphen" that featured correspondents Steve Carell and Stephen Colbert debating through issues via ad hominem attacks and insults. While certainly related, the occasion under scrutiny here is Jon Stewart's appearance on *Crossfire* on October 15, 2004. Introduced under the guise of promoting his new book, *America (The Book): A Citizen's Guide to Democracy Inaction,* Stewart instead spends his time on the episode arguing with the hosts about the merits of their program. Both Carlson and Begala defend the program as asking "pointed questions" and Carlson goes to great lengths to compare *Crossfire* to *The Daily Show,* an issue I will explore in more depth later in this essay. Famously, Stewart attacks the ethos of the program, calling out its claims to hard-hitting questions, calling its hosts "partisan hacks." As a consequence of Stewart's appearance, at least in part, CNN pulled *Crossfire* from its programming and cut ties with Tucker Carlson (Carter, 2005), displaying the power of the argument that is constructed through *The Daily Show*.

Second, Jon Stewart has appeared on two occasions on *The O'Reilly Factor* on Fox News. Host of the program, Bill O'Reilly, is well known for having strong, conservative positions as well as going after Jon Stewart and *The Daily Show*. Generally, the demeanor between the two was friendly yet pointed, with O'Reilly consistently calling the audience of *The Daily Show* "stoned slackers" and Jon Stewart frequently arguing that Fox News and O'Reilly are mouthpieces for conservativism. Two episodes of *The O'Reilly Factor* are under investigation here. On September 17, 2004, Jon Stewart was a guest on *The O'Reilly Factor* while promoting *America (The Book)*. In the thick of the 2004 presidential election, the interview with O'Reilly included a number of topics such as the election, the influence of *The Daily Show* on the news, and candidate John Kerry bypassing O'Reilly and appearing on *The Daily Show*. During the discussion of Kerry, Stewart claimed that "we're not competitors in terms of content. You're a news show, and we are a comedy show." He continued to discuss how *The Daily Show* is at heart a comedy show that is "informed by relevant issues and important information." Stewart appeared on *The O'Reilly Factor* again on February 3, 2010. This time, the topic was largely about President Barack Obama and his first year in office as well as the influence of Fox News. Stewart attacked Fox News, as he has on his own program, for being a voice of the conservative movement, for being "able to mainstream conservative talk radio." In the full version of the interview found on Fox News' website, O'Reilly challenged Stewart for using clips of Fox News out of context. Stewart argued with O'Reilly about the false narrative of Fox News, calling it a "cyclonic perpetual emotion machine that is a twenty-four-hour a day, seven-day a week—They've taken reasonable concerns about this president and this economy and turned it into a full-fledged panic attack about the next coming of Chairman Mao." Overall, the interview showed a considerable amount of clash between the two anchors.

Third, as host of the program *Mad Money* on the financial network CNBC, Jim Cramer is well-known for being a performative personality. His show features frequent sound effects and silly props as he discusses financial markets. After the collapse of the market and bursting of the housing bubble in 2008, Jon Stewart and *The Daily Show* took aim at the financial network for promoting stocks that tanked in the crash while having CEO's of major companies as guests, who seemingly lied while on the air. The March 4, 2009 episode of *The Daily Show* featured a clip of Rick Santelli ranting about the proposed bailouts of foreclosures with a subsequent set of clips from Santelli's network that promoted companies such as Bear Stearns, Lehman Brothers, Merrill Lynch, Bank of America, and AIG. Stewart then discussed how CNBC promotes itself as the top source of financial news, while also not investigating the underhanded business practices of top investment firms. At the end of the segment, Stewart resoundingly exclaimed[2] "fuck you" to the network and its poor handling of the financial meltdown. In the March 9, 2009 episode of *The Daily Show*, Stewart recapped the previous controversy, noting that CNBC and Jim Cramer were upset at *The Daily Show* for supposedly taking clips out of context. Stewart then displayed a fuller context for Cramer's promotion of Bear Stearns, ending the clips, again, with a "fuck you." On the following day, *The Daily Show* devoted another act to the controversy, now discussing how Cramer had been touring other NBC programs to muster support for his financial reporting. In response, Stewart went on his own "Viacom tour," including a stop with Dora the Explorer and a mock conversation with the cast of *The Hills* on MTV. The controversy ended with Cramer being a guest on the March 12, 2009 episode of *The Daily Show* and responding to Stewart's criticism directly.

Fourth, and most recently, Jon Stewart and Bernie Goldberg have traded barbs about generalizing comments that Goldberg made about liberals. *The Daily Show* called Goldberg out on the generalization, and Goldberg responded on *The O'Reilly Factor* by calling Stewart a "safe Jay Leno with a much smaller audience" who can drop "the f-bomb" to an "unsophisticated audience." Stewart responded by offering a bitter apology and called the news organization cynical and disingenuous. Stewart then broke into song with gospel singers in the background who make fun of both Goldberg and Stewart. He rails against Goldberg and Fox News, eventually calling their reaction to the supposed liberal bias in other news organizations as being like an auto-immune disorder, that Fox News is the lupus of the modern news industry, and finally, although "bleeped" out, "go fuck yourself." The end of the song had Stewart dancing while the singers continue to sing in (bleeping) harmony, "Go fuck yourself." Goldberg responded on a variety of Fox News programs by attacking Stewart and his fans. He explained that the hardcore fans of *The Daily Show* flooded his website with nasty emails and comments, which displays the type of person that watches the show and the nature of the show in general.

Each of these encounters indicates that *The Daily Show* has a reach beyond its usual satire. In the case of Tucker Carlson and *Crossfire*, the implications of Jon Stewart's critique are quite real world. In other cases, such as with the Jim Cramer dispute, both networks enjoyed a boost in viewership because of the controversies. Yet, the real questions remain: How does *The Daily Show* position its critique against twenty-four-hour news networks? What is the nature of its strategy of argumentation? To answer these questions, I engage in a rhetorical analysis of argument, looking specifically to how such radical critique found on *The Daily Show* and how Jon Stewart positions the program in a manner that defies rational discussion about the merits of the show. While Stewart certainly engages in political discussion with guests (Baym, 2007) and when on other programs, *The Daily Show* itself is remarkably immune to arguments against its production of satire, largely due to its ability to engage in self-parody and carnivalesque as a form of argument scheme. To understand how such a premise is created, I examine *The Daily Show* through Perelman's notion of argument schemes. From this framework, I contend that *The Daily Show* utilizes carnivalesque as a strategy. When challenged, *The Daily Show* can rely and rest upon its ridiculousness and comedy. This position allows *The Daily Show* to remain a remarkably critical force of creative farce that is difficult to refute in its pointed critique. So long as the program instills a self-reflective laughter in its audience, it will live up to its promise. Before getting to my analysis, a brief review of the three concepts of Perelman's argument schemes, carnivalesque, and self-parody are necessary.

PERELMAN'S STARTING POINTS

In their establishment of the new rhetoric, Perelman and Olbrechts-Tyteca (1969) refocus the practice of argumentation within rhetoric as being more than mere style. Rather, they intend to reposition rationality and reasonableness as primary forms of argumentation in rhetoric (Foss, Foss, and Trapp, 2002). Importantly, they delineate between formal, logical demonstration and argumentation, believing that argumentation is more akin to what is reasonable within a particular audience. Gross and Dearin (2003) argue that the new rhetoric sought to "find a rational basis for decision making in the fields of human endeavor where the doctrines of Cartesian rationalism, the canons of formal logic, and the procedures of modern mathematics have proven to be ineffectual" (pp. 13–14). While a thorough review of the new rhetoric is well beyond the scope of this essay, a few items are important for consideration: the primacy of the audience, starting points for argumentation, and argument schemes.

The new rhetoric reaffirmed the focus of not only rhetoric but argumentation on the audience. "Argumentation is intended to act upon an audience, to modify an audience's convictions or dispositions through discourse, and it tries to gain a meeting of minds instead of imposing its will through constraint or conditioning" (Perelman, 1982, p. 11). Differentiating between the concept of audience under rhetoric and under formal logic, "Their concept of audience refers to the speaker's mental conception of the audience rather than to the physical presence of a group of people assembled to hear a speech" (Foss, Foss, and Trapp, 2002, p. 88). Perelman and Olbrechts-Tyteca conceptualize audience as both universal and particular. The universal audience is understood as all reasonable and competent people and the particular audience is that which is exposed to or targeted by the act of persuasion through argumentation (Foss, Foss, and Trapp, 2002; Gross and Dearin, 2003). The universal audience is one of fact, truth, and presumption of an established reality, whereas the particular audience is one that is understood through adherence to values. In the new rhetoric, Perelman and Olbrechts-Tyteca argue that philosophy and logic are those endeavors aimed at universal audiences, while rhetoric is one that is concerned with the particular: "the philosopher appeals to common sense of common opinion, to intuition or to self-evidence . . ." (Perelman, 1982, p. 17) but rhetorical appeals to the values are inherent to the audience at hand.

In turn, the particular audience, as understood by the speaker, is one that has at its foundation a set of values. These values become the premises or starting points for argumentation. Perelman and Olbrechts-Tyteca contend that argumentation with a particular audience entails displaying adherence to established values as starting points for argumentation, and then moving the audience along toward preferable values that the speaker would like the audience to have. "Once the audience accepts the premises, the next step is to encourage the members of the audience to adhere to the conclusion in the same way it agrees with the premises" (Foss, Foss, and Trapp, 2002, p. 90). Values are best understood as either concrete or abstract, depending on the goals of the orator. Individuals who argue for the status quo . . . are more likely to begin their arguments with concrete values because such values are more persuasive when the goal is to preserve institutions rather than to reform them" (p. 92). However, as I will contend in the case of *The Daily Show*, "those who argue for change are more likely to begin their argumentation with abstract values" (p. 92–93). Skilled speakers will utilize such value constructions in larger schemas, which inform their overall approach to the argument.

Warnick and Kline (1992) argue that while much of the controversy about new rhetoric has focused on the conception of the universal and particular audience, the central idea of the theory is about how argument is developed from audiences through starting points or premises into larger schemes.

> For instance, the starting points of argument—facts, truths, presumptions, values, hierarchies, and the loci of the preferable—are derived from premises to which the arguer's anticipated audience presumably subscribes. The conventions for conducting arguments also grow out of practices and norms mutually accepted by interlocutors who participate together in a common culture. Likewise, the inferential schemes that move the audience to accept the arguer's claims are generated through commonplaces and structures recognized and accepted by Western society. Over two-thirds of The New Rhetoric was devoted to describing these agreed-upon liaisons

that make inferences possible, for Perelman and Olbrechts-Tyteca believed that in practical reasoning, inferential moves are made possible rhetorically. (Warnick and Kline, 1992, p. 2)

In other words, the starting points for argument can be developed into larger schemes and can be understood, in one form or another, as the bulk of how argumentation operates under the new rhetoric. Argumentation occurs when there is dispute about how a scheme adheres deductively or quasi-logically (and how the audience adheres) to a notion of reality. Also under possible dispute in debate, therefore, is the establishment of starting points for discourses. Gross and Dearin (2003) explore this concept as "the means by which a speaker or writer seeks to bring about an adherence of minds whenever an existing view of reality cannot be invoked as an argumentative starting point" (p. 65). In this case, the speaker must inductively connect the argument to the nature of reality that he or she would like as a starting point (and conclusion) for the claim. The establishment of and use of schemes is critical to *The Daily Show* when it speaks outward in its satire. However, *The Daily Show*'s "reality" is one that is quite fake, or at least surreal. To enact its starting point, *The Daily Show* and its host Jon Stewart engage in carnivalesque and self-parody as the primary form through which the program is to be read.

THE CARNIVALESQUE

Bakhtin's (1984a, 1984b) notion of the carnival and carnivalesque serve as primary starting points for arguments in *The Daily Show*, as I will display below. As a part of his approach to speech communication as dialogic, Bakhtin's (1984a, 1984b) carnival explores and upends the components of hierarchy, power, and relationships between people. In contrast to many approaches to communication that focused on the speech act, Bakhtin argues that communication is best understood as the dialogic moment between people and structures, as dialogue between speakers and the negotiation of meaning between them. Understood in this way, dialogue "is both the source of meaningful life and an orientation that permeates one's external responses to others as well as one's self-consciousness; it is inherent in both the written and spoken word, in inner and outer consciousness, and in action" (Shields, 2007, p. 65). Connecting this notion to rhetoric and the examination of texts, the dialogic method is a "way of recognizing (a) the speaker's or writer's (rhetorical) intention to move the audience to action and (b) the audience's active role in interpreting utterances in order to reply or react, a role that the speaker or writer is well aware of" (Bizzell and Herzberg, 2001, p. 1209). Used in conjunction, as I am here, with Perelman's argumentative schemes, both approaches to rhetoric underscore the audience-centered approach and the contextual nature of argument. However, my purpose here is not to focus solely on the dialogic approach; Bakhtin's notion of carnival is a much closer match for *The Daily Show*.

The carnival, for Bakhtin, resembles the medieval conception of carnival more than the modern one. As a festival, the carnival was a public gathering of participating in upending hierarchy and structures of governance. It was a time when positions of power were temporarily frozen and hierarchies turned upside down:

> Civil and social ceremonies and rituals took on a comic aspect as clowns and fools, constant participants in these festivals, mimicked serious rituals such as the tribute rendered to the victors at tournaments, the transfer of feudal rights, or the initiation of a knight. Minor occasions were also marked by comic protocol, as for instance the election of a king and queen to preside at a banquet "for laughter's sake." (Bakhtin, 1984b, p. 5)

In doing so, the carnival creates a moment of dialogue between the established forms and their carnivalesque counterparts. Through the privileging of the grotesque and the wearing of masks, participants in the carnival would lose their previous markers of social class and status. Forms of expression were turned over and opposites explored through parody (Shields, 2007). From critical reflection upon the old forms, new ideas about structure, communication, and hierarchy emerge:

> Carnival is the place for working out, in concretely sensuous, half-real and half-play-acted form, a *new mode of interrelationship between individuals,* counterposed to the all-powerful socio-hierarchical relationships of noncarnival life. The behavior, gesture, and discourse of a person are freed from the authority of all hierarchical positions (social estate, rank, age, property) defining them totally in noncarnival life, and thus from the vantage point of noncarnival life become eccentric and inappropriate. (Bakhtin, 1984a, p. 123)

In turn, the carnivalesque display has been understood in a number of ways. Olbrys (2006) examines the carnivalesque performance of Chris Farley on *Saturday Night Live,* noting his disciplining through the "yoking" of laughter. Martin and Renegar (2007) find social critique in the film, *The Big Lebowski*, arguing that it questions "the norms upon which we base our lives and positions" (p. 309). Chvasta (2006) sees the carnival through the performance of street protests against the war on terror and the Iraq War. Finally, and most closely related to *The Daily Show,* Hariman (2008) sees a vital component of public discourse as formed through the notion of humor and parody through carnival: "By doubling discourse into a self-consciously comic image of itself, and then casting that image before the most democratic, undisciplined, and irreverent conception of a public audience, parodic performance recasts the hermeneutics of public discourse" (p. 255). Certainly, parody is a key component in the carnivalesque; however, looking one step further, the notion of *self-parody* also appears as an argumentative form within the carnival.

SELF-PARODY AT THE CARNIVAL

Bakhtin (1984b) sees the performance of the carnival as enjoyed by all. In the modern sense of the carnival, the audience may be merely spectators; however, in medieval carnival, all were participants. Bakhtin (1984b) constructs participation through the positioning of the "footlights" of the show:

> In fact, carnival does not know footlights, in the sense that it does not acknowledge any distinction between actors and spectators. Footlights would destroy a carnival, as the absence of footlights would destroy a theatrical performance. Carnival is not a spectacle seen by the people; they live in it, and everyone participates because its very idea embraces all the people. (p. 7)

Indeed, the lights shine on all participants in the carnival. And, as such, the light is shined upon ourselves. Thus, parody, as a form within the carnival, is pointed at the self as well as others. When used strategically, self-parody through an argumentative form of carnival can bolster the critique. Hutcheon (2000) locates self-parody thusly: "Such art could almost be considered self-parodic in that it calls into question not only its relation to other art, but its own identity" (p. 10). The aim of critique is in all directions, and especially upon the self. Such disavowal of form entails a radical questioning of the production of knowledge or representation at all. "Self parody in this sense is not just an artist's way of disowning earlier mannerisms by externalizations. . . . It is a way of creating a form out of the questions of the very act of aesthetic production" (p. 10).

Conducted with social criticism, self-parody arguably provides either a powerful position to argue, or leads to a path of nihilism. Parody as a form invites a reflexive character through its "capacity to reflect critically back upon itself, not merely upon its character (Hannoosh, 1989, p. 113). Poirier (1968) sees self-parody in literature as "a species of critical analysis" (p. 351). However, as Conway (1992) recognizes, Nietzsche's self-parody "forfeits the epistemic privilege of the philosophical critic, thus ensuring that his own critique appeals exclusively to immanent standards of evaluation" (p. 343). Bennett (1985) describes postmodern parody not only as displaying modernist representational parody, but also as using techniques of self-subversion, self-skepticism, and a meta-parodic manner. As such, the postmodern parodist is fully skeptical of all forms of expression, not deeming even her or himself as the acceptable form in which understanding is found. This radical skepticism finds no comfort in any genre or category of form and continuously blurs the boundaries between them, seeking to "subvert the foundations of our accepted modes of thought and experience . . . [in] an effort to subvert the foundations of language itself, so as to show that its seeming meaningfulness dissipates, to an unillusioned inquirer, into a play of irresolvable indeterminacies" (p. 32). In short, self-parody offers a strategic position for the critic to apply standards of evaluation that subvert in all directions, including those of the critic.

THE CARNIVALESQUE AS ARGUMENT SCHEME

Working from these three lines of thinking, I now turn to *The Daily Show* and its rhetorical construction of argument. In this section, I analyze the program and its argument, paying special attention to the aforementioned examples of Jon Stewart critiquing particular people and programs of the twenty-four-hour news industry. To begin, I focus on how *The Daily Show* constructs its premise or starting point for argumentation. Largely, the program exists as a social critique and satire of the twenty-four-hour news industry. To add to this, I identify elements of the program that embody the carnival. Second, I discuss the use of self-parody as an argumentation technique, especially when speaking out against other news programs. Finally, I locate the moments of clash between *The Daily Show* and other news programs to trace the power and presence of self-parody through the carnivalesque.

A Premise of the Carnival

The Daily Show has been widely recognized as being a social critique and satire of the modern news industry (Baym, 2005, 2007; Hariman, 2007; Waisanen, 2009). Waisanen (2009) notes that the dual hosts, Jon Stewart of *The Daily Show* and Stephen Colbert of *The Colbert Report*, operate as rhetorical critics who critically examine the production of news through a Burkean comic perspective. Certainly, that is the case; however, the argumentative style of the critique on *The Daily Show* also embodies the notion of the carnival. To understand this construction, I draw on examples from the program as well as Jon Stewart's positioning of the show when debating other hosts of news programs. The carnival is best understood as an inversion of social hierarchy and normalcy, largely constructed through laughter. Recall that Bakhtin (1984a) points to the disruption of the hierarchies of noncarnival life. He also argues that the carnival "brings together, unifies, weds, and combines the sacred with the profane, the lofty with the low, the great with the insignificant, the wise with the stupid" (p. 123). *The Daily Show* constructs similar disruptions. For example, in the clip that criticizes Jim Cramer and the financial experts at CNBC, Stewart orients the discussion of the profoundly serious collapse of the market with crass descriptions of the talking heads at CNBC. Stewart says he would be happy to talk to the individuals that represent the financial network, who he lists with ridiculous names and visuals of animals who offer financial advice. In this gesture, *The Daily Show* combines the (serious) expertise and wisdom with the stupid and ridiculous. In the same controversy with CNBC, when Jim Cramer traverses the NBC network to gain support for his program against Stewart's criticism, *The Daily Show* answers with Stewart appearing on *Dora the Explorer*. In this moment, the cartoon child character Dora explains the controversy, saying that the issue is not Cramer's specific actions, but that he represents a general movement in financial news that helped create the economic problems in the first place. In this example, the seemingly unwise (cartoon child) explains the complex argument offered by *The Daily Show*, again inverting conventional wisdom.

As a primary device of *The Daily Show*, laughter operates as voice against the seriousness of oppression. Bakhtin (1984b) argues that laughter "liberates not only from external censorship but first of all from the great interior censor; it liberates from the fear that developed in man during thousands of years: fear of the sacred, of prohibitions, of the past, of power" (p. 94). *The Daily Show's* self-professed aim is to laugh at the absurdity of the news industry. Accented with a primed studio audience, the program is framed as funny before social critique, although the critique is not far behind. In his 2010 exchange with Bill O'Reilly, Stewart explains the show and its audience: "Here's the thing about the show, we don't think about who's receiving it. We just do what we think is funny to us" ("Interview: Jon Stewart," 2010) In the same exchange, O'Reilly pushes Stewart and his portrayal of Fox News, asking if Stewart was personally offended about Fox News' decision to cut a presentation from President Obama short. Stewart responds: "I wasn't offended. I thought it was funny" ("Interview: Jon Stewart," 2010). In these exchanges, the overly serious O'Reilly is faced with Stewart's preference for laughter above all else. In characterizing the medieval carnival, Bakhtin (1984b) contrasts seriousness with laughter:

> Seriousness had an official tone and was treated like all that was official. It oppressed, frightened, bound, lied, and wore the mask of hypocrisy. . . . When its mask was dropped in the festive square and at the banquet table, another truth was heard in the form of laughter, foolishness, improprieties, curses, parodies, and travesties. (p. 94)

Laughter and comedy, for Stewart and *The Daily Show*, is not just a reaction; it is a mode of being. It operates as a primary frame of reference against the official tone of CNBC, Bill O'Reilly, Jim Cramer and others. By bringing these serious issues to the "festive square" of Comedy Central, Stewart and his team speak "another truth."

One final element of *The Daily Show's* carnival is its preference for the profane. Bakhtin (1984a) labels one of his carnivalistic categories *profanation*: "carnivalistic blasphemies, a whole system of carnivalistic debasing and bringing down to earth, carnivalistic obscenities linked with . . . carnivalistic parodies on sacred texts and sayings" (p. 123). The act of profanation pairs blasphemy with the sacred. On *The Daily Show,* the sacred text of the twenty-four-hour news networks and industry is spoken about with all that is crass. Reflecting on the CNBC dispute, Jon Stewart sums up his critique of the financial network with a simple: "Fuck you." In his tour of Viacom programs, Jon Stewart joins Dora the Explorer in calling Cramer and his colleagues *pendejos*. And, in his tearing down of Fox News and Bernie Goldberg, Stewart and his gospel choir sing to Fox News a chorus line of "Go Fuck Yourself." Such performances of overt profanity speak to the premise of the show as carnivalesque, but they also serve another purpose. Given that the starting point for argumentation in the case of *The Daily Show* is laughter and carnival, grotesque profanity and sensationalized performances provide powerful answers to the reasoning offered by Fox News or other targets of the satire. While I will explore this in more detail below, the point is that when challenged for its aim of social critique and satire, the profane most always becomes a style of refutation. *The Daily Show*, through laughter and excess, effectively rebukes its critics. Coupled with acts of self-parody, the program remains in a powerful social position of radical critique.

Self-Parody and Puppets Making Crank Phone Calls

Conway (1992) notes that Nietzsche engaged in self-parody "in order to discredit his own claim to a privileged critical perspective" (p. 347). Through it, he argues, Nietzsche was able to "deploy a strategically self-referential method of philosophical criticism" (p. 348). Similarly, self-parody operates strategically in *The Daily Show*, providing Jon Stewart a position to critically argue against the modern construction of journalism without ever having to answer to his own criticism. Frequently, Stewart, both on air on *The Daily Show* or meeting with other news entities, criticizes the twenty-four-hour news networks for not living up to their own credos. In his dispute with Tucker Carlson, Stewart told the two hosts that he came on the program "because I have privately, amongst my friends and also in occasional newspapers and television shows, mentioned this show as being bad . . . it's not so much that it's bad, as it's hurting America" ("CNN Crossfire," 2004). He goes on in the interview to discuss why *Crossfire* portends and also pretends to be a debate show that asks hard-hitting questions, but actually only repeats the talking points of pundits and politicians. Similarly, in his dispute with CNBC, Stewart calls out the network for claiming that their financial broadcasting is synonymous with credible expertise, especially in a promo for Jim Cramer's show that displays: "In Cramer We Trust." During the Cramer controversy, Stewart called out the slogan, explaining that he would not take issue with the slogan if it provided a qualifier for his expertise or if he was portrayed as a talking dartboard. Simultaneously, *The Daily Show* constantly debases its own existence as a "news" show. To carve out this position, *The Daily Show* structures its strategic argument in two primary ways. First, when confronted by other news casters in controversy, Stewart and *The Daily Show* will argue back with verbal dismissals of claims of journalistic ethos coupled with direct comparisons to the *idea* of *The Daily Show*. Second, the show performs its position of comedy, coupled with self-deprecation, back at its target.

In making its criticism against the modern news industry, *The Daily Show* frequently calls out the construction of journalistic goodwill and ethos that is purported by the twenty-four-hour news networks. However, since the premise of *The Daily Show* is carnival, arguing back at it is difficult. This is especially apparent when Stewart speaks out against particular individuals. In his taking down of *Crossfire*, Stewart debases the program for not being as hard-hitting as the hosts believe it to be. Tucker Carlson argues back, saying "I want to contrast our questions with some questions you asked John Kerry recently," and, "You had John Kerry on your show and you sniff his throne and you're accusing us of partisan hackery?" ("CNN Crossfire," 2004). Jon Stewart responds to Carlson saying, "If you want to compare your show to a comedy show, you're more than welcome to." Famously, Stewart quips that Carlson and Begala have a responsibility to good journalism, whereas *The Daily Show* does not: "You're on CNN. The show that leads into me is puppets making crank phone calls" ("CNN Crossfire" 2004). In a similar exchange with Bernie Goldberg, Goldberg goes after Stewart for wanting to be more than a comedian, for wanting to "be a social commentator" and that to be a good one, he should "find some guts" ("Interview: O'Reilly . . ." 2010). Stewart responded by saying that comedians do not have to decide between comedy and social commentary because comedy is best understood as a type of social commentary. He also explains that, if anything, news programming is becoming more like comedy. Similar to his dispute with *Crossfire* and CNBC, he calls out Bernie Goldberg for trying to apply Fox News' slogan of "Fair and Balanced" to *The Daily Show*. These examples indicate that Jon Stewart and *The Daily Show* will frequently leverage its position as a carnival news program against its targets. In so doing, Stewart lays bare the differing responsibilities of each program.

To accent the foundation of the critical argument, the premise of the show, *The Daily Show* will perform its act of self-parody. Returning to the Bernie Goldberg dispute, Goldberg calls out the audience of *The Daily Show* for being "unsophisticated" because of the use of the "f-bomb" on television. To answer this charge, Stewart is interrupted by a supposed audience member who is a huge fan of the show named Toppington von Monocle. The audience plant quotes, in Latin, a line of profanity by Catalus, and ends his bit by farting into his chair. Later, in the same exchange, Stewart breaks into song with a gospel and sings along with them. His background singers make fun of Stewart, saying that he makes things up, calling him lactose intolerant, a communist, and a monarchist. At one point, a background singer calls Stewart's interviews incoherent and not funny. A dancing, dramatic Stewart closes the song, telling Goldberg that *The Daily Show* does not need to adhere to what others believe satire is supposed to be, nor does it need to live up to the Fox News tagline of "Fair and Balanced."

In another performative example, in the Jim Cramer/CNBC debate, *The Daily Show* provided a special episode (of sorts) for the interview with Cramer on the show. While the interview contained quite a bit of discussion via comparison, the writers of the program created a special introduction to the show that used flashy graphics and powerful language to introduce the interview, similar to that of the major news networks' coverage of the Stewart vs. Cramer debate. In the case of *The Daily Show*, however, the introductory voiceover blatantly claims that the interview is a way to increase ratings and advertising charges for its programming. This moment of satire pokes fun of the mainstream coverage of the dispute, but also provides fodder against parent network Comedy Central. When the interview finally occurs, Stewart has vitally important questions for Cramer, even getting emotional at times. Arguably, however, with such a self-parodic backdrop, Cramer has little recourse for argument back at Stewart.

Clashing Premises: Comedy vs. "The News"

Working from the premise of comedy and laughter, and coupled with not-too-subtle self-parodic reminders of the construction of *The Daily Show*, Stewart and his cadre of writers have crafted an argumentation strategy that provokes social critique and is difficult to refute. In this final section, I explore how the establishment of the argument scheme operates to position the show as radical critique. To do so, I follow up on those individuals that have been in disputes with Stewart to examine how they attempt to refute such arguments. While Tucker Carlson was able to trade jabs with Stewart in person, other news personalities take to other programs to publicly condemn Stewart. Jim Cramer appeared on Joe Scarborough's program; Bernie Goldberg visits with Bill O'Reilly and Megyn Kelly on Fox News; and, Bill

O'Reilly discusses Stewart with Nancy Skinner. Each of these moments displays the difficulty in answering the claims of *The Daily Show*. Often, the pundits look for other ways of categorizing *The Daily Show* or Jon Stewart, such as being a liberal or focusing on Stewart's audience, to make their argument. Ultimately, the critique that is offered from the news satire powerfully stands against the twenty-four-hour news programs.

In order to actively refute the construction of *The Daily Show*, targets of the program will often categorize Stewart in ways that deem it possible to have some ground in the debate. This strategy intends to discursively sever the comedic portion of the show in favor of finding another premise to dispute. The most common characterization is that of *liberal*. In Stewart's interviews on *The O'Reilly Factor*, O'Reilly calls the audience of *The Daily Show* left-leaning or Obama supporters. In a discussion with Nancy Skinner about the Goldberg dispute, O'Reilly calls Stewart a "liberal comedian" and a "committed liberal who likes President Obama" when discussing his tactics on *The Daily Show*. In discussing his arguments against Fox News, O'Reilly says that "he is and isn't" doing comedy, struggling to articulate Stewart's argument premise and scheme (nancyskinnerlive.com, 2010). This attempted refutation of Stewart grapples with the difficulty of pinning down exactly what *The Daily Show* is doing.

While certainly satire, *The Daily Show* offers something more. Its premise of comedy stretches into contemporary social issues, which beg for stock argumentation of those issues. However, Stewart is always able to revert back to comedy and laughter to bolster his position. Problematically, respondents to Stewart and *The Daily Show* will be unlikely to refute that premise, which means they turn to other characterizations. O'Reilly's use of liberal here is a way to focus his conservatively based talk show against *The Daily Show*. Similarly, Goldberg's refutation to Stewart focuses not on the issues, but on Stewart's audience. To damage the credibility of the show, Goldberg claims that after being lambasted on *The Daily Show*, the "most loyal fans" of the program flooded his website with nasty and vulgar comments (Interview: O'Reilly . . . part 2, 2010). He calls the Internet a "sewer" and fans of *The Daily Show* "sewer rats" who disparaged him on his website ("Bernie Goldberg . . ." 2010). This discursive shift attempts to deflect attention from the core argument that Stewart made on *The Daily Show*, and instead, focus on the behavior of the program's audience. Again, in this case, targets of *The Daily Show* struggle to argue back at the program's satire.

One notable moment of possible refutation to the argument of *The Daily Show* is a discussion between Bernie Goldberg and Megyn Kelly ("Bernie Goldberg . . ." 2010). To frame the exchange, Fox News displays a graphic that calls the argument and Stewart's gospel singing performance "Political Debate Degenerates into Coarse Name Calling." Kelly opens the discussion with Goldberg asking him if he finds the performance funny. Goldberg dodges the question, and instead discusses the response that he received on his website. To push on the issue, Kelly compares the ratings and viewership of *The Daily Show* with "other big titans," likely referring to Fox News. She continues, saying that Stewart "maintains that he is a comedian and that he has no obligation to be fair and balanced, and he's never made any promises about being fair, and he's not a journalist, and he basically likes to make fun of news people. But do you think that his audience understands that?" Goldberg, rather than discussing the construction of the show and its audience, reverts back to the issue of generalizing, which was at the heart of the initial dispute. "Man up, Jon. Man the hell up. You can't criticize us at Fox for generalizing about liberals and then you do the same thing or ignore it when it happens and then say, 'Well, I'm not a news man.' No, I'm not buying that; I'm not buying that for a second" ("Bernie Goldberg . . ." 2010).

This discussion underscores the difficulty in answering the comedic aspect of Stewart's critique. Stewart boldly claims that he needs not be "fair and balanced," yet Goldberg cannot reconcile this criticism. Thinking back to the argument schemes, Perelman (1982) argues that those speakers that rely on presumptions about reality favor the status quo and those who favor change work from abstract values. Stewart constructs his argument with comedy as its premise, eschewing any presumed journalistic responsibility; Goldberg constructs his premise through journalism ethics. At their foundation, however, Goldberg will need to abide by his own premise, while Stewart will not have to follow Goldberg's. Since Goldberg only attempts to answer Stewart's comedy with journalistic standards of fair critique, he largely fails to respond to Stewart's argument. As a result, if Stewart creates laughter as a consequence of his performance, he is already successful in his argument. And, if he stirs controversy and critical social thinking about issues, then he has furthered his success. As such, *The Daily Show* need not persuade beyond laughter. Additionally, to answer Megyn Kelly's question, the audience of *The Daily Show* absolutely understands the ironic construction of the show as argument from comedy/carnival; the audience would not "get the joke" otherwise (Hutcheon, 1995, 2000). Yet, Goldberg attempts to establish the premise of the show as through journalistic standards largely for the Fox News audience, which would require some level of fairness. While the Fox News audience may appreciate Goldberg's standards, they also recognize (as Kelly introduces and Goldberg acknowledges) that Stewart is a comedian. In this way, Goldberg's audience may disbelieve his evaluation of the dispute.

CONCLUSION

From this analysis, I have argued that *The Daily Show* constructs an argument scheme devoted to the carnivalesque inversion of modern broadcasting, which disallows many of its victims of satire to respond to the biting critiques offered by Jon Stewart. As a premise for argumentation, Stewart begins his critique without presumption of ethics, fairness, and balanced reporting. Rather, he argues with the abstract values of radical critique, seeking to challenge the modern news industry's claims of "Fair and Balanced," financial expertise, and supposed devotion to hard-hitting debate on issues. Through self-parody, *The Daily Show* even makes fun of itself, insulting Stewart openly on the program, making fun of its audience, and discussing the advertising dollars generated through the public disputes. Entranced by his targeted critique, members of the news industry argue back, operating from a premise of journalism; however, Stewart nimbly offers further proof of its premise: more laughter. Because of the competing premises of these arguments, *The Daily Show* is unlikely to be answered. Ultimately, Stewart is right when he describes the show to Bill O'Reilly: "If we have influence, it is peripheral. And I don't imagine that people who watch the show are watching it to make up their minds in terms of who they think would best prosecute the war on terror. I think they watch to see who would maybe have the best jokes on the war on terror" (Interview: The Jon Stewart . . . 2004).

As a consequence, two lessons can be learned through an understanding of *The Daily Show*'s argument scheme. First, radical critique is multidirectional. *The Daily Show*, as many have noted, will target anyone, regardless of their political beliefs or position. Just as in the carnival, hierarchies are upended on *The Daily Show*. Arguing back at a program that dismisses even its own content is unlikely to be successful. Just as Bakhtin (1984b) speaks of "clowns and fools" mimicking "serious rituals," so, too, does *The Daily Show* offer its own cadre of performers who lash out in laughter at the sacraments of the news. Self-parody also offers an additional layer of protection for Stewart, which allows all to be questioned and all to be victims of strong satire. Instead of answering the call, those who are targeted by *The Daily Show* would be better served with silence, knowing that to answer back only invites additional critical laughter. As radical critique, *The Daily Show* offers a position of constant pointing; pointing at its own flaws, pointing out the flaws of others, and pointing out the flaws in all of us. Arguably, *The Daily Show* does not argue for anything; rather, the program offers a carnival funhouse mirror for both the audience and authors of the news industry to view.

Second, *The Daily Show*, as carnival, provides a vital, comic social service. Indeed, its performances do not necessarily invite rational discourse (although Stewart's interviews often do [see Baym, 2007]). However, they do offer a corrective. Again, Bakhtin (1984b) offers insight into the power of the comic:

> Laughter purifies from dogmatism, from the intolerant and the petrified; it liberates from fanaticism and pedantry, from fear and intimidation, from didacticism, naïveté and illusion, from the single meaning, the single level, from sentimentality. Laughter does not permit seriousness to atrophy and to be torn away from the one being, forever incomplete. It restores this ambivalent wholeness. Such is the function of laughter in the historical development of culture and literature. (p. 123)

In our (post)modern development of culture, Jon Stewart offers laughter in response to the construction of news that promotes an agenda of partisan hackery, dubious financial expertise, and false claims to fairness. Laughter, for Stewart, purifies our modern obsession with twenty-four-hour news and punditry through personality.

NOTES

1. In all instances of the programs, I either use transcriptions found at the corresponding news websites ("CNN Crossfire...," 2004; "Interview: Jon Stewart...," 2010; "Interview: The Jon Stewart...," 2004) or paraphrasing from the episodes of *The Daily Show* in which they were broadcast or found on *The Daily Show's* website.
2. All instances of swearing on the show are "bleeped" out.

REFERENCES

Bakhtin, M. M. (1984a). *Problems of Dostoevsky's poetics*. Minneapolis, MN: University of Minnesota Press.
———. (1984b). *Rabelais and his world* (H. Iswolsky, Trans.). Bloomington, IN: Indiana University Press.
Baym, G. (2005). *The Daily Show:* Discursive integration and the reinvention of political journalism. *Political Communication, 22,* 259–276.
———. (2007). Crafting new communicative models in the televisual sphere: Political interviews on *The Daily Show*. *The Communication Review, 10,* 93–115.
Bennett, D. (1985). Parody, postmodernism, and the politics of reading. *Critical Inquiry, 27,* 27–43.
Bernie Goldberg vs. Jon Stewart (2010, April 21). *Fox News*. Retrieved from http://video.foxnews.com/v/4160824/bernie-goldberg-vs-jon-stewart.
Bizzell, P. and Herzberg, B. (2001). *The rhetorical tradition*. New York: Bedford/St. Martin's.
Carter, B. (2005, Jan 6). CNN will cancel 'Crossfire' and cut ties with commentator. *New York Times*. Retrieved from http://www.nytimes.com/2005/01/06/business/media/06crossfire.html?_r=1.
Chvasta, M. (2006). Anger, irony, and protest: Confronting the issue of efficacy, again. *Text and Performance Quarterly, 26,* 5–16.
CNN Crossfire: Jon Stewart's America. (2004, Oct 15). *CNN.com*. Retrieved from http://transcripts.cnn.com/TRANSCRIPTS/0410/15/cf.01.html.

Conway, D. W. (1992). Nietzsche's art of this-worldly comfort: Self-reference and strategic self-parody. *History of Philosophy Quarterly, 9,* 343–357.

Foss, S. K., Foss, K. A., and Trapp, R. (2002). *Contemporary perspectives on rhetoric.* Long Grove, IL: Waveland Press.

Gross, A. G. and Dearin, R. D. (2003). *Chaim Perelman.* New York: SUNY Press.

Hannoosh, M. (1989). The reflexive function of parody. *Comparative Literature, 41,* 113–126.

Hariman, R. (2008). Political parody and public culture. *Quarterly Journal of Speech, 94,* 247–272.

Hutcheon, L. (1995). *Irony's edge: The theory and politics of irony.* London: Routledge

———. (2000). *A theory of parody: The teachings of twentieth-century art forms.* Chicago, IL: University of Illinois Press.

Interview: O'Reilly and Bernie Goldberg respond to Jon Stewart's criticism of Fox News. (2010, April 20). *Fox News.*Retrieved from http://www.foxnews.com/story/ 0,2933,591304,00.html.

Interview: O'Reilly and Bernie Goldberg respond to Jon Stewart's criticism of Fox News, part 2. (2010, April 20). *Fox News.*Retrieved from http://www.foxnews.com/story/ 0,2933,591385,00.html.

Interview: Jon Stewart in the no spin zone. (2010, Feb 4). *Fox News.*Retrieved from http:// www.foxnews.com/story/0,2933,584805,00.html.

Interview: The Jon Stewart and undecided voter connection. (2004, Sept 20). *Fox News.*Retrieved from http://www.foxnews.com/story/0,2933,132946,00.html.

Martin, P. and Renegar, V. (2007). "The man for his time"*The Big Lebowski* as carnivalesque social critique. *Communication Studies, 58,* 299–313.

nancyskinnerlive.com (2010, April 22). Skinner on O'Reilly talking Jon Stewart vs Fox.mpg. *YouTube, Inc.* Retrieved from http://www.youtube.com/watch?v=0s6-SKAC_cQ.

Olbrys, S. G. (2006). Disciplining the carnivalesque: Chris Farley's exotic dance. *Communication and critical/cultural studies, 3,* 240–259.

Perelman, C. (1982). *The realm of rhetoric.* London: University of Notre Dame Press.

Perelman, C. and Olbrechts-Tyteca, L. (1969). *The new rhetoric: A treatise on argumentation* (J. Wilkinson and P. Weaver, Trans.). Notre Dame: University of Notre Dame Press.

Poirier, R. (1968). The politics of self-parody. *Partisan Review, 35,* 339–353.

Shields, C. M. (2007). *Bakhtin primer.* New York: Peter Lang.

Waisanen, D. J. (2009). A citizen's guides to democracy inaction: Jon Stewart and Stephen Colbert's comic rhetorical criticism. *Southern Communication Journal, 74,* 119–140.

Warnick, B., and Kline, S. (1992). The New Rhetoric's argument schemes: A rhetorical view of practical reasoning. *Argumentation and Advocacy,* 29(1), 1. Retrieved from Communication and Mass Media Complete database.

Weisman, J. (2008, Oct 31). The groundbreakers: Television: Jon Stewart. *Daily Variety.* Retrieved May 13, 2010 from LexisNexis Academic.

Chapter Seven

The Voice of the People: Jon Stewart, Public Argument, and Political Satire

Ryan McGeough

"The ramification of the issues before the public is so wide and intricate, the technical matters involved are so specialized, the details are so many and so shifting, that the public cannot for any length of time identify and hold itself." —John Dewey (1927, p. 137)

"A class of experts is inevitably so removed from common interests as to become a class with private interests and private knowledge." —John Dewey (1927, p. 207)

Since the industrial revolution, the complexity of public matters from commerce to international relations has been beyond the understanding of the average citizen. To expect a public to command the technical knowledge necessary to formulate a detailed energy policy or repair a spiraling economy is asking for both the impossible and unreasonable. On a variety of issues, publics have had little choice but to turn over control of matters beyond their own understanding to technocratic elites. Yet offering the reins to an elite class of experts seems not only contrary to the principles of a democratic culture, but potentially dangerous as well. The potential that experts could act in their own interests rather than the interests of the public contributed to Dewey's (1927) struggle with how the increasing complexity of modern society could be reconciled with democratic public deliberation. The challenges of finding the appropriate role of specialized knowledge in deliberative democracy have only increased since Dewey's era. Thomas Goodnight (1982) laments "[t]hat the media could be employed to extend knowledgeable debate but do not [is evidence] of the decline of deliberative practice" (p. 260). He claims the media increasingly allow expert discourse to dominate in areas that should be subject to concentrated public deliberation.

Coming at the end of the "golden age" of broadcast news media of the 1960s and 1970s, Goodnight's words proved prophetic. Few would argue that Goodnight's call for the media to improve public deliberation and public understanding of complex issues has been sufficiently answered. Meanwhile, the role of the expert in public affairs has increased. *The Daily Show* offers a nightly critique of how this trend has led to the creation of mock experts, as every *Daily Show* correspondent is introduced as *The Daily Show*'s Senior (fill-in-the-blank) Correspondent. These titles are different every episode, and ironically introduce the correspondents with incredibly story-specific areas of expertise, which sometimes change mid-segment. A single corre-spondent may be introduced as *The Daily Show*'s Senior Black Correspon-dent for one segment, and reintroduced as *The Daily Show*'s Senior Oil Spill Correspondent in the next. The trend they satirize is a symptom of the reli-ance on experts and technocrats that Goodnight suggests has very serious effects on debate in the public sphere. As such, a reexamination of the prob-lem posed by Goodnight would be valuable in determining how we might preserve and improve contemporary public deliberation. To do so, I further elaborate on Goodnight's problem and explore a possible solution in the notion of the *dialectical vernacular*.

Etymologically rooted in the Latin term *verna*, meaning "home-born slave," the term vernacular generally serves to mark something as common, non-institutional, or both (Howard, 2008). The phrase has become popular in critical and rhetorical scholarship, but its potential as an argumentative locus in a mediated environment has yet to be thoroughly explored. This paper expands on the possibilities of vernacular argumentation by addressing the intersection of vernacular argument and multimedia technology. To see what this solution would look like in action, I analyze Jon Stewart's highly touted March 12, 2009 exchange with *Mad Money* host Jim Cramer. I focus specifi-cally on Stewart's use of multimedia to be able to argue in a technical language in which he himself has little or no expertise, as well as with a common indignation typically absent from expert debate. I argue that Stew-art's strategy offers great potential as a method of holding technocrats ac-countable in the public sphere, as well as a call contained within it to fulfill an ideal role of the press: providing the public with sufficient information to revive the democratic ideal of the informed citizen capable of public deliber-ation.

PRIVATE, TECHNICAL, AND PUBLIC SPHERES

Goodnight (1982) claims that contemporary public deliberation occurs in and across three distinct spheres: the personal, technical and public. The spheres are distinct because of the norms and expectations associated with deliberation within each. He notes that "'Sphere' denotes branches of activity—the grounds upon which arguments are built and the authorities to which arguers appeal" (p. 253). Though arguments may move between the spheres, Goodnight suggests U.S. deliberation is unique as a result of the intentional separation of the spheres (e.g., Constitutional protection of private debate from governmental interference).

Those with specialized expertise in a matter of debate tend to deliberate in the technical sphere. Academics and other specialized experts engage in debate over the particular interests of their community. Unlike the personal sphere, the standards for evidence and the formal expectations of argument are generally rigid. Argument in the technical sphere is often conducted using the specialized vocabulary of a given field. When debating in the technical sphere (as opposed to importing its language into the public sphere) the primary goal is the advance of specialized knowledge of a complex topic. However, such specialized knowledge is increasingly essential to matters of public policy, as publics need to address problems relating to highly complex fields such as economics or foreign policy.

In contrast, argument in the personal sphere is typified by informality. No preparation is required to enter into personal argument, and the statements of arguers are ephemeral insofar as they are unlikely to be preserved. In these situations, "evidence is discovered within memory or adduced by pointing to whatever is at hand" (Goodnight, 1982, p. 254). Standards for evaluating arguments in the personal sphere are correspondingly lax—rather than the rigid standards of a given expert community, arguments in the personal sphere are adjudicated by arguers using informal standards. Whether occurring between interlocutors in an airport bar or coffee shop, these encounters do not require specialized expertise in order to make judgments on the topic of conversation.

Transcending both private and technical is the public sphere. In the public sphere, standards of evidence are more fluid and relaxed than in the technical sphere, yet the technical language of the community may still be deployed and mixed with "common language, values, and reasoning" (p. 255). The public sphere contains more formalized modes of deliberation than conversations in the personal sphere. Goodnight's conception of the public sphere is neither the formal requirements for rational-critical debate Habermas describes, nor the quotidian dialogues of Hauser's reticulate public sphere. Goodnight conceives of deliberation in the public sphere as characterized by its focus on stakes that transcend both private and technical concerns, and affect the interests of the broader community.

The problem Goodnight poses lies in the need to deal with the incursion of the private and technical into the public sphere. Deliberative democracy is troubled by "argument practices arising from the personal and technical spheres [that] presently substitute the semblance of deliberative discourse for actual deliberation, thereby diminishing public life" (p. 252). As private and technical modes of argument become the predominant loci for deliberation, the public sphere erodes. Goodnight makes specific note of the increasing tendency of news media to turn to technical modes of discussion, causing "questions of public significance themselves [to] become increasingly difficult to recognize, much less address, because of the intricate roles, procedures, and terminologies of the specialized forums" (p. 259). The reliance on specialized discourse is itself debilitating to the public, as those without a mastery of it are unable to move much beyond the statements of the expert.

This reliance becomes even more dangerous in the inevitable cases where those commanding expert discourse are decidedly wrong. Journalism scholar John Zaller (2003), who argues for a much lower requirement of citizens and public debate, suggests that citizens simply need to be given enough information to hold elected officials accountable at election time. Yet, when public leaders on a topic are unelected technocrats, holding them accountable is far more difficult. If the public is unable even to speak the technical language, it borders on impossible. This possibility adds yet another dimension to the problem of the encroachment of the technical into the public sphere. Examples such as President George W. Bush's use of classified information to both justify the invasion of Iraq, and deflect criticism after that information turned out to be false, evidence a larger trend emerging from the incursion of the technical into the public: retreat to the technical sphere to escape public accountability. The mystification of any given field (whether it be foreign intelligence, economics, or science) renders those with access to knowledge a particularly powerful place in deliberation and informing the public. However, should those experts' statements prove incorrect or misleading, that same mystification denies the public access to the vocabularies necessary to hold the experts accountable. Imagined as a Venn diagram, although the technical sphere is increasingly encroaching into the public sphere (as experts make decisions about matters of public concern), the technical sphere also retains enough outside room for those experts who speak the technical language to retreat out of the realm of public accountability.

Exactly what Goodnight would have us do about this problem is unclear. To the broader problem of the erosion of the public sphere, he suggests "those practices which replace deliberative rhetoric by substituting alternative modes of invention and restricting subject matter need to be uncovered and critiqued" (p. 261). However, thirty years after Goodnight's call, it seems that scholars pointing out the technical sphere's infiltration of the public sphere has been of little avail. These days, the solution of unmasking feels somewhat unfulfilling. To offer a more specific solution to the problem of retreating to the technical, I now turn to the *dialectical vernacular*. Robert Howard (2008) claims that new media technologies allow for the creation of a vernacular rhetoric, offering powerful "possibility[ies] for transformation" (p. 509). Yet, exactly what problems such rhetoric is well-suited to address remains ill-defined. In the next few pages I seek to explain the dialectical vernacular as an argumentative strategy appropriate for the problems Goodnight poses.

DIALECTICAL VERNACULAR

Howard (2008) suggests that vernacular rhetoric has always been recognized as a powerful agency to enact social change. However, to understand how this agency works, it is necessary to return to the origins of the term, which has been lost in contemporary scholarship:

> On the one hand, vernacular forms are those available to individuals or groups who are subordinated to institutions, and, on the other, they are a common resource made available to everyone through informal social interaction. . . . As the concept emerged in communication studies however, it became bifurcated along these two lines. On the one hand, the vernacular is imagined as local discourse that is distinct from larger institutional discourses. In this "subaltern" view, the vernacular voice is that of the subordinate counteragent seeking to be heard over hegemony. On the other hand, the vernacular is imagined as a shared resource, a sensus communis, or community doxa. In this "common" view, the vernacular is a communal chorus that emerges from the multiplicity of voices speaking in the noninstitutional discursive spaces of quotidian life. Both of these conceptions, however, rely on a strict division that fails to fully account for the vernacular's hybrid characteristics. (p. 491)

In other words, both "subaltern" and "common" notions of the vernacular reflect a contemporary division of the term that neglect that it is both of these, and more.

The subaltern vernacular suggests a discourse distinct from institutional discourse, created by the marginal's cooptation of that dominant discourse. Ono and Sloop (1995) describe the subaltern vernacular as a "syncretic" pastiche that "constructs a unique discursive from out of cultural fragments," that, rather than serving the interests of the institution, often subvert and work against the dominant (p. 23). In contrast, the notion of "common" vernacular connotes the local language and nomenclature of a community. Hauser (1999) suggests that the bonds of a public are maintained by its shared language, which contains within the ability to call a people together for action. Howard (2008) claims that the common "vernacular is equated with the doxa, sensus communis or 'common sense' that is maintained and taught within a local community but held separate from institutional power structures" (p. 495). Thus, the common vernacular refers to a set of language and modes of thought common to a people that are maintained outside of institutional power.

These divergent definitions of vernacular sell short its significant social power by forgetting its original meaning. As I noted above, the term verna (or the Greek *oikotrips*) referred to a slave born in the Roman household. These slaves were more valuable because although the Empire was so vast that most slaves spoke some sort of vulgar Latin, verna tended to be fluent speakers of both Latin and their native languages. The ability to speak the native and institutional languages made the verna both valuable and potentially dangerous. Whether in supporting or contesting those in power, the "noninstitutional aspect of the verna was seen as powerful by institutional Rome precisely because it was able to act both in institutional modes of communication, and because it had access to something beyond the control of those institutional powers. . . . The vernacular is powerful because it can introduce something other than the institutional into an institutional realm" (Howard, 2008, p. 496). As the Romans recognized, the ability to speak multiple languages and import the common modes of thought and argument from one into the other can serve as a potent challenge to institutional discourse.

The term is *dialectical* precisely because it creates a clash of two separate modes of thought and language. The user of the dialectical vernacular invokes his/her status as both part of and outside of the marginal and dominant communities. In doing so, he/she engages in "a complicit means to power where the vernacular gains an alternate authority by participating in its own subordination" (Howard, 2008, p. 497). Unlike the subaltern or common conceptions of vernacular, this mode of argument is available only because the user has some authentic membership to both the marginal and dominant communities and is recognized as an outsider as well as part of the establishment.

DIALECTICAL VERNACULAR ON *THE DAILY SHOW*

On February 19, 2009, CNBC's Rick Santelli issued an impassioned rant on the floor of the Chicago Mercantile exchange in which he decried the Obama administration's Making Home Affordable mortgage relief program as an attempt to "subsidize the losers' mortgages" (Blumer, 2009). As the traders around him jeered and shouted, Santelli compared the mortgage program to Cuban socialism that would make the founding fathers "roll over in their graves" (Blumer, 2009). After Santelli failed to attend a scheduled appearance on *The Daily Show*, Stewart responded with an eight-minute segment which began by berating Santelli for his outburst and for having cancelled on his *Daily Show* appearance. He then turned on CNBC by ironically mocking all of the loser homeowners who were optimistic enough to accept money offered to them by large banks and replaying CNBC's ad claiming to offer the information and expertise necessary for the complex financial world. Stewart followed this with a montage of CNBC commentators and reporters making optimistic recommendations on major financial stocks such as Bear Stearns and Lehman Brothers, or on the market as a whole. Following each dated clip was the date that each respective company defaulted or the steadily declining Dow Jones Industrial Average. *Mad Money* host Jim Cramer accused Stewart of being unfair, and other NBC affiliate hosts, such as MSNBC's conservative commentator Joe Scarborough, began criticizing *The Daily Show*'s treatment of CNBC. Stewart responded with a montage calling on the support of *The Daily Show* parent company Viacom's other "personalities" such as Bob the Builder and Dora the Explorer. After a series of exchanges made on each of their programs, Cramer agreed to appear on *The Daily Show*.

I focus on a few specific moments in Stewart's (Bodow and O'Neill, 2009) interview with Cramer to demonstrate Stewart's use of the dialectical vernacular as an argumentative strategy to counter Cramer's attempts to retreat from the public to the technical sphere. Where Stewart has no personal expertise, he is able to turn to a multimediated response. Stewart uses video clips of Cramer to respond to Cramer's use of technical discourse, combined with a performance of indignation toward CNBC and Cramer for failing to protect those without expert knowledge of the economy. Although common indignation might seem an irrational response to expert argument, when coupled with Cramer's own statements, it becomes a powerful tool by positioning Stewart as a member of the public Cramer and CNBC have failed. Certainly not the first to speak in the name of the people, Stewart's debate with Cramer is unique in that his responses to Cramer's arguments are intertextual—a mix of common indignation, a sufficient degree of technical knowledge to engage in the debate, and, most strikingly, a fluid pastiche of video clips from Cramer's television program *Mad Money*.

The episode begins with Stewart claiming to be intimidated by the complexities of engaging in a financial debate. He opens the show by stating that he spent the day training, and the screen cuts to a mock boot-camp segment showing Stewart answering (sometimes incorrectly) a rapid barrage of technical questions on financial topics such as the number of stocks in the Dow, the largest hardware and software components, and the meaning of financial terms such as tier-one capital and P/E ratio. The camera cuts back to Stewart, who ironically reaffirms his newfound financial expertise by noting that the person on the back of the twenty dollar bill is a president but the person on the back of the hundred dollar bill is just some guy, and claiming to not have known that before his training.

After Cramer makes his way on stage, Stewart begins by making clear that his concern is with CNBC rather than Cramer himself. Stewart recounts his criticism of Santelli for working at a network which praised the banks and financial practices that led to the financial collapse, then criticizing people who had lost their homes. He notes his frustration with CNBC and Santelli for failing to recognize how they had contributed to the problems leading up to the collapse. Although Stewart lambastes Cramer throughout the interview, he consistently reiterates that Cramer is simply one member of a larger financial news media failing to uphold its responsibilities to the public.

In response to Stewart's criticism, Cramer repeatedly attempts to retreat from responsibility for his and CNBC's role in the recession by blaming others for economic maneuvering that contributed to the overvaluing of stocks, and adopting an expert persona that qualifies him to tell the public how incredibly complex the market is. Stewart airs a clip from a financial radio show in which Cramer states: "You know a lot of times when I was short at my hedge fund and I was position short, meaning I needed it down, I would create a level of activity beforehand that could drive the futures. It doesn't take much money" (Bodow and O'Neill, 2009). When Stewart asks Cramer to explain this technical statement, Cramer claims that his statement on the radio program was simply an exaggerated example. He then claims that he has actually been working to reduce short selling (the practice described above), and rather than engaging in the practice himself, he has been attempting to publicize such practices and the financial risks of engaging in them. Stewart notes that in the clip, Cramer sounds as though he was admitting to engaging in short selling. In response, Cramer states that he must have been inarticulate in the clip, because he did not engage in short selling, but rather tried to get financial regulators to monitor the practice.

Stewart simply responds by asking for the next clip. In it, Cramer tells the host that he would encourage hedge fund managers to engage in short selling because it is a legal, satisfying and fast way to make a profit. Following the clip, Cramer is left looking around uncomfortably for a moment, and as the studio audience groans, Stewart suggests an interesting goal for CNBC and *Mad Money* in pleading for protection from the Cramer he sees on the video clips (Bodow and O'Neill, 2009).

In this exchange, Stewart answers Cramer's attempt to renegotiate the meaning of past technical statements by simply replaying Cramer's own words. Cramer attempts to describe his field as technical and difficult to understand, and then misleadingly translates his past statements by claiming that he was trying to encourage regulation of short selling. However, by juxtaposing multiple video clips of Cramer's past statements, Stewart allows the audience to evaluate technical claims (Cramer's claim that although it is difficult to understand his past statements, what he was really saying was that more regulation is necessary) by the standards of the personal sphere (in this case, is Cramer being honest?). The groans of the audience do not suggest they have a greater understanding of the technical intricacies of short selling or financial markets, but rather that they now have the knowledge to evaluate his arguments using criterion from the personal sphere—he is clearly lying. The ability to hold experts accountable using the criteria of the personal sphere may be the best mechanism of accountability such satire allows. It is unreasonable, after all, to expect a public, a studio audience or even a host to have the technical knowledge necessary to contest the technical claims of various experts. However, Stewart demonstrates the possibility of equipping the public to judge the experts themselves, by using multimedia to demonstrate the contradictions between Cramer's statements.

Cramer describes himself as helping to curb dangerous Wall Street practices, noting he has been working with members of congress to implement legislation known as uptick rule (though he fails to explain it, the rule regulates the short selling Cramer had just admitted to engaging in). Rather than explain what the regulation means, Cramer again simply labels it as something technical and claims it as evidence he is trying to help with the problems Stewart accuses him of contributing to. Again, Cramer positions himself as an expert but overtly avoids explaining what he claims to have done to protect consumers. Further skirting any responsibility, he repeatedly describes the economic downturn as so complex and unpredictable that even the best financial minds could not have seen it coming. Cramer then attempts to absolve himself of responsibility by blaming the insiders that provided him with his own expert information. He states that the CEOs who appear on *Mad Money* sometimes lie to him, and claims that without subpoena power it is difficult to know if experts are providing him with accurate information.

Again Stewart counters Cramer with his own language, rejecting Cramer's repeated attempts to blame his own failures on technical conversations with dishonest elites on and off of *Mad Money*. He responds by rolling a clip in which Cramer states "You can't foment. You can't create, yourself, an impression that a stock's down, but you do it anyway because the SEC doesn't understand it" (Bodow and O'Neill, 2009). The camera cuts back to Stewart, who asks for another clip. In the next clip, Cramer states:

> Apple is [sic] very important to spread the rumor that both Verizon and AT&T have decided that they don't like the phone. That's a very easy one to do. You also want to spread the rumor that it is not going to be ready for MacWorld and this is very easy because the people who write about Apple want that story, and you can claim that it is credible because you spoke to someone at Apple. (Bodow and O'Neill, 2009)

Following the fomenting clip, Stewart expresses a frustration with Cramer, not as someone able to answer back Cramer's expert claim that the 2008 financial collapse was unforeseeable, but as a member of the public disgusted with the media's failure. Having already identified himself as speaking only as a layperson he responds to the video by seemingly losing his temper and chastising Cramer for making finance into a game. Despite Cramer's attempts to describe the market as complex and unpredictable, Stewart states that seeing these videos of Cramer makes him believe that Cramer and other CNBC personalities do understand how they contributed to the financial collapse, and that pretending it is the result of a one-in-a-million confluence of complex and unforeseeable factors is lying and potentially criminal. Stewart then seems visibly angry at Cramer's claim that he wants indictments for those responsible, Stewart compares the corruption and financial mismanagement leading to the collapse with Sherman's March, and berates Cramer (and other financial commentators) for knowing this corruption was occurring, but failing to do anything.

These moments of indignation are important because they serve to punctuate Stewart's repeated positioning of himself as a layperson counting on the media establishment to do its job. Stewart invokes the vernacular, despite being a media figure, by marking his communication as alternate to the institutional. His discussion of the money lost in the collapse consistently polarizes the people (including himself and his family) whose money was lost and the financial insiders (including financial media) responsible for this loss. Stewart consistently criticizes Cramer for contributing to the loss of *our* pensions and retirement funds. In so doing, he is able to counter Cramer's attempts to use technical language to absolve himself of guilt by both enabling his audience to evaluate Cramer's technical claims through more informal and personal criteria, as well as by translating the technical causes Cramer offers for the financial collapse into its effects in the personal sphere. When Cramer argues that the collapse was unforeseeable and that CNBC is trying to offer interesting programming about a dry and technical field, Stewart responds that they were complicit in the practices leading to the collapse, and emphasizes the personal costs of this complicity. He closes the interview by telling Cramer that his seventy-five-year-old mother lost her savings in the financial collapse.

THE PRESS AND THE PUBLIC

Though Stewart debates Cramer on technical issues, enabling his audience to evaluate them using personal criteria and by enumerating personal costs, he consistently returns the debate to the public stakes of the CNBC's failures. Stewart's self-assumed role as a watchdog of journalism has been well recognized amongst both scholars and the press itself. National Public Radio contributor David Folkenflik (2009) claims "at times, Stewart crystallizes the frustration others have with the failings of the media with near-perfect pitch" (para. 15). Obviously, Stewart is himself an important member of the press, yet his popularity seems to partially stem from the frustration he shares with his viewers about the failings of politicians and the press.

Stewart utilizes the dialectical vernacular in part through his repeated positioning of himself as a "layperson" and non-expert member of the general public. Yet accompanying Stewart's statements on how CNBC has failed himself and other members of the public counting on the financial news media is a recurrent call to fulfill the public duties of the press. He chastises Cramer by comparing his calm and rational demeanor in media appearances outside of *Mad Money* with his *Mad Money* persona who throws cream pies and plastic cows and pushes a large red button that shouts "Sell! Sell! Sell!" Stewart states that he is unable to reconcile the expertise and technical knowledge of financial markets Cramer possesses with the dramatic and eccentric persona he portrays on his program.

The opening of *The Daily Show* on the day of Cramer's appearance offers a not so subtle critique of the spectacular form much financial (and other) news comes in, with an explosion laden introduction leading into what commercials for the episode had labeled the "week-long feud of the century." Throughout the interview, Stewart condemns Cramer for a spectacular show in which he honks horns, throws cows, and orders viewers to "Buy! Buy! Buy!" He drives this point home early in the interview by showing and then criticizing a *Mad Money* promo in which viewers are told not to panic about an "economy in free-fall" because "When you don't know what to do, don't panic, Cramer's got your back!" (Bodow and O'Neill, 2009) This spectacular brand of news is part of what Goodnight (1982) sees as diminishing the public sphere. News media "artfully capture the drama of public debate even while systematically stripping public argument of consequences beyond the captured attention given to the media itself. And the media's own patterns of argument create a view of life where the trivial and mundane eternally interchange with the tragic and spectacular by the hour" (p. 260). Stewart's critique of Cramer echoes Goodnight's concern that in its reliance on spectacular news coverage, the news media is failing to properly equip its viewership to deal with complex issues.

Though numerous scholars have explored the potentially dangerous effects of such spectacular news framing (Bennett et. al, 2008; Capella and Jamieson, 1997; Entman, 2003; Hamilton, 2004), Stewart uses the dual positioning of the dialectical vernacular to both satirize and earnestly criticize the failings of financial news to one of its most famous personalities.

Having recounted the personal costs of CNBC's failures, Stewart leaves Cramer little room for maneuver when he asks whether Cramer is responsible to working people who take advice from *Mad Money* when investing their pensions and 401(k)s, or to Wall Street executives and traders. After getting

Cramer to repeatedly state that he wished he had done better for his audience, Stewart turns to suggesting the public responsibilities of the financial media. Stewart suggests an ideal for the financial news media reminiscent of his now famous 2004 appearance on CNN's *Crossfire*—asking for a less theatrical and spectacular press in favor of one focused on equipping viewers to better understand complex issues and holding financial experts/insiders accountable.

Critics such as Baym (2005) have posited that Stewart's blend of news, comedy and political commentary advances a "deliberative model of democracy based on civility of exchange, complexity of argument and the goal of mutual understanding" (p. 273). Stewart's suggestions to Cramer describing the role of the financial media support this read of *The Daily Show*. Stewart consistently calls on Cramer to explain the financial realm to a public with little knowledge of its inner workings. At least in this way, his call is like that of Walter Lippmann's (1922)—the role of the press is to provide the public with the knowledge they need on matters "too big, too complex, and too fleeting for direct acquaintance" (p. 8). Yet, unlike Lippmann, Stewart does not seem to think it is too much to ask of the press to provide individuals with the information necessary to at least *better* understand complex financial markets. Responding to Cramer's attempts to deflect blame to financial regulators, Stewart notes this potential when he asks Cramer why he blames regulators when CNBC could have exposed the practices leading to the financial collapse. His responses to Cramer seem to suggest an ideal for the financial news media of not only serving as a tool of illumination for the public, but also engaging in investigative journalism necessary to hold financial experts accountable.

Near the end of the interview Stewart notes that the clips he aired in response to Cramer make clear there is a difference between the intent and letter of the law. Speaking as a member of a public depending upon the financial media to perform a watchdog role, Stewart tells Cramer the American public would benefit from an organization beyond the SEC holding financial companies and technocrats accountable and exposing when the spirit of the law was being broken. He describes a financial news media capable of illuminating unethical financial dealings such as what Cramer advocates in the earlier clip in which Cramer notes that although fomenting is illegal, investors should "do it anyway because the SEC doesn't understand it" (Bodow and O'Neill, 2009). Stewart tells Cramer that he desperately wishes insiders like Cramer would expose the dangerous practices that financial insiders engage in. The public role Stewart describes for the financial news media is not unlike his own use of the dialectical vernacular—a group of reporters who speak both the language of financial markets and that of the public, translate the language of the markets into something understandable to their viewers, and are capable of introducing something from outside of the institution (in this case, accountability) into the institutional realm.

CONCLUSION

Thomas Goodnight (1982) notes that "argumentation offers a momentary pause in the flow of events, an opportunity to look down the present road as well as paths untaken" (p. 251). A look down the present road indicates that Goodnight's fear of the technical sphere's incursion into the public sphere has proven well founded. Yet because of the inaccessibility of technical discourses, the same experts who the news media allow to replace public deliberation are able to enter and exit the public sphere without the accountability that generally typifies public sphere deliberation. In the wake of the 2008 market collapse, financial experts hoped to make a similar escape. Jon Stewart's feud with *Mad Money* host Jim Cramer demonstrates one example of maintaining this accountability. Though other critics should continue to analyze the concept of the dialectical vernacular in more depth, a cursory view of Stewart's deployment of multimedia evidenced a unique strategy for holding elites accountable, and performing the difficult but important task of translating technical language into the public sphere (Fabj and Sobnosky, 1995). By using Cramer's own words to access his technical language, playing the role of a citizen betrayed by Cramer and CNBC, and constantly refocusing the discussion onto the public stakes of having a healthy financial news media, Stewart is able to invoke the dialectical vernacular as a strategy to hold Cramer and CNBC accountable in the public sphere.

Beyond cudgeling Cramer and his employer for their acquiescence to Wall Street traders and their part in his elderly mother's financial difficulties, Stewart's clash with Cramer offers an entry point into some interesting insights into the role of news media in democracy. When Stewart calls out Cramer for the spectacular, dramatic framing of *Mad Money*, Cramer replies that like Stewart, he is trying to make a successful television program. He notes that viewers are not interested in the sorts of technical issues Stewart was rehearsing at the beginning of the episode, that he tries to have an educational segment in each show, but if he focused entirely on such topics, viewers would simply tune out. Stewart further lambastes him for failing to provide individuals with the base knowledge to make investment decisions, but Cramer's argument raises an important point—market/economic pressures often inhibit the press from fulfilling its optimal role. Again, Goodnight's (1982) call to unmask the failures of experts and the press, even when done well and done publicly, may be insufficient to overcome the market pressures for spectacular journalism that neither informs the public nor holds experts and insiders accountable.

However, Stewart does not seem to think the spectacular journalism Goodnight criticizes is necessary, as evidenced by his past statement: "For some reason, people think that solid, good, in-depth [reporting] equals dull, low ratings, low profitability." He states "I don't think that's the case. I think you can make really exciting, interesting television news that could become the medium of record for reasonable, moderate people" (Schlosser, 2003). Whether this is an attainable goal for news media in general, and financial news media in particular, is beyond the scope of this essay. As a member of the press, it is a goal Stewart contributes to while claiming it is not his responsibility; as a member of the public, it is a goal he seems to wish did not fall to him. Yet through his use of the dialectical vernacular, it is a goal Stewart often fulfills—finally getting Cramer to agree to return to fundamentals of reporting, so that Stewart can return to comedy.

REFERENCES

Baym, G. (2005). *The Daily Show*: Discursive integration and the reinvention of political journalism. *Political Communication, 22*(2), p. 259–276.

Bennett, W.L., Lawrence, R. G., and Livingston, S. (2008). *When the press fails: Political power and the news media from Iraq to Hurricane Katrina.* Chicago: University of Chicago Press.

Blumer, T. (2009, February 19). Rant for the Ages: CNBC's Rick Santelli Goes Off; Studio Hosts Invoke 'Mob Rule' to Downplay. Retrieved from: http://newsbusters.org/blogs/tom-blumer/2009/02/19/rant-ages-cnbcs-rick-santelli-goes-studio-hosts-invoke-mob-rule-down-play.

Bodow, S. (Head Writer) and O'Neill, C. (Director). (2009, March 12). [Television series episode]. In J. Stewart (Executive producer), *The Daily Show with Jon Stewart.* New York: Viacom.

Capella, J.N. and Jamieson, K.H. (1997). *The spiral of cynicism: The press and the public good.* NY: Oxford University Press.

Dewey, J. (1927). *The public and its problems.* New York: Holt.

Entman. R. (2003). Projections of power: *News framing, public opinion, and U.S. foreign policy.* Chicago: University of Chicago Press.

Fabj, V., and Sobnosky, M.J. (1995). Aids activism and the rejuvenation of the public sphere. *Argumentation and Advocacy*, 31(1), 163–184.

Folkenflik, D. (2009). *On 'Daily Show' Stewart, Cramer get serious.* Retrieved from: http://www.npr.org/templates/story/story.php?storyId=101888064.

Gans, Herbert, J. (2004). *Deciding What's News: A Study of CBS Evening News, NBC Nightly News, Newsweek and Time.* (25th Anniversary Edition). Evanston, IL: Northwestern University Press.

Goodnight, G.T. (1982). The persona, technical, and public spheres of argument: A speculative inquiry into the art of public deliberation. *Argumentation and Advocacy, 18*, 214–227.

Hamilton, J.T. (2004). *All the news that's fit to sell.* Princeton, NJ: Princeton University Press.

Hauser, G.A. (1999). *Vernacular voices: The rhetoric of publics and public sphere.* Columbia: University of South Carolina Press.

Howard, R.G. (2008). The vernacular web of participatory media. *Critical Studies in Media Communication*, 25(5), 490–513.

Lippmann, W. (1922). *Public opinion.* NY: Harcourt and Brace.

Ono, K.A., and Sloop, J.M. (1995). The critique of vernacular discourse. *Communication Monographs, 62*(1), 19–46.

Schlosser, E. (2003). The kids are alright. *Columbia Journalism Review,* 41, 27–30.

Zaller, J. (2003). A new standard for news quality: The burglar alarm and the monitorial citizen. *Political Communication, 20*(3), 109–130.

III

Strategies

Chapter Eight

We Frame to Please: A Preliminary Examination of *The Daily Show*'s Use of Frames

Penina Wiesman

There has been a lot of buzz about Comedy Central's satirical news program *The Daily Show* and its estimable host, Jon Stewart. This attention is warranted, as the program has not only won countless entertainment awards, but has also captured two Peabody awards for its coverage of the 2000 and 2004 presidential elections. In addition to Stewart's and *The Daily Show*'s contribution to contemporary political discourse, research has shown that *The Daily Show* has become an important (though not the only) news source for the younger generation (Pew Research Center, 2004).

The Daily Show has also received significant praise from the academic world. Far from "fake," scholars and journalists have extended their analyses to praise *The Daily Show* as an innovative critique of the techniques used by both politicians and the News[1] to manipulate the public (Alterman, 2009; Day, 2009; McKain, 2005), purveyor of truth (Alterman, 2009; Cornfield, 2005), a method of encouraging critical thinking (Morreale, 2009; Trier, 2008(a), 2008(b)), a facilitator of democracy (Baym, 2005; Hariman, 2007; Warner, 2007), a subversive political tool (Warner, 2007), a way to draw more people into politics and News consumption (Baym, 2005; Mutz, 2004), and even as a model for an evolved form of journalism (Baym, 2005).

Based on this nearly unbridled praise, the function of *The Daily Show*, in the eyes of many journalists and scholars, can be summed up with the following: *The Daily Show* reveals "the artificiality of real newscasts" (Day, 2009, p. 86), alerting the viewer to the highly constructed nature of News presentations of reality (by editors, media consultants and spin doctors), prompting a more skeptical consumption of these products, and possibly even political action. That *The Daily Show* operates as a satirical parody of mainstream television News is noted by nearly all sources. However, most are content to identify what the show is parodying before moving on to the business of proving why, based on their theoretical analysis, the program merits such praise. In other words, the discourse surrounding *The Daily Show* uses its parodic text as a springboard to suggest more panoptic implications of the effects of *The Daily Show* as a unit.

A closer examination of what exactly *The Daily Show* is parodying reveals a unifying element that is a characteristic of both that which *The Daily Show* is criticizing and the form of critique itself: framing. The aforementioned analyses of *The Daily Show* performed by these scholars (in particular, Baym, 2005; Day, 2009; McKain, 2005; Smolkin, 2007; and Warner, 2007) lend support to the observation that *The Daily Show* exposes the framing activities performed by mainstream News (and by extension, politicians, who have learned to adjust their strategy to take advantage of the News' modus operandi (Jamieson and Waldman, 2003; Warner, 2007). As a result, it can be (and has been) argued that *The Daily Show*'s audiences learn to be aware of the constructed nature of packaged information from News and politicians, and are judged to be better off for it.

Such praise focuses wholly on *The Daily Show*'s encouraging contributions to political communication and journalism, domains that are perceived to be in crisis. While the accolades *The Daily Show* receives in this area are certainly justified, there seems to be an absence of discussion centering on the program'sown relationship to framing as a process it uses itself. The comedic nature of *The Daily Show*'s content is often discounted as having little to no importance to the show's greater social purposes, but this paper will show how *The Daily Show*'s framing activities are actually intended to satisfy its own comic agenda. In fact, as I will argue below, on *The Daily Show,* framing for comedy takes precedence over the other functions for which the show has been commended.

FRAMING

There has been quite a bit of scholarly discourse on framing in an effort to explicate and organize the concept of framing. Simply put, framing is a method of organizing and presenting information (de Vreese, 2005; Nelson et al, 1997). Entman (1993) defined framing as a process involving the choosing of certain components of "a perceived reality" and then highlighting those elements, or "mak[ing] them more salient," in the message communication, with the goal of advancing a specific interpretation of the particular situation under discussion (p. 52). Entman (1993) did not specifically limit frames to the domain of the text producer, instead postulated that frames operate along four nodes of the communication process: the communicator, the text, the receiver, and the culture. Building on this suggestion, de Vreese (2005) posed an integrated process model of framing that identifies three stages of framing: "frame building, frame setting, and individual and societal level consequences of framing" (p. 52). The model suggests the overlapping of the four locations posed by Entman (1993) in the process of framing. Frame-building is the determination of the frame by the communication source and its subsequent creation in the text. "*Frame-setting* refers to the interaction between media frames and individuals' prior knowledge and pre-dispositions," both of which are determined by cultural norms as well as personal experience (de Vreese, 2005, p. 52). Consequences, the final stage in the model, are the effects of these frames on individual attitudes and broader social processes.

In the context of this examination of framing in News and on *The Daily Show*, the focus is primarily on the frame-building stage, with some emphasis on the frame-setting stage. When a frame is created for the presentation of an issue, its constructor intends to communicate a specific interpretation of that issue. The preferred interpretation might be driven by a simple narrative ("Pilot makes safe emergency landing"), or it might seek to achieve a broad influence, as with a political ideology (i.e. conservative or liberal). Additionally, the perspective of the assumed audience is to some extent taken into account, as the successful transmission and acceptance of information through a constructed frame will depend on its resonance with the audience's extant understandings of the world around them. The final, completed frame will integrate both the intentions of the producer and the assumed prior knowledge of the audience. Since framing here relates to the communicative power inherent in the way a text is constructed (Entman, 1993), frames are therefore ideal tools for controlling information when constructed within a News text, as well as defining the boundaries of discussion for any issue (Jamieson and Waldman, 2003; Nelson et al, 1997).

The complexity of frame construction can be basically understood to consist of processes that can be classified as either structural or rhetorical. On structural level, in the interest of privileging one interpretation, a frame might be designed to deliberately exclude information that does not support the stressed focus (Jamieson and Waldman, 2003; Nelson et al, 1997). Here, the frame can be seen as a rather literal construct, determining "what information is included and what is ignored" (Jamieson and Waldman, 2003, p. xiii), thus delineating the parameters of that issue. Rhetorically, a frame promotes its preferred perception by linking information to corresponding "culturally familiar symbols" present in the audience's knowledge structure "that guide individuals' processing of information" (Entman, 1993, p. 53). In other words, frames will also utilize certain culturally dependent constructs, such as stereotypes or provocative wording, in its presentation of information in order to evoke a specific reaction intended to further guide the audience to acceptance of the frame's highlighted perspective.

FRAMES IN NEWS

The simplest practical examples of the rhetorical and structural components of the framing process used in News production are word choice and video editing, respectively. Word choice is important in the construction of frames because language is the foundation of how we define and understand our surroundings. Therefore, both the newsmaker and the News deliberately choose words and phrases based on their semiotic and emotional characteristics. As a structural process of framing, video editing for a News story admits certain pieces of information and excludes others through the physical cutting and organization of content (Jamieson and Waldman, 2003). By cutting down lengthy footage of a political speech, for example, a video editor at a news station can choose which images and words will represent the entire event to the public.

As a way to organize large amounts of information for presentation, frames are an ideal tool for News programming because they offer predictable categories of interpretation that help to simplify the journalist's job (Jamieson and Waldman, 2003). However, structural and rhetorical processes of frame construction give these organizations an additional degree of power. The rhetorical ability to trigger extant knowledge constructs and cultural beliefs is a key element of a frame's power over audience reactions (Entman, 1993; Nelson et al., 1997). Moreover, because structurally News frames literally "determine the content of the news," they control what constitutes reality for the average citizen (Jamieson and Waldman, 2003, p. xii). Given the power the use of frames offers over audience interpretation, as well as the News' general reliance on them, it is therefore not surprising that politicians have since adopted frames as a valuable communication technique (Entman, 1993; Jamieson and Waldman, 2003; Nelson, et al, 1997).

Frames can be problematic in News because they are seen as interfering with journalism's duties to the public (Entman, 1993; Jamieson and Waldman, 2003). Contemporary critics have charged the mainstream News with journalistic malpractice in the form of behaviors and tendencies believed to not be in the American public's best interest (Gaines, 2007; Kellner, 2004; Warner, 2007). The charges include, but are not limited to, complaints of misplaced focus (Jamieson and Waldman, 2003; Kellner, 2004), a defective sense of "balance" (Day, 2009; Entman, 1993; Nelson et al, 1997), unquestioningly adopting politically constructed frames for News coverage (Jamieson and Waldman, 2003; Kellner, 2004; Trier, 2008a), and a lack of critical analysis in News coverage (Baym, 2005; Kellner, 2004). Although some of these critics do not explicitly say so, these criticisms are all issues concerning framing.

FRAMING IN *THE DAILY SHOW*

The praise that *The Daily Show* has received has been focused, in part, on the show's ability to fulfill the roles the News has been neglecting, specifically, its ability to take the News and politicians to task for their use of frames to manipulate or even shortchange the public (Colapinto, 2004; Day, 2009; Solomon, 2008). *The Daily Show* devotes significant energy to criticizing the News' and political actors' use of structural and rhetorical framing techniques to support interpretations of an issue that agree with their underlying agenda. However, there seems to be an absence of discussion centering on *The Daily Show*'s relationship to framing as a technique it uses itself rather than a practice performed by "others."

In order to assess how *The Daily Show* uses framing, the program's primary agenda must first be identified. The discourse surrounding *The Daily Show* interprets the show's "agenda" to be related to its attacks on media and politics, only paying lip service to the show's comic elements. I argue, however, that the comedy that others have essentially dismissed is actually *The Daily Show*'s primary agenda. If *The Daily Show* was *primarily* driven by the critical agendas scholars have attributed to it, the tone and content of all its content would be guided by frames constructed to reflect these goals. However, while scholars each chose to cite specific examples from *The Daily Show* to illustrate the different goals they ascribe to the show, the examples used throughout the discourse are similar in that they are *all* humorous. As the common denominator, therefore, it is reasonable to propose that comedy is *The Daily Show*'s primary agenda.

Additionally, despite the buzz in academic, journalistic, and political arenas, *The Daily Show* continues to defend its identity as a comedy program. Although frames can be constructed to fulfill a variety of motives, in order to determine the primary agenda driving the framing tactics of *The Daily Show*, one need look no further than the words of Jon Stewart: "Ultimately," he said in an interview for *Rolling Stone* magazine, "I'm judged on whether or not the show is funny" (Colapinto, 2004, p. 64). This particular quotation is certainly not the only time Stewart has identified comedy as the primary goal of the show. The most famous example, cited by a number of articles, occurred during his 2004 appearance on the now defunct CNN program *Crossfire* (see Alterman, 2009; Baym, 2005; Day, 2009; Hart and Hartelius, 2007;

Kakutani, 2008; Morreale, 2009). After levying an unexpected attack on the program, host Tucker Carlson countered by criticizing Stewart for not asking tough questions of then presidential candidate John Kerry when he appeared on *The Daily Show*. Stewart's responded with the now infamous "You're on CNN. The show that leads into me is puppets making crank phone calls" (quoted in Hart and Hartelius, 2007, p. 267). The steadfastness with which *The Daily Show* defends its "fake" News designation is further indication that comedy is the program's primary agenda.

The identification of comedy as *The Daily Show*'s primary agenda determines that all other political, critical, or social agendas attributed to the show are secondary, and that their effects on the show's frame-building activities will ultimately be subordinate to the comic agenda. It is therefore reasonable to suggest that all framing efforts undertaken by *The Daily Show* will be chiefly geared toward maximizing its comedic output. This comedic output I have termed *The Daily Show*'s Comic Frame. The term "comic frame" was originally coined by theorist Kenneth Burke, though it carries a slightly different meaning and application in literary and dramatic rhetoric (Burke, 1984). In the context of this chapter, however, the Comic Frame will refer to the comic interpretation *The Daily Show* seeks to convey in its treatment of all content which is constructed through the use of various framing techniques.

Upon reviewing research focusing on *The Daily Show*'s function in political media, analyses of the program was found to vary in terms of overall objective and choice of *The Daily Show*'s techniques evaluated to that end. It was deemed beyond the scope of this chapter to embark on a lengthy, in-depth investigation of the myriad ways *The Daily Show* employs its Comic Frame. However, both word choice and video editing are ideal points of analysis from which to begin. As discussed above, they are basic examples of the rhetorical and structural components of frame construction, respectively. In addition to being used by News programming, these techniques are also used by *The Daily Show*, in part due to its parodic and critical activities (Day, 2009), but also to fulfill its comic agenda. Therefore, this study will analyze the *The Daily Show*'s use of word choice and video editing as the site of introductory evidence of the show's Comic Frame.

WORD CHOICE

According to Andrea DeCapua (2007), it is the surrounding social and cultural milieus that establish the meaning of words and phrases that otherwise would just be "arbitrary systems of sounds and sound patterns" (p. 70). Since meaning in language is, at its core, subjectively determined, the descriptions it constructs of the world are therefore equally subjective. This logic leads DeCapua (2007) to conclude that "there is no absolute objective reality," only that which has been produced by language (p. 77).

Because language is the foundation of how we define and understand our surroundings, word choice is an important part of any frame. Jamieson and Waldman (2003) specifically identify language choice as a key framing strategy in political communication:

> Tax cuts or tax relief? Religious or faith-based? Death penalty or execution? Estate tax or death tax? Civilian deaths or collateral damage? In the early stages of almost any policy debate, one can find a battle over which terms will be chosen. Because the terms we use to describe the world determine the ways we see it, those who control the language control the argument, and those who control the argument are more likely to successfully translate belief into policy (p. xiv).

The truth of this statement leads both the newsmaker and the News to deliberately select specific words and phrases for their semiotic value and any sentiments they are understood to provoke. Word choice has the power to delineate the frame of interpretation for an issue. Controlling the language used in a discussion sets both the boundaries of understanding and the emotional tone of the issue.

Consider, for example, the tragic events that took place on November 5, 2009, when Army psychiatrist Nidal Malik Hassan opened fire into a crowd of soldiers (Jayson and Reed, 2009). In his News-oriented discussion of the event, Fox News host Glenn Beck noted that, while most news sources had chosen to refer to Hassan as a *gunman*, Beck himself preferred the designation of *terrorist* (Striegel, 2009). Comparing the two descriptors, we can see they each convey specific meanings and emotions to an audience informed only by their consumption of the event through news reports. *Gunman* connotes a perpetrator whose actions are the result of cognitive or emotional motivations, such as the desire for money or revenge. The crime can therefore be comprehended as one that was driven by a discernable component found in society and relationships. Although the gunman is seen as responsible for his behavior, the outcome of such an incident evokes mainly a sense of regret at the destruction of human life, but the fact that there is a recognizably human cycle of cause and effect allows the audience a degree of distance from the danger. *Terrorist*, on the other hand, is a word that connotes a perpetrator whose actions may be the result of hatred towards Americans and association with al Qaeda. Here, the crime is contextualized in terms of the audience's identity as an American and therefore a potential target of a similar attack at an unspecified future time. Labeling Hassan as a terrorist removes the safety of distance between the audience and the threat, evoking fear.

As this example shows, the simple choice of one word over another has the capacity to frame an entire event by defining its context and tone. *The Daily Show*'s writers are fully aware of the power word choice can have in the framing process. One of the simplest ways *The Daily Show* uses word choice as part of its Comic Frame is the sudden juxtaposition of "serious" news content with coarse vulgarity, where the source of the humor is the incongruity of the two opposing elements. By faithfully mimicking the atmosphere of a mainstream News program (set, costumes, demeanor), the façade *The Daily Show* erects is an image of serious news reporting begging to be shattered by a casually placed vulgarity (Day, 2009; Warner, 2007). The destruction of the "respectability" of the News has been highlighted as a testament to *The Daily Show*'s critique of the "objectivity and credibility crisis besetting mainstream media" (Cornfield, 2005, p. 34; Smolkin, 2007). However, this method of producing comic incongruity is also a form of framing through word choice.

Although using profanities or other crude language is not uncommon on *The Daily Show*, the cast deliberately insert such expressions into their reporting as a contrast to any segment with an overwhelmingly sensible tone. Stewart is particularly adept at this method. For example, in a segment covering President Barack Obama's trip to China, Stewart comments on America's immense financial debt to China, a country whose relationship with the United States is not particularly strong, yet who is our largest debtor. Immediately after painting this rather humorless picture of the situation, Stewart shifts his tone, speaking directly to President Obama, calling upon him to "shine that turd up" for Stewart and his audience (Bodow and O'Neill, 2009g). The decision to introduce coarse language into what otherwise appears to be a more serious commentary serves to frame the segment in terms of its primary agenda of comedy, grounding more somber critique within the context of the "fake" News designation. Another, more explicit example of this can be found looking at another segment on *The Daily Show* discussing net neutrality (Bodow and O'Neill, 2009d).

Stewart spends a decent amount of air time seriously explaining that right now, information travelling through the Internet moves at the same speed, regardless of whether the source is a huge multi-million dollar corporation or a small-scale, relatively unknown business. Offering examples, Stewart names Google to represent a large, well-known company, but for the smaller business, his example suddenly shifts to the comically absurd, as he quickly recites the website's name, and then pauses for laughter: "JonStewartsheadonMarioLopezsbodygettingf***edbyaunicorn.net."

Upon revealing the name of the website, the over-the-shoulder (OTS)[2] graphic to Stewart's right immediately changes to display the literal image described by the fictitious domain name, and Stewart pauses in his explanation of net neutrality to pursue a brief comic sidebar, where he explains that his site's domain name was assigned the .net extension because the more common .com version was already in use. After soaking up the laughter elicited by the ludicrous idea that someone else had already thought of this particular website, Stewart fishes for more, noting that the only part of the OTS image that he had to construct was putting his own head on Mario Lopez's body, which comically suggests that the rest of the image was real.

Stewart then resumes a serious demeanor as he continues to explain how Internet service providers would prefer if the FCC decided against net neutrality because without it, ISPs would be able to control which websites (such as ones the ISP owns) would receive faster delivery service of their content to Internet users, and which sites would receive slower delivery (such as competing websites). This explanation goes on for even longer than the first bout of serious information, and he once again brings a hypothetical example using real companies like Comcast, NBC and ABC to illustrate his point. He concludes by noting that this example considers websites by major, well-financed corporations, which suggests that sites without such funds might receive even worse treatment. The example Stewart brings for such a disadvantaged site? The fictitious JonStewartsheadonMarioLopezsbodygettingf***edbyaunicorn.net, which he pronounces with added vocal emphasis and speed, as if the outrageous name was not enough to catch his audience's attention.

Stewart's lengthy explanation of net neutrality coupled by the fact that the majority of this treatment sounds more like what one might find on serious News suggests that net neutrality is a legitimate and important issue. The sobriety of Stewart's discussion of the issue is broken up, however, by the verbal and visual conjuring of his ludicrous website. The first mention of the site is incongruous in the same way as Stewart's "shine that turd up" remark in the previous example. The second interruption comes after a description of net neutrality that is significantly more protracted and in depth, ostensibly for the purpose of drawing the audience into the serious discussion in order to enhance the comic shock when Stewart suddenly reinvigorates the vulgar concept by reproducing both the verbal web address and its image representation. In addition to framing the segment within the context of *The Daily Show*'s comic agenda, the repetition of the vulgar image operates on the referential level of frames. The second exposure triggers the same feelings (most likely some combination of shock and laughter) evoked by the audience's first encounter with the fake site, while strengthening their overall appreciation and acceptance of *The Daily Show*'s comic agenda.

Another technique *The Daily Show* uses to frame information through word choice is through the packaging titles it creates for its segments. The titles on *The Daily Show* are, of course, parodies of similar titles used heavily by televised News. By creating story titles using specific, culturally determined emotional and cognitive cues, television News is able to direct its audience to its preferred frame. As noted above, connecting information to what Entman (1993) described as "culturally familiar symbols" is fundamental to the rhetorical function of frames (p. 53). *The Daily Show*'s parodied version of these titles also relies heavily on cultural symbols, in the form of references to common culture and popular entertainment. The show's writers select familiar phrases from popular culture (usually the title of a popular media product, a well-known adage, or a popular catch-phrase) and combine them with puns to create these titles.

There are three types of titles on *The Daily Show*, all of which use puns: to headline ongoing segments, to identify individual news items, and as lower thirds, also known as chyrons,[3] during the discussion of a news story. Ongoing segments are comprised of stories which are related in a particular way. They are all linked together by the title of the ongoing segment, which is presented prior to each story in an extended introduction featuring animated graphics and text accompanied by music. During Stewart's onscreen anchor reporting on these stories, a still image of the ongoing segment's title is shown in the OTS graphic. For stories that aren't part of an ongoing segment, *The Daily Show* creates individual titles. These titles do not receive any introduction, but they all appear in Stewart's OTS graphic as he discusses the story. Lower thirds are used on *The Daily Show* to identify the reporter delivering a story and also to identify the action occurring in onscreen footage that doesn't feature a reporter. *The Daily Show*'s lower thirds consist of two lines, or tiers of text. The text in the first tier plainly identifies the story at hand. The second tier is the comic element of the title, featuring the pop culture phrase, modified for punning purposes.

Puns, one of the simplest forms of wordplay, are entirely dependent on double entendre for their humor, and *The Daily Show* is, of course, able to exploit this quality by choosing popular culture references that can also double as clever satire. For example, when discussing the spate of television interviews given by former Vice President Dick Cheney, *The Daily Show* titled the story "Interview with a Vampire" (Bodow and O'Neill, 2009a). The primary meaning of the phrase refers to the titles of both a popular 1994 film starring Brad Pitt and Tom Cruise and the famous 1973 novel by Anne Rice on which it was based. The secondary meaning is created by linking the content of the news story—a television interview with Dick Cheney—with the book/film title, which also mentions an interview, only with a vampire. The title implies a satirical analogy, suggesting that Dick Cheney is an evil, cold-hearted, blood-sucking individual (a characterization made on *The Daily Show* repeatedly).

The title described above was an example of *The Daily Show* creating a humorous secondary meaning for a popular culture reference simply by linking it, untouched,[4] to a given news item. However, many pop culture phrases don't lend themselves to punning current events in their original form. *The*

Daily Show's solution is to replace one or two words in the original phrase with ones specifically chosen to link the phrase to the news story without completely obscuring its referential power to popular culture. Examples of this type of punning is abundant in *The Daily Show*'s titles, such as "White Men Can't Judge," (Bodow and O'Neill, 2009c) which modified the title of the 1992 movie *White Men Can't Jump* to headline the story on the 2009 Supreme Court confirmation hearings of Judge Sonia Sotomayor, "From Here to Neutrality" (Bodow and O'Neill, 2009d), linking a discussion of net neutrality to the 1953 film *From Here to Eternity*, "Queer Eye for the Hawk-eye" (Bodow and O'Neill, 2009b) altering the title of the popular television program *Queer Eye for the Straight Guy* (2003–2007) to cover the story of the Iowa State Supreme Court declaring a ban on gay marriage to be unconstitutional, "Jobba the Hunt" (Bodow and O'Neill, 2009i), which plays off the name of amorphous *Star Wars* character Jabba the Hutt for a lower third title displayed during a story about government efforts to spur job growth, and "World of WarmCraft" (Bodow and O'Neill, 2009k), punning the popular videogame *World of WarCraft* as a title for a discussion on the debate over global warming. These titles all contain a popular culture reference that has been modified in order to link it to a news story. The change, however, is minor enough so that the new phrase still retains the cadence of the original, which preserves the cultural relevance for the viewer.

While these titles are all clever and entertaining, it should also be noted that they lack the satirical sting present in the initial example ("Interview with a Vampire"). As we have seen with that example, in which the original reference to popular culture (*Interview with the Vampire*) was used to critique the subject of the news story (Dick Cheney) through direct analogy, the program's writers can use puns to construct titles that produce both comic entertainment and satirical critique. However, many of the puns in the titles on *The Daily Show* do not result in such strongly visible commentary. In fact, it is not uncommon for *The Daily Show*'s titles to offer no discernable critique at all, as in the other examples listed above. The content of these titles generally have little to no deeper meaning beyond the simplistic laughter the pun evokes.

Jon Stewart himself occasionally acknowledges the inanity of these punned titles, such as when he paused and asked "Really?" when the audience loudly laughed at the title "The Men Who Stare At Votes" (Bodow and O'Neill, 2009e), which played off the 2009 film *The Men Who Stare At Goats* for a story about the House of Representatives passing the health care bill. Stewart reacted with similar disbelief to the audience's abundant approval for the title "Scary Plotter" (Bodow and O'Neill, 2009j), which referred to a story about the arrest of a Chicago man in connection with terrorist attacks in India by modifying the title of the popular book/film series *Harry Potter*. These reactions, though rare, are not surprising. Most titles on

The Daily Show contain virtually no critique of the news item they represent, but instead are primarily devices highlighting simplistic word play of puns and mindless pop culture to produce purely fatuous comedy. However, puns are not only simplistic, but are also culturally despised as one of the lowest and most bromidic classes of humor (Tartakovsky, 2009). The implication is clear: *The Daily Show*'s writers (a group of which Stewart is himself a member) might not consider these titles to be more than a method of drawing cheap laughs. It is precisely for this reason that the prominent use of puns in *The Daily Show*'s titles can be considered an element of the program's Comic Frame.

VIDEO EDITING

Although News is usually televised live, not all content being aired transpires simultaneously with the broadcast. A percentage of News consists of prerecorded video footage of newsworthy events, officials' speeches, and journalists' on-location reports. Inevitably, more footage is created than can actually be used during the time allotted for the program, and so it must be cut and rearranged into a final product that is significantly shorter, yet must communicate the essence of the event (Jamieson and Waldman, 2003). This is the primary, stated purpose of video editing. However, as noted above, video editing is also an example of the structural framing process, where the external structure of a segment defines its frame of interpretation. Since editing entails the cutting and organization of extended footage, programs have the power to literally determine "what information is included and what is ignored" in the News story for which it is produced (Jamieson and Waldman, 2003, p. xiii). In this case, *The Daily Show* uses the structural framing power of video editing to ensure that the only material included is that which will support its Comic Frame.

The two steps in video editing that aid in the framing process are the selection and cutting of raw footage and the later organization of the selected shots. *The Daily Show*, as well as mainstream News, use both these steps, exemplified (respectively) by its use of two different forms[5] : the sound bite and the originally produced segment.

Strictly speaking, a sound bite is a video or audio "segment, within a news story, showing someone speaking" (Hallin, 1992, p. 5). It is created by cutting down extended footage of (usually) one person talking, but the editing decisions made in its construction are often determined by the desired final frame. Editing footage of speeches and statements into short sound bites determines that a large portion of the footage will likely have a very small human audience, if any at all (Baym, 2005). Yet the fraction of material compiled into the final sound bite is meant to represent the entire text.

The Daily Show has received a significant amount of praise for its treatment of prepackaged sound bites, the favorite method of both News and politicians for summing up a specific position or story[6] (Baym, 2005; Trier, 2008b; Warner, 2007). In particular, *The Daily Show* has been commended for highlighting the fact that mainstream News relies heavily on editing to craft its sound bites (Baym, 2005; Day, 2009; McKain, 2005; Trier, 2008b; Warner, 2007), and further, for illuminating that despite being presented as such, the finished sound bite is often not representative of the actual speech or exchange (e.g. Baym, 2005; McKain, 2005).

Although this important function deserves recognition, equally deserving is how *The Daily Show*'s video editing feeds into its Comic Frame. *The Daily Show* will creatively cut existing footage gleaned from News or public proceedings into sound bites for comic purposes. This is illuminated by the following example from a segment covering the twentieth anniversary of the fall of the Berlin Wall, which included a montage of clips in which various News anchors reminisced about their own coverage of the event in 1989 (Bodow and O'Neill, 2009f). The montage concludes with a 1989 clip of CNN correspondent Jim Clancy signing off from Berlin that dissolves into a shot of present-day Jim Clancy joking, "Who was that guy?" The camera cuts to Stewart, sporting a mildly confused look. He then pretends to converse with both versions of Jim Clancy, saying that he doesn't recognize either the present-day Jim Clancy or the 1989 Clancy, whose 1980s clothes and mustache Stewart compares to a producer of pornography. Following this joke, Stewart then sets up for the next one, saying that even though *he* may not recognize Clancy, there's one fellow CNN newscaster who seems to only have eyes for the veteran reporter.

The shot immediately following Stewart's words is a clip featuring CNN anchor Wolf Blitzer in dialogue with Clancy:

Blitzer: Nice mustache, Jim. Uh, very nice mustache, twenty years ago, uh, you ever think of getting that mustache back?

Clancy: I miss that mustache.

Blitzer: I know you do. I remember that mustache, cause I, I used to watch you all the time. (DeDaykis, 2009)

The clip cuts here, while Blitzer is ostensibly mid-sentence, and the focus returns to Stewart, who jolts his head up and opens his eyes wide in an expression of uncomfortable surprise. After a moment's pause, Stewart acts as a television announcer signaling to the audience that there is about to be a commercial break. However, he delivers this message as if he's an innocent bystander witness to a major social faux pas, stutteringly announcing that the "Incredibly Awkward Social Situation Room" will return shortly.

Here, Stewart is playing on the title of Blitzer's show, *The Situation Room*, for comic effect. But more important is the structural framing of this video clip through cutting. It is highly unlikely that the meaning proposed by Stewart was what was originally intended by Blitzer. Common logic suggests that when Blitzer said that he "used to watch" Clancy "all the time," he actually meant that he used to view Clancy's broadcast reports, and was not admitting to stalking Clancy. Rather, the choice to cut the video clip immediately after Blitzer utters the words "I used to watch you all the time," was a deliberate effort to frame the footage in a specifically comic way. In addition, by sandwiching the clip between a deliberate setup and a comic play on words, Stewart actively channels the sequence's interpretation through *The Daily Show*'s Comic Frame. Thus, in much the same manner as News, *The Daily Show* decides the point at which to cut extended footage so that the interpretation (accurate or otherwise) of the resulting sound bite will correspond to the program's primary agenda.

The arrangement of the cut footage, the second step to structural framing used by *The Daily Show* to construct its Comic Frame, is exemplified in original segments produced by the program's cast of "reporters" and "correspondents." Like the sound bite, original segments are also edited by physically cutting raw footage for time. However, original segments are more complex forms in that they entail a large number of these cut shots that are organized to communicate a coherent narrative. Original segments also differ from sound bites on *The Daily Show* in terms of the measure of control they offer over the frame.

Sound bites are generally clips that have been designed and produced by sources either in mainstream News or political speechwriters (Baym, 2005; McKain, 2005). The images and speech they contain are therefore fixed. Though the interpretation of a sound bite from the State of the Union Address can be modified by changing the point at which the shot is cut, the clip cannot be edited to depict anything other than the President delivering a speech. As a result, the control *The Daily Show* has over the framing of sound bites is somewhat limited. Original segments, however, are composed primarily of content written, filmed, and edited by *The Daily Show* personnel. Here, the show's staff controls both the content production *and* editing and therefore are able to exercise complete power over structural framing. Such control enables *The Daily Show* to determine the comedic output of any original content it produces. The primary focus of scholarly discourse concerning these original segments addresses their function as a critical parody of highly edited and predictably framed News segments (McKain, 2005; Morreale, 2009). However, if, as I argue, the production of an original segment on *The Daily Show* is primarily guided by the show's Comic Frame, the finished product will reflect a drive to maximize comedic output.

A clear example of this comic amplification is an original segment covering the reaction to the November 2009 release of the book *Going Rogue*, written by former vice presidential nominee Sarah Palin (Bodow and O'Neill, 2009h). The piece, starring cast member John Oliver, satirizes the media hype that Palin's book is "flying off the shelves" and generating long lines of excited fans. Oliver theorizes that, not unlike *Harry Potter* enthusiasts, people around New York City celebrated the release of Palin's book by showing up to bookstores in costume.

The bulk of the segment features a montage of Oliver interviewing a number of individuals at a bookstore in New York City, trying to guess which character from the book they are trying to mimic. Because none of the interview subjects are actually impersonating anyone from Palin's book, Oliver's suggestion that they are is instantly humorous, and because Oliver's guesses are based purely on visual stereotyping, they take on an additional quality of insult comedy. Oliver's stereotyping ranges from the simple, such as guessing that a white-haired man in his sixties came as John McCain or that a pregnant woman came as Bristol Palin, the author's pregnant teenage daughter, to the offensive, like when he guessed that a short, pudgy white man was supposed to be Cindy McCain, if she were gay.

However, the decision to have Oliver personally interview the subjects on camera rather than to guess their costumes in a voiceover attached during editing adds further levels of comedy to the sequence. Delivering his stereotypical and generally impertinent comments directly to his subjects' faces first affords the opportunity to film their reactions, which is independently humorous. Moreover, Oliver's interaction with his subjects allows him to engage in comic improvisation, playing off their responses to his questions and their reactions to his insulting guesses. For example, when one slightly overweight white man plays along and claims he's come dressed as Levi, the father of Bristol Palin's baby, Oliver immediately plays off this answer and the man's appearance by suggesting that this version of Levi is one where he suffered from depression and consoled himself with food.

Cutting these interviews and linking them together in a montage stresses the comic purpose of the interviews. The filming of each interview undoubtedly took at least several minutes. Oliver had to ask questions and his subjects had to give their answers. Yet most of the interviewed exchange is eliminated in each case, resulting in the majority of the shots in the montage lasting only long enough for Oliver to offer his guess as to his subject's "costume." In only a few instances are the subjects' responses shown. The responses that are used in the montage are either ones whose reactions and responses were particularly humorous or whose replies were followed by a (sometimes) impromptu comedic quip from Oliver. In one of the longer shots in the montage, for example, Oliver briefly chats with a thin white man about his hair before proclaiming his sudden realization that this man is dressed as a Jew. As the man laughs and nods in agreement with Oliver's assessment, Oliver nonchalantly remarks that Jews are one of the book's evil characters.

The montage offers a clear example of structural framing. It can be reasonably assumed that the footage that was excluded was done so purposely, because it did not fit with the Comic Frame. In other words, although we can only speculate what was in the footage that was left on the cutting room floor, its content was probably not funny at all or not funny enough for *The Daily Show*'s purposes.

Oliver eventually concludes that the majority of patrons at this bookstore preferred to dress as one of the villains in Palin's book, whom he identifies as the "liberal elite." This observation prompts another round of cheeky observations at the expense of random book store patrons. The segment is clearly meant to poke fun at both Palin's book and the subsequent news coverage through parody, but it focuses equal (if not more) time on Oliver's rapid-fire ridicule of innocent bystanders than on lampooning the news outlets or even Palin's book. This is further evidence of the Comic Frame taking priority in *The Daily Show*'s production practices.

Similar to the technique described earlier of juxtaposing incongruous verbal cues for comic purposes, comedy in this sequence is also created by structurally linking together Oliver's voiceover narration and shots that present the opposing reality. For example, in a voiceover during a few shots of b-roll footage of the bookstore interior, Oliver notes that the sheer popularity of Palin's book has this particular bookstore preparing itself to be inundated by customer orders. In the very next sequence, Oliver is interviewing a clerk at the bookstore, asking him how many copies of the book the store expects to sell. The clerk's replies that the store originally ordered eight copies, adding that he doesn't think there will be much interest in the book beyond this week. As if he can't believe that the store would only order eight copies, Oliver proposes that when the clerk said eight, what he really meant was eight thousand. The clerk shoots down Oliver's suggestion with a definitive, one-worded restatement of the actual number of copies ordered: eight. Pressing the issue, Oliver clarifies that the bookstore only ordered eight books. The clerk confirms that by parroting Oliver's words back to him. After a brief pause, Oliver exclaims that the bookstore decided to order at least more than seven copies of Palin's book, as seven were a pathetically minuscule order for a newly published book, but ordering eight copies is significantly less pathetic. Nodding, the clerk agrees that eight is indeed one more than seven copies.

Oliver's voiceover claim that the bookstore was preparing for a barrage of sales of Palin's book was meant to align with the actual news reports describing the consumer frenzy surrounding the its release. The organization of this voiceover followed immediately by the clerk's matter-of-fact contradiction of this assertion is an extension of the technique, prevalent on *The Daily Show*, of showcasing inconsistencies for comic purposes. In addition, the extra effort Oliver puts into clarifying for himself, and therefore for the audience, that the bookstore only ordered an insignificant number of copies further highlights the contrast between the media hype about the book and the reality of the situation at this bookstore. Moreover, Oliver allows his rapid exchange with the clerk over the number of copies ordered to drag out, drawing greater attention to it, milking the comic element of the structural juxtaposition as much as possible.

The comedy produced by this technique is further intensified in the final sequence of the segment, where Oliver reads *Going Rogue* to a group of children in the bookstore, because, as he explains in voiceover, Palin's book was written for the youngest members of society, the future citizens of our country. This sequence, once again, plays on the contradiction between unexpected extremes to generate comedy. *Going Rogue* was clearly written for an adult audience, therefore the idea that it would appeal to young children, who prefer books with simple stories, words and illustrations, is undoubtedly absurd. At one point, the children even revolt and select a different book for John to read instead of Palin's. Even if you've never heard of *Chicka Chicka Boom Boom*, the physical appearance of the book the kids choose is large and brightly colored, visibly contrasting to Palin's book. This brief instance highlights the fact that *Going Rogue* is very much *not* a book for children, and additionally reinforces the ludicrousness of the idea of reading it to a group of children. The decision to do so was very likely motivated by the humor such an absurd contradiction creates for *The Daily Show*'s audience. However, the sequence builds further on this initial contradiction, as Oliver only pretends to agree to the children's request. Like a boy reading a Superman comic behind his history book, he mischievously opens *Going Rogue* behind the larger frame of *Chicka Chicka Boom Boom* and continues to read Palin's book aloud. The children's frustrated reactions to Oliver's practical joke provide another level of comedy for the audience to enjoy.

As explained above, that the children find *Going Rogue* boring is quite expected, and indeed, as Oliver first begins to read aloud, some of them literally fall over from boredom, which is humorous on its own. To illustrate what Oliver calls the "undeniable impact" of Palin's book, the segment closes with a montage of the children expressing how they would prefer to be tortured rather than having to read *Going Rogue*. The children conjure a number of deadly situations into which they'd throw themselves, include a volcano, boiling hot lava, a house set to explode, and shark-infested waters. One boy thumps his fist against his chest, then without explanation, claims that he would do exactly that rather than have to listen to one more word of the book. When asked what his mimed act represents, he explains that he feels such a great hatred for the book that he'd willingly stab himself in the chest with a knife. Similar to the example with the bookstore clerk, this sequence sets up a comic juxtaposition between the tonal extremes of childhood innocence and purity (represented by adorable children) and animated loathing (expressed in the form of multiple characterizations of violent suicide in response to Sarah Palin's book).

However, the physical arrangement of the shots in this concluding sequence adds an additional degree of comedy to the children's reactions. This sequence is not one long shot. Rather, it was the composition of a number of shots taken during Oliver's interaction with the children. These shots were arranged into the coherent narrative presented in the final product. The narrative that has been constructed, however, conveys a set of children's reactions that are unexpectedly reflective of the audience's (supposed) distaste for Palin. The comedy is in the children's unwitting articulation of the adult audience's opinion of Palin as an author and a political figure as they express their own violent hatred toward a book they simply consider to be torturously boring.

As demonstrated by this example, original segments provide *The Daily Show* with complete control, which allows it one of the best opportunities to maximize comic output through structural framing. Adding multiple levels of comedy to a single sequence reflects an objective of amplifying the humorous output of its segments. This focus on comedy over other types of content (i.e. political or journalistic critique) further strengthens the notion of the primacy of the Comic Frame on *The Daily Show*.

CONCLUSION

This chapter has argued that *The Daily Show*'s primary agenda is comedy, reflected in its consistent efforts to fit its content into a Comic Frame of interpretation. I must stress, however, that the goal here was *not* to suggest that *The Daily Show* has no value beyond its comic appeal. My argument does not invalidate the important democratic and critical services scholars suggest *The Daily Show* performs for the American public (or at least their own audiences). The show does indeed act as a counterpoint to political spin and traditional news media presentations and conventions. The recognition of *The Daily Show*'s primary comic agenda merely stands as a fact independent from judgment.

It is important to recognize the primacy of *The Daily Show*'s Comic Frame because its existence is the shield which allows *The Daily Show* to perform all the valuable functions for which it has been praised for so effectively. Examining how *The Daily Show* both uses and reveals the framing process is an important part of the discussion of the show's function as a critique of mainstream News and political communication. However, we must acknowledge and study *The Daily Show*'s Comic Frame (and its other comedic strategies) in order to safeguard it, because it is the seat of the program's identity a humorous, "fake" news program, and it is this identity that both allows it to conduct its criticism and makes those critiques particularly resonating. The loss of the comic element on *The Daily Show* would render it impotent—declaw it, so to speak. And choosing to ignore *The Daily Show*'s Comic Frame runs the risk of allowing the show to devolve into just another News program, manufacturing frames that can all too easily manipulate the unwitting public.

In addition, the acknowledgment that *The Daily Show*, just like the institutions it critiques, uses framing may initiate a beneficial shift in the status of the framing process itself. So often, framing is discussed as a one of News' fatal flaws which *The Daily Show* has worked hard to expose. However, the recognition that *The Daily Show* also relies on frames (comic or otherwise) highlights the fact that framing is, to some extent, a necessary element of news presentation. Although News framing often results in misled audiences, it is important to distinguish that not all framing is performed with malicious intent to control perception, nor does the use of framing, by definition, determine the exclusion of pertinent information. Every significant event that occurs in this world is connected to an immense amount of information (factual, contextual, historical, etc.). However, spatial and temporal constraints in the transmission of news are present in every form of news media. Television and radio are subservient to predetermined time slots, while print and Internet-based publications must focus on space in the context of economic concerns and limited audience attention. On the most basic of levels, framing helps journalists manage and organize the massive quantities of information connected to any given event (Jamieson and Waldman, 2003; Nelson et al, 1997). Indeed, it is not the mere act of framing that should be seen as dangerous, but the underlying conventions and convictions that might govern the process and seek to manipulate the public. *The Daily Show* is unlike News in this respect because it openly acknowledges the comic (and other) motivations guiding its framing, and this acknowledgment further solidifies the show's worthiness for the praise it has received.

NOTES

1. This paper will adhere to the distinction made by McKain (2005) between news and News, where the former refers to the content, or "that which is news*worthy,*" while the latter will indicate the media that transmits the content (p. 416, italics in original).

2. When an anchor on a televised newscast reports on a story, an OTS graphic related to the story is displayed. The OTS graphic generally appears in a box that is located over the (usually right) shoulder of the news anchor as (s)he is delivering the story.

3. Lower thirds, or chyrons, are identifying graphics that appear at the bottom of the screen (covering the bottom third of the frame) whenever the camera is not focused on the news anchors.

4. The title of both the book and the film is actually "Interview with *the* Vampire," but the modification for *The Daily Show* title is so minor as to be insignificant in this case.

5. Although both of these steps can be found in each form, cutting footage is more prominently demonstrated by the sound bite, while the construction of meaning in original segments is more heavily dependent upon the arrangement of the shots.

6. The heavy use of language to control the nature of press coverage by politicians began with the Reagan administration's conscious blend of the brand advertising slogan with political communication. This has since evolved into the common political practice of repeating talking points in public addresses in the hopes that the media will pick them up and incorporate them into their News frame (Raphael, 2009; Warner, 2007).

REFERENCES

Alterman, E. (2009, April 13). Is Jon Stewart our Ed Murrow? Maybe . . . *The Nation*, 9.

Baym, G. (2005). *The Daily Show*: Discursive integration and the reinvention of political journalism. *Political Communication*, 22 (3), 259–276.

Bodow, S. (Head Writer) and O'Neill, C. (Director). (2009a, March 18). [Television series episode]. In J. Stewart (Executive producer), *The Daily Show with Jon Stewart*. New York: Viacom.

———. (2009b, April 6). [Television series episode]. In J. Stewart (Executive producer), *The Daily Show with Jon Stewart*. New York: Viacom.

———. (2009c, July 14). [Television series episode]. In J. Stewart (Executive producer), *The Daily Show with Jon Stewart*. New York: Viacom.

———. (2009d, October 26). [Television series episode]. In J. Stewart (Executive producer), *The Daily Show with Jon Stewart*. New York: Viacom.

———. (2009e, November 9). [Television series episode]. In J. Stewart (Executive producer), *The Daily Show with Jon Stewart*. New York: Viacom.

———. (2009f, November 10). [Television series episode]. In J. Stewart (Executive producer), *The Daily Show with Jon Stewart*. New York: Viacom.

———. (2009g, November 17). [Television series episode]. In J. Stewart (Executive producer), *The Daily Show with Jon Stewart*. New York: Viacom.

———. (2009h, November 18). [Television series episode]. In J. Stewart (Executive producer), *The Daily Show with Jon Stewart*. New York: Viacom.

———. (2009i, December 7). [Television series episode]. In J. Stewart (Executive producer), *The Daily Show with Jon Stewart*. New York: Viacom.

———. (2009j, December 8). [Television series episode]. In J. Stewart (Executive producer), *The Daily Show with Jon Stewart*. New York: Viacom.

———. (2009k, December 14). [Television series episode]. In J. Stewart (Executive producer), *The Daily Show with Jon Stewart*. New York: Viacom.

Burke, K. (1984). *Attitudes toward history* (3rd ed.). Berkeley: University of California Press.

Colapinto, J. (2004, October 28). The most trusted name in news. *Rolling Stone*, (960), 58–64. Retrieved from Academic Search Premier.

Cornfield, M. (2005). "The Daily Show" revolution. *Campaigns and Elections*, 26(8), 34.

Day, A. (2009). And now . . . the news?: Mimesis and the real in *The Daily Show*. In J. Gray, J. Jones, and E. Thompson (Eds.). *Satire TV: Politics and comedy in the post-network era* (pp. 85–103). New York: New York University Press.

de Vreese, C. (2005). News framing: Theory and typology. *Information Design Journal + Document Design*, 13(1), 51–62.

DeCapua, A. (2007). The use of language to create realities: The example of Good Bye, Lenin! *Semiotica*,166(1–4), 69–79.

DeDaykis, J. (Writer). (2009). Episode dated 9 November 2009. In E. Sherling (Executive Producer), *The Situation Room with Wolf Blitzer*. Washington, D.C.: CNN.

Entman, R. (1993). Framing: Toward a clarification of a fractured paradigm. *Journal of Communication*, 43(4), 51–58.

Gaines, E. (2007). The narrative semiotics of The Daily Show. *Semiotica*, 166, 81–96.

Hallin, D. (1992). Sound bite news: Television coverage of elections, 1968–1988. *Journal of Communication*, 42(2), 5–24.

Hariman, R. (2007). In defense of Jon Stewart. *Critical Studies in Media Communication*, 24(3), 273–277.

Hart, R.P. and Hartelius, J. (2007). The political sins of Jon Stewart. *Critical Studies in Media Communication*, 24(3), 263–272.

Jamieson, K.H. and Waldman, P. (2003). *The press effect: Politicians, journalists and the stories that shape the political world*. New York: Oxford University Press.

Jayson, S. and Reed, D. (2009, November 5). In 'horrific' rampage, 12 killed at Ft. Hood. *USA Today* (Arlington, VA), p. ARC. Retrieved from NewsBank on-line database (Access World News).

Kakutani, M. (2008, August 17). The most trusted man in America? *The New York Times*, p. 1.

Kellner, D. (2004). The media and the crisis of democracy in the age of Bush 2. *Communication and Critical/Cultural Studies*, 1(1), 29–58.

McKain, A. (2005). Not necessarily not the news: Gatekeeping, remediation, and *The Daily Show*. *Journal of American Culture*, 28(4), 415–430.

Miller, J. (Writer) and O'Neill, C. (Director). (2009, December 14). [Television series episode]. In J. Stewart (Executive producer), *The Daily Show with Jon Stewart*. New York: Viacom.

Morreale, J. (2009). Jon Stewart and *The Daily Show*: I thought you were going to be funny! In J. Gray, J.P. Jones, and E. Thompson (Eds.), *Satire TV: Politics and comedy in the post-network era* (pp.104–121). New York: New York University Press.

Mutz, D. (2004). Leading horses to water: Confessions of a Daily Show junkie. *Journalism and Mass Communication Educator*, 59(1), 31–35.

Nelson, T.E., Oxley, Z.M., and Clawson, R.A. (1997). Toward a psychology of framing effects. *Political Behavior*, 19(3), 221–246.

Pew Research Center (2004). *Cable and internet loom large in fragmented political news*. Retrieved from http://people-press.org/report/200/cable-and-internet-loom-large-in-fragmented-political-news-universe.

Raphael, T. (2009). The body electric: GE, TV, and the Reagan brand. *Drama Review*, 53(2), 113–138.

Smolkin, R. (2007). What the mainstream media can learn from Jon Stewart. *American Journalism Review*, 29(3), 19–25.

Solomon, N. (2008, November/December). Dubious praise for The Daily Show. *The Humanist*, 38.

Striegel, G (Executive Producer). (2009, November 11). *Glenn Beck* [Television broadcast]. New York: Fox News Network.

Tartakovsky, J. (2009, March, 28). Pun for the ages. *The New York Times*, p. A21.

Trier, J. (2008a). *The Daily Show with Jon Stewart*: Part 1. *Journal of Adolescent and Adult Literacy*, 51(5), 424–427.

Trier, J. (2008b). *The Daily Show with Jon Stewart*: Part 2. *Journal of Adolescent and Adult Literacy*, 51(7), 600–605.

Warner, J. (2007). Political culture jamming: The dissident humor of *The Daily Show with Jon Stewart*. *Popular Communication*, 5(1), 17–36.

Chapter Nine

Breaking News: A Postmodern Rhetorical Analysis of *The Daily Show*

Aaron Hess

Jon Stewart's face adorned the cover of the October 2009 issue of the *Atlantic*, coupled with the title "Who is killing the media?" The question is seemingly pointed at Stewart, and even lists "fake news" as one of many causes of the death of journalism. While provocative, the author largely misses the point of the late night comedy show. Simultaneously, while Jon Stewart has not always been celebrated throughout the communication discipline (Hart and Hartelius, 2007), he and his cast at *The Daily Show* have often been recognized for their prowess in delivering a strong message of incredulity toward the twenty-four-hour news programming offered on a number of television networks (Baym, 2005, 2007; Hariman, 2007; Waisanen, 2009). The question asked by the *Atlantic* "Who is killing the media?" is certainly a pertinent one, but misses the subtly of *The Daily Show's* construction of news parody and satire. Rather, the proper question to be asked of Jon Stewart and his band of merry correspondents is "Who is *subverting* the media?"

This chapter traces the subversive use of irony, parody, and satire on *The Daily Show*. Well known for its parodic and satiric import, *The Daily Show* continues to challenge mainstream news organizations and their commitment to "fair and balanced" news and infotainment. Through a postmodern rhetorical criticism, I analyze *The Daily Show* and its use of structural and stylistic satiric parody. Through the approach, I argue that the program's success is intricately tied to its ability to utilize irony as "repetition with critical difference" (Hutcheon, 1995, 2000) to structure a news program that highlights the problematic purpose of modern news organizations. Moreover, I trace *The Daily Show* through the past decade, noting significant changes in the program that indicate that its postmodern audience has become solidified as welcome and appreciative recipients of satire. To complete this analysis, I will first examine the overlapping ideas of irony, parody and satire, making connections to how *The Daily Show* has been labeled as such. Second, I outline how a postmodern rhetorical analysis assists in displaying the intertextual relationships between *The Daily Show* as a parody and twenty-four-hour news networks as parodied texts. Finally, I analyze *The Daily Show,* paying close attention to structural and stylistic devices, simultaneously attending to the changing structure of the program through time in order to display how it continues to rely on its own reputation and ethos. It has cultivated an audience that tends to already "get the joke," which has allowed *The Daily Show* to creatively strengthen its satire.

IRONY, PARODY, AND SATIRE

The Daily Show has been recognized as illustrating the ideas of irony, parody and/or satire by both popular media (Ganahl, 2002; Segal, 2002; LeDuc, 2002) and in scholarship (Baym, 2005, 2007; Hariman, 2007; Waisanen, 2009). While some may believe that *The Daily Show* merely reeks of cynicism (Hart and Hartelius, 2007), I agree with Hariman (2007), who sees Jon Stewart as "a parodist, a satirist, a comic engaging in political humor" (p. 274). The three ideas of irony, parody, and satire have considerable overlap between them; yet, to treat those as similar may miss the nuance of each. While defining irony, parody, or satire is as slippery as trope is to use, Hutcheon's (2000) notion of "repetition with difference" captures much of the essence of these ideas. While the discussion of irony is vast, my purpose in this section is to highlight four relevant ideas for the purpose of this chapter. First, irony is an explicitly audience-centered act. In conversational irony, the utterance is tagged as such to signal something that it is not. Second, in conjunction with satire and parody, irony can be used as a critical device. Drawing from Linda Hutcheon's (1995) work on "irony's edge," I underscore the critical side of irony and its transgressive ability. Third, and certainly related, is the intertextual relationship created through irony and parody. Looking between the parody and the parodied text, the critical element of irony appears in the form of an argument unpacked through a dialectical reading of the two texts. Finally, I consider Hutcheon's (1995) arguments regarding the parallel tropes of parody and satire.

While many theorists agree that defining irony, parody, and satire is tricky or even impossible (Hutcheon, 1995; Booth, 1974, 1983), I offer the following definition of each. Irony is the construction of discourse that means something different than and often contradictory of what is said. Parody, according to Hutcheon (2000), is understood as repetition with difference, a wonderfully simple definition for a form that is exceptionally complex. The "difference" in the repetition is often constructed through the trope of irony. Finally, satire, again according to Hutcheon (2000), is related to parody, but tends to carry an element of social critique through ridicule. Irony operates as a central discourse within both parody and satire, and examining and recognizing its relationship to them assists in recognizing the rhetorical value of the trope. Irony has a broad base of theorists behind it (Booth, 1974, 1983; Burke, 1945; Kaufer, 1977; Hutcheon, 1995; Tindale and Gough, 1987). First, verbal or conversational irony offers a starting point for realizing the audience-centered nature of irony and parody. Verbal irony is largely understood through the dependence of both realization and interpretation of the ironic message. It seems, therefore, that the interpreter is "the one who decides whether the utterance is ironic (or not), and then what *particular* ironic meaning it might have" (Hutcheon, 1995, p. 11). Comments about how beautiful the weather is in the middle of a nasty, windy snowstorm would embody a simple exchange of ironic messaging. The meaning here is not to express delight in the meteorological conditions, but instead to connect with the audience at hand through an implicit recognition of the bad weather through an inverse explicit message. Thus, verbal irony has an element of unification because "the little intellectual dance we must perform to understand it brings us into a tight bonding with the ironist" (Booth, 1983, p. 729). Burke (1945) sees irony as dialectic, which "requires that all the sub-certainties be considered as neither true nor false, but *contributory*" (p. 513). In other words, the range of meaning offered through an ironic utterance asks the listener to consider all possible meanings and their relationship to the ironic message and messenger. Through the audience-centered message of irony, assuming that the recipient recognizes the ironic intent, the interlocutors share the meaning of the moment.

Second, and certainly related, is the critical and rhetorical character of irony. Hutcheon (1995) largely believes that this element of the trope allows it to stand apart from other, similar types of communication. Set apart from expressions such as a puns, metaphors, or metonymy, "the 'transideological' (White 1973, p. 38) nature of irony . . . function[s] tactically in the service of a wide range of political positions" (Hutcheon, 1995, p. 10). This transideological purpose seeks to undermine dominant modes of expression and meaning, which, as Hariman (2008) argues, are essential to engaging audiences in complex considerations of meaning and for a healthy public discourse. This type of irony is both subversive and transgressive, meaning that such irony invites dialectical reading (Burke, 1945) of any text that asks a reader to discover a wide range of meaning which may question the content of the message. When working against a dominant perspective, irony can, therefore, undermine and contest the established meanings and ideologies (Hutcheon, 1995, p. 16). McClure and McClure (2001) contend that irony through "postmodern parody installs and subverts the meaning-making conventions and processes (rhetorical practices) of our culture (modernism) and thereby exposes those conventions while simultaneously inviting an interrogation of these taken-for-granted conventions" (p. 81–82). In other words, as an act of meaning-making, the form of irony invites a critical stance toward its target.

Central to the ideas of irony, parody, and satire is the intertextual relationship between two or more texts. Within any parodic text, an intertextual negotiation exists between the original text and the parody itself. This exchange between texts is a crucial aspect of parody, which then must be seen in its contextual light. Hutcheon (2000) describes intertextuality as "the complexity of the meeting of two texts combined with the meeting of a painter and a viewer" (p. 12). Intertextual negotiation appears in both the incorporation of an original text through mimicry or mirroring, as well as through the stylistic reconstruction of the other text through structure and form. Beyond mere reproduction or pastiche, the recreation of form and content through ironic (and often critical) differentiation is at the heart of parody. Critical to the incorporation of a previous text or work is the audience recognition of the older text. Indeed, as Shugart (1999) fears, for those audiences that are not versed in the irony of the text, their reading may "reify the very qualities and characteristics it is attempting to challenge" (p. 453). Thus, audience foreknowledge of the text, or familiarity with the form or structure that is being parodied, becomes a precursor of success for the author of parody. The recognition of the repetition with difference comes through an active cognitive process of discovery. The consideration of the original authored text, including its context and purpose, is compared to the parodied version, finding a sense of incongruities between the two. "Such incongruities no doubt make a parodic reading of a text both easier and more plausible" (Bennett, 1985, p. 29). Thus, the audience's ability to realize the parody and the parodied, and the difference between the two, is critical to the success of the author.

Because of the intertextual relationship between texts, Bennett (1985) argues that mimicry through parody or satire can never be neutral. The intertextual incorporation of other texts within discourse carries with it political baggage. At its very core, the transcontextual nature of imitation attempts to redefine the possible meanings of previous texts. As such, parody must be marked as such to allow its audience to "get the joke." Titles will mimic older texts, older texts are actually repeated within the new text, and other markers may be used. McClure and McClure (2001) analyze the use of parody in *Zelig*, paying close attention to the ability of the film to play with generic and conventional filmmaking stylistics. They contend that the comparison of the two forms allows the parodic form to criticize and perhaps even negate the conventional form. Shugart (1999) examines the structural and stylistic components of a parodic interpretation of da Vinci's *The Last Supper* by Susan White's *The First Supper*. In this case, the use of postmodern irony and parody assists in the unpacking of the patriarchal message of the original message, but also dangerously supports a hegemonic interpretation if the irony is missed. For *The Daily Show,* the audience must be well versed in modern structures of news media in order to fully appreciate its parodic nature. Also, as I will show in my analysis, *The Daily Show* has become increasingly reliant on the audience's foreknowledge of both "real" and fake news.

Parody, according to Hutcheon (2000) is ideologically suspect because it "implicitly reinforces even as it ironically debunks" (p. xii). Through textual reproduction, parody inherently supports its target; it borrows, yet also criticizes. With the addition of subversive irony, parody can take a satiric tone, even though parody and satire are often interchangeably used. Hutcheon (2000) contends that "the difference between these two forms lies not so much in their perspective on human behavior . . . but in what is being made into a "target." In other words, parody is not extramural in its aim; satire is" (p. 43). The extramural target emerges in the form of social criticism, as the satiric representation aims to situate itself in larger contexts, while the parodic many only interplay within the original and parodied texts. Parody is about textual form and genre; satire is about social commentary (Druick, 2009). Of course, these two genres are not mutually exclusive. Both overlap, especially with their utilization of ironic representations and critical distancing. Furthermore, "satire frequently uses parodic art forms for either expository or aggressive purposes" (Hutcheon, 2000, p. 43). Recognizing then that *The Daily Show* contains a controversial tone while incorporating formal elements of modern broadcasting, the program is best understood as satiric parody. Its parody is contained in its formal appropriation of news structures; its satire located through its style of ridicule of twenty-four-hour news networks.

In sum, irony, parody, and satire offer complex, audience-centered rhetorical tropes that call for dialectical consideration and speculation from its witnesses. *The Daily Show* has often been named as an irony-laden program, and has been previously examined as such (Baym, 2005, 2007; Hariman, 2007; Waisanen, 2009). Yet, while many have recognized the power of its parodic interpretation of the nightly news, few have recognized the changing structural and stylistic components of the program. Indeed, as the program has evolved over the past decade, its focus on the audience has also transformed. *The Daily Show* has altered its form to increase its reliance on the perceived knowledge of the audience. Hutcheon (1995) notes that there exists a "special relationship in ironic discourse between the ironist and the interpreter . . . it is irony itself that is said to *create* that relationship" (p. 89). Over time, *The Daily Show* has fostered and created a relationship with its audience, which has allowed the program to be more forceful and biting in its critique. Less and less, the program relies on parodic markings. Instead, the program has become more focused in its use of satire. In other words, the program has become less parodic, and more satiric. This shift illustrates *The Daily Show's* ability to create a "discursive community" out of irony in its audience (Hutcheon, 1995, pp. 89–101). To display this shift, I chart *The Daily Show's* decreased use of structural parody and reinforced stylistic satire over the past decade, noting early and now declining use of markers that assist the audience in getting its joke. To do so, I engage in a postmodern rhetorical criticism, paying special attention to the changing intertextual character of the program.

METHOD: POSTMODERN RHETORICAL CRITICISM

In the shift toward critical rhetoric, a number of rhetorical theorists reflected on the increasingly fragmentary nature of public discourse (Ceccarelli, 1998; Charland, 1991; Condit, 1990; Hariman, 1991; McKerrow, 1989, 1991; McGee, 1990). Of primary concern of critical rhetoric is the increasingly problematic nature of the critic, the text, and the relationship between the two. "Critical rhetoric does not *begin* with a finished text in need of interpretation; rather, texts are understood to be larger than the apparently finished discourse that presents itself as transparent" (McGee, 1990, p. 279). Critics, thus, become inventors of texts that are suitable for criticism. Through this act, critics recognize the vast webs of intertextual relationships that exist in public discourse. Burgchardt (2000) reflects on this notion and critical rhetorical approaches in relation to postmodernism: "postmodern theory challenges traditional assumptions about what constitutes a 'text,' whether the creator of a work can make authoritative claims about what the critical object means, and whether interpretation of rhetorical objects can be free from politics"(p. 603). Critical postmodern rhetorical theorists contend that texts are free and open for multiple forms of interpretation (Ceccarelli, 1998), and that postmodern discourse can be playful in nature, oscillating from various interpretations and considerations of meaning. "[A] critical rhetoric allows one to 'make sense' out of the pastiche of discourses that mark our postmodern experience" (McKerrow, 1991, p. 76). In the case of *The Daily Show*, the intertextual relationship between parody and parodied requires a perspective that appreciates such fluid and polysemic markers.

One prominent feature of postmodern rhetorical criticism is the expansion of the notion of what constitutes a text. Blair, Jeppeson, and Pucci (1991) argue that the Vietnam Veteran's Memorial embodies this type of textual interpretation: "it is inclusive; it does not suggest one reading or the other, but embraces even contradictory interpretations" (p. 281). These contradictory and competing interpretations of the same artifact are understood through complex polysemic readings: "The Memorial stands as a commemoration of veterans of the war, *and* as a monument to political struggle" (p. 281). Methods in critical rhetoric seek to contextualize discourse within its potential interpretations and relationships with other texts. No text is devoid of references to other texts and should be realized within its fuller context of intertextual references. Other instances of postmodern rhetorical criticism feature voices that are outside the normal realm of discourse. Michael Hyde (1993) examines the discourse of euthanasia, paying particular attention to an anonymous letter entitled "It's Over, Debbie," which reveals a narrative that talks of a hospital worker who assisted with the suicide of a young patient suffering from ovarian cancer. Multiple readings and interpretations of the letter are found within its text, as revealed by the controversy following its publication in the *Journal of the American Medical Association.* "In telling the story of 'Debbie,' the author not only is presenting something that is supposed to be totally unpresentable, but is presenting it in a way filled with uncertainty" (p. 208). Once again, this type of rhetorical interpretation highlights the various readings that one can find within a text.

Drawing from these ideas of intertextuality and the fluidity of fragmentary texts, I structure my analysis in three parts. First, looking within the text and content of the show, I uncover the stylistic uses of irony and satire, both verbally and visually, to understand how the program intertextually relates to and critiques the twenty-four-hour news networks. Second, by examining the structural parody of the show, I compare *The Daily Show* to the various other texts that are being parodied. Understanding the fullest intent of the parody and especially its intertextual nature will require an investigation into both the parody and the parodied. Finally, I discuss the structural and stylistic changes that the program has undergone in the past decade. Looking at current examples of episodes of the program illustrates the increasing reliance of the program on its audience as a discursive community with foreknowledge of parody in order to display its argument about modern news broadcasting. Throughout my analysis, I draw from episodes taken from three time periods in the program's history: early 2000s, mid-2000s, and recent episodes in 2010. Examining these time periods assists in seeing the changes that *The Daily Show* has undergone and how they relate to its parodic form and satiric end.

ANALYSIS

Stylistic Satire

The Daily Show is a "fake" news organization in the sense that the program does not actually *conduct* journalism. Instead, the show appropriates major headlines of the day (Segal, 2002) and re-presents them ironically in order to make its argument. Visual and verbal markers, along with a parodic structure, assist viewers in "getting the joke" of the show. Investigating the "fake" portions of the program provides insight into the ways the show uses irony and parody. Baym (2005) has noted that the label "fake" for *The Daily Show* is highly problematic because it "fails to acknowledge the increasingly central role the show is playing in the domain of serious political communication" (p. 260). From winning Peabody awards to Jon Stewart being named as the most trusted newscaster in the country ("Poll results," 2009), to say that *The Daily Show* is not real misses the mark. Baym (2005) also argues that to label *The Daily Show* as fake would mean that the label "real" could be applied to the other types of mainstream journalism. Instead, Baym (2005) argues, *The Daily Show* should be seen as a form of experimental journalism. Certainly this is the case, and with Baym (2005), I argue that the stylistic use of irony and satire is both experimental *and* interrogatory of the assumptions of modernist news practices. Through the use of irony, *The Daily Show* hyperbolically portrays the news in order to expose the inherent flaws of the news industry.

The social satire of *The Daily Show* expresses one general premise: Driven by ratings and the impossible twenty-four-hour timeslot, the modern news industry reports and presents the world in an excessively stylistic manner that lacks real substance. News networks as "infotainment" construct a fearful world in turmoil, packaged in flashy graphics and "brought-to-you-by" consumer products. In an interview with Connie Chung, Jon Stewart remarks that: "It's more what makes us sad or angry about the news and then we try to turn that into something that could be considered humor or satire . . ." Continuing on in the interview, Stewart describes how the excess of the news is something to be satirized. "The [news] people have forgotten that these are tragic images [of September 11th] and they are using them as bumpers. So by overloading that, we make fun of those kinds of things" (Perlmutter, 2002). This criticism of news reporting is a prevalent theme in most of the program's episodes.

Through this general critique of excess, *The Daily Show* constantly plays with styles of news reporting. The parodying of news structures is hyperbolically and ironically represented through the use of developed visual cues. The first act of the program, which is devoted to recent headlines, uses clips from the day's news and major headlines. As will be discussed below, the structure of the program uses picture boxes in the top-left corner of the screen much like those of major new organizations. As a visual repetition with difference, however, *The Daily Show* alters either the title of the headline or the picture being featured, accenting it with studio audience laughter. For example, the June 27, 2002 episode of the program featured a story on the constitutional challenge of the Pledge of Allegiance statement "under God." The visual box featured the title, "In God we Fuss," playing on American currency. On the September 9, 2002 episode, Stewart describes the UN World Summit on Sustainable Development. The text box in this headline superimposed upon a picture of the globe reads "We Scar the World," referencing the '80s hit song, "We Are the World." More recently in the April 13, 2010 episode about the changes in tax law, the visual caption of "That's Tariffic" adorns the screen.

This ironic tactic of displaying ridiculous headlines has continued throughout the program's run, which feeds the overall ironic theme of the program and allows the audience to recognize the ironic utterances. In some cases, *The Daily Show* makes direct references to similar ridiculous types of visual displays found in mainstream news. On the February 10, 2010 episode, *The Daily Show* reported on the large snowstorm that hit the east coast of the United States. Stewart, displaying the program's usually ridiculous use of language about the storm, began to call it "snowmageddon" and "snowpocalypse" but interrupts himself with clips of news agencies calling the storm exactly those terms. Eventually, Stewart "one-ups" the news agencies making up "snowtorious B.I.G." with a graphic of a dancing snowman to boot. Of course, he then cuts to CNN who has him beat already by quoting a comment to the CNN message boards on the air of "snowtorious B.I.G." Stewart gives up and reverts to calling the weather "unusually large snowstorm." Similarly, on the April 19, 2010 episode, reporting on the volcano eruption that interrupted flights across Europe, Jon Stewart jokingly called out news agencies for lacking the same fervor in discussing the natural disaster. Again, *The Daily Show* pushes the boundaries with "Volcanolypse 2010," replete with a fire-blazing screen and blockbuster-film sounding music. While seemingly inane displays of excess, such ironic visuals craft a critical argument about the sensationalized and excessive nature of mainstream news organizations.

Outside of visuals, *The Daily Show*'s use of being "on location" also parodies the style of mainstream news, poking fun at the emphasis of on-the-ground reporting. When correspondents report from scenes all over the world, they are obviously within the studio standing in front of a digitally created backdrop. On multiple occasions the program plays with this notion, pushing it to the limit of hyperbolic expression. For example, in the July 23, 2002 episode, Steve Carell reports from the French Alps about the Tour de France. "Live" on the scene, Carell reports on the cycling, saying that he was suffering from altitude sickness and was excited about seeing the race. On the January 31, 2005 episode, Samantha Bee reports "on location" from Saddam Hussein's campaign headquarters after the Iraqi election. And, on September 6, 2005, Ed Helms reports live from Giants stadium (not the Superdome) on the aftermath of Hurricane Katrina. These scenes illustrate *The Daily Show's* playful inversions of the twenty-four-hour news media. Too often, CNN, Fox News, or other news networks attempt to increase their credibility from such in-the-trenches styles of reporting. *The Daily Show's* satire of being live on the scene, twists the notion of this importance, laying clear the absurdity of reporting, for instance, on extreme weather while standing in it.

Finally, *The Daily Show* stylistically replicates many of the news features found in mainstream media. One powerful example of this is the special report "Even Stevphan," a bit from the early 2000s which was comprised of a debate between two correspondents, Steve Carell and Stephen Colbert. A major news issue is offered and the two correspondents argue and discuss it, parodying CNN's now-defunct debate program *Crossfire*. The parodic twist found in *The Daily Show* appears in the form of personal insults, which are frequent and the primary source of actual debate in the feature. The two correspondentsonly tangentially discuss major issues and instead litter their debate with insults, rancor, and attacks. In the August 19, 2002 episode, Steve Carell, apparently on leave, was replaced by Ed Helms in an "Even Stevphen" segment. This special "Even Stevphen" focused on the looming invasion of Iraq. Helms, who has never previously appeared in this particular bit, performs using actual reasons as to why invading Iraq would be a preferable option for the United States. Colbert, with his usual wit, refutes Helms' argument with a series of ad hominem attacks. A confused Helms asks why Colbert makes fun of him; he thought they were friends. Colbert stops the argument to explain to Helms how the special works, laying out a direct comparison between the segment and CNN's *Crossfire*. He notes that the subject, in shows such as these, is irrelevant; it's all about the debate and game aspect of the program. After this explanation, Helms attacks Colbert's personal life about his wife leaving him for another woman, after which Colbert begins crying because of this "real" event. When compared to programs such as *Crossfire*, this clip exposes the falsely constructed debates that occur. The real issues are a façade, used only to highlight partisan differences between correspondents. By juxtaposing itself with *Crossfire*, *The Daily Show's*satire unpacks the contrivance of such talking head programs.

The ironic style and satire of *The Daily Show* has been well-documented as having profound effects on journalism and political communication (Baym, 2005). My intent here is only to display how the visual and verbal satire of the show illustrates the argument that Stewart and his band of correspondents are making. By ironically inverting the stylistic devices of twenty-four-hour news networks and their devotion to ratings-driven info-tainment, *The Daily Show* unpacks these devices to display their excess. The postmodern irony subverts the claims of modern journalism, laying bare their claims to truth. Certainly, *The Daily Show* relies on irony to mark and make its "repetition with difference;" however, as seen above, *The Daily Show* engages in "hyperbolic explosion" of the journalistic style of modern news. By overloading the constructs of major news networks, *The Daily Show* pushes such reporting to an extreme until it bursts. As such, the program situates itself on a continuum of absurdity; a continuum that twenty-four-hour news networks have already been on for quite some time. Coupled with irony as an audience-centered discourse (Shugart, 1999), the program invites its audience to consider and ultimately reject the style of the modern news industry. To assist in this reading, *The Daily Show* has fostered its audience through structural changes as it has gained prominence.

Structural Parody

Coupled with satire, the parodic form of *The Daily Show* underscores its argument against the twenty-four-hour news networks. Recall that parody operates as a discursive repetition of another text (Hutcheon, 2000, p. 43), and as an intertextual transference of form, without necessarily referring to the content of the original text. *The Daily Show* operates as structural parody in the sense that it appropriates the common structure of news reporting, including special reports, breaking news, and headlines. "Irony participates in parodic discourse as a strategy . . . which allows the decoder to interpret and evaluate" (Hutcheon, 2000, p. 31) the original message. *The Daily Show* includes ironic difference and satire through strategies of hyperbolic representation and explosion in its content, but such representations are grounded in a structure that reads as the news would. As social critique, *The Daily Show* has been recognized for subverting the modernist portrayals of news and broadcasting, as "an important experiment in journalism, one that contains much significance for the ongoing redefinition of news" (Baym, 2005, p. 273). Within *The Daily Show*, the modernist structures of news reporting and representations of world affairs from the dominant news industry perspective are critically examined. Using the same format allows *The Daily Show* to interact with these structures, both subverting them and engaging them simultaneously. Full recognition and appreciation of this transideological process can be accomplished through an analysis of each of the parts of the program and unpacking of the portions of the show that have specific parodic references. My intent here is not to break down the show into parts in order to dissect them, but instead to understand the intertextual relationships that the show constructs.

Throughout its tenure, *The Daily Show* has most often used a three act structure. Usually, the show begins with a short monologue from Jon Stewart to introduce the first act. After his speech, the host will discuss the major news of the day. In the second act, the program will either continue to speak of news events, or have a special report from a correspondent. Finally, the last act includes a guest for the program, which ranges from musical artists and actors, to world leaders, politicians, and other media pundits. The show closes with a "Moment of Zen," usually related to the day's content. In this format, the postmodern ironic elements of the show invert and twist the "real" news, demanding the audience rethink the cultural and social constructions of more mainstream news programs. A decade ago, these parts of the program were explicitly marked as "Headlines," "This Just In/Breaking News/Other News," "Special Reports," and the introduction of guests. The label of "Headlines," constructed as a segue device, inspired by "bumpers" between segments in twenty-four-hour news, assists the audience in considering the formal qualities of the parodied text. The other acts of the program use similar features. In its current form, the sections are not labeled in the same manner. While the show has maintained the basic three part structure, the audience has become accustomed to its progression.

The "Headlines" feature of *The Daily Show* utilizes, in form, many techniques from news broadcasting. First, the show employs the standard anchor format, using Stewart as a verbal vehicle to report. Along with Stewart as a "talking head" the show uses visual cues that are common in twenty-four-hour news reporting, such as the use of a picture box located at the top-left corner of the screen that includes visual imagery to illustrate the headline being discussed. This tactic of structural parody interacts with dominant news broadcasting by appropriating the style of visual representation and adding an ironic and comedic twist and has been seen in other programs such as *Weekend Update* on *Saturday Night Live*. Second, along with the picture box and its ironic inversion, *The Daily Show* uses correspondents much in the same way that any normal news program does. As Stewart reports on the day's headlines, he will include correspondents as specialists on the topic, or jump to his correspondents who are "live on scene" reporting. For example, the August 22, 2002 episode featured updates on the Enron scandal and trials, as well as new videos released by CNN in the war on terror. Ed Helms offers insight as a "media analyst" on the tapes released by CNN.

One prominent structural feature of the program is its slippery generic qualities. Kellner (1999) terms such genre-playing as "genre implosion and hybridity" in his examination of *The X-Files*. He notes:

> *The X-Files* thus takes the postmodern strategies of genre pastiche, quotation, appropriation, and hybridity to new levels, drawing heavily on previous genres, redoing old stories and formulas, mixing generic codes, playing on the audience's knowl-

edge of traditional folklore, the occult, and media culture, quoting its codes, iconography, plots, and themes, but often reworking traditional material to question it critically, using it to interrogate the institutions and society affirmed—for the most part—in earlier genre productions of media culture. (Kellner, 1999, p. 167)

Similarly, *The Daily Show* structurally draws from a variety of genres. Such playfulness has been noted by a number of academics, who label the show a political culture jamming news parody (Warner, 2007), a late-night comedy show (Baym, 2007), and alternative journalism (Baym, 2005). The difficulty in determining the generic structure of the program appears at its intersection of self-professed "fakeness" and its drawing from late-night comedy, sketch comedy, news programming, and talk show forms. The use of multiple genres of television programming allows the audience to draw upon a wide array of familiar forms, including those of late night television, stand-up comedy, and news broadcasting. No static categorization of form can be found within *The Daily Show*, which is much like Kellner's (1999) examination of *The X-Files*. Also similar to Kellner's analysis, the program plays upon the audience's knowledge of each of those forms through critical interrogation. However, over time, the form of *The Daily Show* has solidified as its audience and public persona has taken shape, an issue I will explore in the final section of this essay.

The featured guests of the show offer a particular moment when the blurring of genres and forms becomes especially problematic. Guests can range from movie actors, to political authors, to famous athletes. This portion of the program blurs the genre between late-night television and news broadcasting. Often, in the news, the use of specialists or experts will sharpen a report and clarify issues for the audience. Similarly, on *The Daily Show*, political pundits and experts on foreign affairs will frequent the program to discuss major issues of the day. Through the interviews, the show defies being categorized into solely a news satire or late-night comedy. Indeed, the postmodern irony and predominant satire of the previous two acts often departs as Stewart engages in thoughtful albeit playful discussion with guests. Baym (2007) sees this moment as carrying an "ethos of democratic dialogue constructed within and across the interviews" and a "blending of postmodern stylistics and a modernist belief in reasoned discourse" (p. 94–95). In other words, the use of guests counterbalances the hyperbole of its satire. Indeed, over time, Stewart's interviews have taken on increased prominence (Baym, 2007). In its current form, *The Daily Show* uses its accompanying website to have longer and unedited versions of interviews, lasting as long as twenty minutes. This preference for thoughtful discussion indicates that *The Daily Show* has recognized its own place and power in the production of news stories.

Overall, the use of both structural parody and genre-blurring adds to *The Daily Show*'s postmodern implications. One feature of postmodern discourse is "leaving behind the assumptions and procedures of modern theory and embracing a dynamic and ongoing encounter with emergent theories, sciences, technologies, cultural forms, communications media, experiences, politics and identities" (Kellner and Best, 2001, p. 7). Modernist representations of reality depicted through news reporting structures are challenged through the appropriation of those same structures in *The Daily Show*. As a postmodern entity, *The Daily Show* enjoys a fluidity of categorization, which feeds the interpretation of the satire as both engaging these genres and challenging them. Using the modernist news frame, adding a twist of postmodern irony, the program undermines the dominant structures of representation through its satire. Put another way, the formal structure of the program operates as a foundation for its argument against the twenty-four-hour news networks and its stylistic satire serves to strengthen its audience's knowledge of the repetition with difference. However, over time, the program has increasingly relied on its satiric style to make its argument.

Changes Over Time

Certainly, *The Daily Show* has been well-known for its powerful critique. Warner (2007) calls the program a form of culture jamming and Waisanen (2009) labels Jon Stewart and Stephen Colbert rhetorical critics who reflect on news programming. Building upon these observations, I argue that the structural changes in the program over time indicate that the audience, forged out of irony, has become something of an "imagined community," constituted by the form and content of *The Daily Show*'sdiscourse (Charland, 1987). Early in the program's run, its satiric style was matched with a number of parodic markers, making its argument plain for its viewership. Over time, however, the program has shed such parodic markings to focus on its satire. Shugart (1999) recognizes that traditional irony is audience centered: "Audience agency, by virtue of participation, is crucial to traditional irony's success" (p. 452). However, in postmodern or subversive irony, "audience agency appears to be constrained. The specifically postmodern nature of subversive irony appears to cater to and thus invite a particularly postmodern audience" (p. 452). Similarly, in the case of *The Daily Show*, the invited audience is one that must be cognizant and appreciative of contemporary news topics and forms. In the early 2000s, *The Daily Show* used a prescripted structure that it followed in nearly every episode; however, since its rise in popularity and parodic appreciation, the program has become less reliant upon the obvious references to the parodied text. In recent episodes, the program merely begins after Jon Stewart's brief monologue, diving into the content of the show without labels of "Headlines" or other parts of the news program. Correspondents have retained their labels as "specialists" in this or that, but the overall "news-like" feel of the program has changed. The current features of the program illustrate the decreased need for the program to be marked as parody. Furthermore, *The Daily Show* has more frequently deviated from its usual program in more recent episodes. While previous deviations were usually limited to election nights (*Indecision 2000, 2004, 2008*), more frequently, the program has devoted its time differently. Two striking examples illustrate the changing form of *The Daily Show.*

In the June 26, 2002 episode, Jon Stewart discusses the ways in which "Breaking News" dominates the twenty-four-hour news networks. Through the special report entitled "I on News" Stewart dismantles these news tactics, explaining that one defining element of the twenty-four-hour news is the idea of "Breaking News." Stewart continues by comparing the types of stories found on such networks, such as the "news alert" or "big story." He then displays CNN's breaking news graphic, which is used as a teaser for the upcoming story, a collection of clips from various news organizations, including Fox News, CNN, and MSNBC, about the "Dirty Bomb" scare, which was a supposed terrorist weapon discovered early in the summer of 2002. The use of fear tactics in these news stories is exposed through Stewart's analysis of the reporting, which grossly overestimates the power and threat of the dirty bomb. Stewart describes a hypothetical, panicked viewer that pleads for answers and solutions to the dirty bomb from the twenty-four-hour news networks. In other words, according to Stewart, the news media constructs fear and provides itself as the means to assuage the very same fear. The intertwining of twenty-four-hour news network clips and commentary from Stewart highlights the inherent excessiveness found in modern American broadcasting. Stewart's comments about the news organization feed the thesis of the program that the common representation of reality through the use of these sorts of reporting tactics creates false depictions and unwarranted responses. Indeed, by *reporting on the reporting*, Stewart uses the same structural form via parody to explain how the news is constructed.

The next example is born out of a reaction to the rise in Fox News as being the most-watched source in news as of 2010, and Jon Stewart's subsequent attack on the conservative news outlet (Stelter, 2010). Both the November 5, 2009 and the March 18, 2010 episodes featured longer monologues aimed at Fox News' Glenn Beck. In these cases, Jon Stewart has shifted the structural parody of the program toward a more ridiculing, satiric stance against Beck, wherein parody becomes mockery and the bite of critique much sharper. His performance outwardly mocks Beck, who is well known for his supposed down-to-earth and overly emotional, even teary-eyed proclamations on Fox News. In the March 2010 performance, Stewart satirizes Beck; he pretends to cry, pokes fun at Beck's use of a chalkboard, and over-gestures as Beck does. He uses clips of Beck's program during his performance, applying Beck's argument to himself as a "progressive." In contrast to his display of "Breaking News" clips in 2002, this caricature of Beck is intended to ridicule him. His use of chalkboards, for example, the form through which Beck frequently deploys his argument, is drastically different than the type of formal parody in which the program usually engages. Beck uses the chalkboards to display arguments in a presumably commonsense manner, one that underscores the "plainness" of his beliefs. In this case, Stewart satirically uses the chalkboards to unpack Beck's claims, mocking Beck's "everyman" persona. He plays with Beck's logic of extremes, which, according to Stewart, means that any argument must be taken to its fullest extreme with every possible negative outcome. In this case, Stewart uses this moment of satire to uncover the ridiculousness of Beck's claims. While the segment draws from clips of Beck's program to assist in the construction of the absurd argument, the use of them only works to undermine Glenn Beck and support Jon Stewart's satiric aim.

The changes in the structure of the program indicate that *The Daily Show* invites an audience that expects parody and especially satire. Just as Shugart (1999) argues that postmodern irony invites a postmodern audience, so, too, does *The Daily Show*. Contemporary viewers are not only knowledgeable of the form and content of the program; they arrive nightly with foreknowledge of vast cultural forms and current events. They are familiar with the blurred and imploded genres that the program uses in its creation. They are cognizant of how Glenn Beck and twenty-four-hour news programs make claims of truth in their presentation of the day's events. And, most importantly, they expect Jon Stewart to ridicule those forms, calling out their content and ideologies. Furthermore, the audience of *The Daily Show* expects the program to produce laughter as well as insight through interviews (Baym, 2007). In other words, while the earlier versions of the program that marked the intertextual relationship between the structures of twenty-four-hour news and *The Daily Show* allowed for a dialectical consideration of parody against parodied, the current version aims for social satire as ridicule, which may not need to invite such consideration, perhaps because the audience already knows them. Yet, for the program to have an audience that understands the use of irony without the same markings, it must have some intelligence of the non-marked parodied text.

CONCLUSION

As many have recognized, *The Daily Show* is not just a laughing matter; it exists as a powerful influence on news making and news reception writ large. Feldman and Young (2008) note that the "audience for *The Daily Show*. . .

maintains high levels of news attention" (p. 417), indicating that to be a consistent viewer of the program, one must have knowledge of the news events of the day. And, the influence of *The Daily Show* has been traced; many eighteen- to thirty-year-olds claimed to get their news from *The Daily Show* and similar programming ("Audience segments," 2008). Rhetorically, this audience has been built out of irony and satire, and established through the parody of news organizations. For viewers to simultaneously get their news and "get" the joke from *The Daily Show*, the intertextual reference must be understood via both its original and parodic reference. In other words, to watch and understand *The Daily Show,* audiences must be aware of current affairs. In this way, the postmodern elements of the show seek to invert the news through ironic twisting, which requires that audience members dialectically (re)think the cultural and social constructions of more mainstream news programs. However, over time, *The Daily Show* has altered its form and structure. It has largely abandoned its devotion to political parody and, instead, focused on sharpening its satire. Largely lost is the moniker "fake news." From and through parody, *The Daily Show* has built its audience as one familiar with the critique of news as a form; from satire and the discursive community of irony, *The Daily Show* has furthered its critique to be pointed at the idea and people of the news.

REFERENCES

Audience segments in a changing news environment: Key news audiences now blend online and traditional sources. (2008, Aug 17). *The Pew Research Center for the People and the Press.* Retrieved from http://people-press.org/reports/pdf/444.pdf.

Baym, G. (2005). *The Daily Show:* Discursive integration and the reinvention of political journalism. *Political Communication, 22,* 259–276.

———. (2007). Crafting new communicative models in the televisual sphere. Political interviews on *The Daily Show. The Communication Review, 10,* 93–115.

Bennett, D. (1985). Parody, postmodernism, and the politics of reading. *Critical Quarterly, 27,* 27–43.

Best, S. and Kellner, D. (1991). *Postmodern theory: Critical interrogations.* New York: Guilford Press.

Blair, C., Jeppeson, M. S. and Pucci Jr., E. (1991). Public memorializing in postmodernity: The Vietnam Veterans memorial as prototype. *Quarterly Journal of Speech, 77,* 263–288.

Booth, W. C. (1974). *A rhetoric of irony.* University of Chicago Press.

———. (1983). The empire of irony. *Georgia Review, 37,* 719 – 737.

Burgchardt, C. (2000). *Readings in Rhetorical Criticism.* State College, PA: Strata Publishing, Inc.

Burke, K. (1945). *A grammar of motives.* Berkeley, CA:University of California Press.

Ceccarelli, L. (1998). Polysemy: Multiple meanings in rhetorical criticism. *Quarterly Journal of Speech, 84,* 395–415.

Charland, M. (1987). Constitutive rhetoric: The case of the Peuple Québécois. *Quarterly Journal of Speech, 73,*133–150.

———. (1991). Finding a horizon and telos: The challenge to critical rhetoric. *Quarterly Journal of Speech, 77,* 71–74.

Condit, C. (1990). Rhetorical criticism and audiences: The extremes of McGee and Leff. *Western Journal of Speech Communication, 54,* 330–345.

Druick, Z. (2009). Dialogic absurdity: TV news parody as a critique of genre. *Television and New Media, 10,* 294–308.

Feldman, L. and Young, D. G. (2008). Late-night comedy as a gateway to traditional news: An analysis of time trends in news attention among late-night comedy viewers during the 2004 Presidential primaries. *Political Communication, 25,* 401–422.

Ganahl, J. (2002, April 23). 'Daily Show' host Jon Stewart is TV's king of irony. *San Francisco Chronicle,* p. D1.

Hariman, R. (1991). Critical rhetoric: Critiques and a response. *Quarterly Journal of Speech, 77,* 67–70.

———. (2007). In defense of Jon Stewart. *Critical Studies in Media Communication, 24,* 273–277.

———. (2008). Political parody and public culture. *Quarterly Journal of Speech, 94,* 247–272.

Hart, R. P. and Hartelius, E. J. (2007). The political sins of Jon Stewart. *Critical Studies in Media Communication, 24,* 263–272.

Hutcheon, L. (1995). *Irony's edge: The theory and politics of irony.* London: Routledge.

———. (2000). *A theory of parody: The teachings of twentieth-century art forms.* New York: Methuen.

Hyde, M. J. (1993). Medicine, rhetoric, and euthanasia: A case study in the workings of a postmodern discourse. *Quarterly Journal of Speech, 79,* 201–224.

Kaufer, D. (1977). Irony and rhetorical strategy. *Philosophy and Rhetoric,* 10(2), 90–110.

Kellner, D. (1999). *The X-Files* and the aesthetics and politics of postmodern pop. *Journal of Aesthics and Art Criticism, 57(2),* 161 – 176.

Kellner, D. and Best, S. (2001). *The postmodern adventure: Science, technology, and cultural studies at the third millennium.* New York: Guilford Press.

LeDuc, D. (2002, February 10). State Senator learns the hard way: Know thy interviewer. *The Washington Post,* p. T05.

McClure, K. R. and McClure, L. L. (2001, Fall). Postmodern parody: *Zelig* and the rhetorical subversion of documentary form. *Qualitative Research Reports in Communication,* 81–88.

McGee, M. C. (1990). Text, context, and the fragmentation of contemporary culture. *Western Journal of Communication, 54,* 274–289.

McKerrow, R. (1989). Critical rhetoric: Theory and praxis. *Communication Monographs, 56,* 91–111.

———. (1991). Critical rhetoric in a postmodern world. *Quarterly Journal of Speech, 77,* 75–78.

Perlmutter, B. (Executive Producer). (2002, June 24). *Connie Chung Tonight* [Television broadcast]. New York: Cable News Network

Poll results: Now that Walter Cronkite has passed on, who is America's most trusted newscaster? (2009). *Time, Inc.* Retrieved from http://www.timepolls.com/hppolls/archive/poll_results_417.html.

Segal, D. (2002, May 2). The seriously funny Jon Stewart; Cable's 'Daily Show' host delivers satire with substance. *The Washington Post,* p. C01.

Shugart, H. A. (1999). Postmodern irony as subversive rhetorical strategy. *Western Journal of Communication, 63,* 433–455.

Stelter, B. (2010, April 23). Jon Stewart's punching bag, Fox News. *New York Times.* Retrieved from http://www.nytimes.com/2010/04/24/arts/television/24stewart.html.

Tindale, C. W. and Gough, J. (1987). The use of irony in argumentation. *Philosophy and Rhetoric, 20,* 1–17.

Waisanen, D. J. (2009). A citizen's guides to democracy inaction: Jon Stewart and Stephen Colbert's comic rhetorical criticism. *Southern Communication Journal, 74,* 119–140.

Warner, J. (2007). Political culture jamming: The dissident humor of *The Daily Show with Jon Stewart. Popular Communication, 5,* 17–36.

White, H. (1973). *Metahistory: The historical imagination in nineteenth-century Europe.* Baltimore: Johns Hopkins University Press.

Chapter Ten

Visual Aspects of *The Daily Show with Jon Stewart*

Lawrence J. Mullen

"I have begun to question whether, even when it is functioning at its highest level, at its most professional, with its greatest degree of journalistic integrity, with its most serious and dedicated reporters (there are a few left), television can ever be seen—as I saw it once—as a medium of enlightenment and as an agent of change, or if it has in fact fulfilled its *true calling* as merely another electronic medium of inane distraction from the harsh realities of life." —Peter K. Fallon (2009, p. 11)

"News isn't so much a report of reality as a form of 'created reality.'" —Berger (1991, p. 149)

The February 27, 2007 broadcast of the Public Broadcasting System's *Frontline* was the third episode in a special series called, "News War." In the introduction to the show the narrator, Will Lyman, states that today's news industry is in crisis. He also acknowledges the public's disdain for journalists and an audience turning to alternative sources for information. Images and sound bites lamenting the state of today's journalism accompany Lyman's commentary. Then there is a transition to pictures from a television studio and we see the production of one of the country's most influential news programs, which isn't a news program at all. It is *The Daily Show with Jon Stewart*. As we watch clips from behind the scenes, Lyman describes how, just a few years ago, "TV critics declared this comedy show the best news show on television to the dismay of the show's producers," and that the show's audience has come to expect "a raucous dissection of the content and conventions of TV news."

Attempting to understand the content and conventions of *The Daily Show*, this chapter dissects the visual aspects of a program that in many ways defies

classification. Some call it parody, others call it fake news, a comedy program, and even a kind of public affairs programming (see Baym, 2005). As a
parody of traditional television news, *The Daily Show* employs satire, sarcasm, irony, comedy, ridicule, discussion, and more to create a hybrid form
of programming. To understand the nature of its visual imagery we need to
understand what *The Daily Show* is. And here I define it in terms of the
obvious: television. As a television phenomenon *The Daily Show* takes on
certain visual characteristics.[1] The rest of the chapter looks more closely at
the "television-ness" of this hard-to-define program in what I'll call a nested
two-by-two critical analysis: 1) historical/critical divided into a) discontinuous aspects and b) repetitive aspects, and 2) visual aesthetics divided into a)
compositional aspects and b) composite imagery.

A TELEVISION SHOW

How is the visual imagery of *The Daily Show* shaped by the fact that it is
mediated by television? In other words, what is television and what makes its
images different from or the same as other ways images are mediated? To
answer these questions we need to understand the nature of the medium
itself. This is, however, such a complex, multi-dimensional undertaking that
any effort is bound to be incomplete. So, two lines of discussion are carved
out here, 1) historical-cultural, and 2) visual aesthetics.[2] These approaches
exclude other ways we could discuss the nature of televisual imagery, most
notably an economics or business approach, which is undeniably important
since much of what we see on television is used to attract viewers to advertisers who, in turn, hope to sell you, the consumer, products and services. This
is evident in the fact that *The Daily Show* has commercial breaks filled with
advertisements that target a particular demographic segment of consumers.
So, the visual "look" of *The Daily Show* functions to bring an audience to
advertisers. Though the economic aspect is not the focus of this chapter, it is
important to remember that the money-making venture of television also
underlies the way *The Daily Show* is visually presented despite its seemingly
anti-establishment/anti-corporate façade. Indeed, it is important to keep in
mind that television is historically a technology created by inventors affiliat-
ed with a broadcasting industry interested in profits. Up until fairly recently
their concern was not with how the televisual image looked, its aesthetic
design, or artistic taste. Their concern was with mass distribution and mass
consumption. Paraphrasing Postman and Powers (1992), the form and content of news programs are designed to keep viewers watching so that they
will be exposed to the commercials. Failure to keep an audience watching
spells the demise for any television show. To this point in time *The Daily*

Show's parodic formula has proven to be successful. Exploring its visual aspects gives us further understanding of its success as a fake news program.

A HISTORICAL-CULTURAL APPROACH

The roots of *The Daily Show* can be traced to the 1960s and the British Broadcasting Corporation's (BBC) *That Was the Week That Was*, a groundbreaking satirical news program starring, among others, David Frost (Fiddy, n.d.). Lampooning the establishment, the program equally satirized British royalty, religion, bigots, and philanderers. Another early "fake news" program was the Canadian Broadcasting Corporation's (CBC) *This Hour Has Seven Days* which broke into the fake news business in 1964 (Wilson-Smith, 2004). These early shows often tried to expose the nature of news production by showing the backstage nuts and bolts of television—the cameras, boom microphones, and flimsy sets used to portray the news. This "behind-the-scenes" perspective was something new to television viewers back in the 1960s. Then in the late 1960s and early 1970s the American comedy variety show, *Rowan and Martin's Laugh-In* featured a satirical news segment "Laugh-In Looks at the News" which was echoed a few years later by *Saturday Night Live's* "Weekend Update" segment. *Laugh-In*'s news segment took a campy approach featuring a chorus line of female cast members who introduced the news with song and dance.[3] What has changed over time is the popularity and influence of fake news. As traditional television news ratings have plummeted, the popularity of fake news has risen to a point where most young people rely on these shows for their news (Wilson-Smith, 2004; Baumgartner and Morris, 2006; Gettings, 2007). In turn, politicians have appeared on fake news and late-night comedy programs to enhance their images and appeal to the audience watching these types of shows. Such appearances have served to legitimize fake news shows and deepened their cultural significance.

As cultural symbols, fake news shows such as *The Daily Show* can be understood as "one of a number of complex sign systems through which we experience and by which we know the world" (Allen, 1987, p. 2). "Perhaps it would be more precise to say that it represents an ever-changing point of convergence" for a variety of sign systems operating in the culture (p. 2). In this way we can understand *The Daily Show* as a sign system that constructs representations of reality through the use of complex conventions—"conventions whose operations are hidden by their transparency" (p. 2). These are the conventions of television production which create the visual images we are concerned with here. They are hidden by the fact that we generally fail to read them, i.e., pay attention to them; camera angles, lighting, and other visual elements. Each of these elements adds layers of meaning to the message. This chapter examines one of these elements (composition) in detail in the section below on the visual aesthetics of the show.

Furthermore, Gitlin (1987) said that, "For the most part, television . . . shows us only what the nation already presumes, focuses on what the culture already knows—or more precisely, enables us to gaze upon something the appointed seers think we need or want to know . . . it is the principle circulator of the cultural mainstream" (p. 3). And so it is with *The Daily Show* as it recasts the things we have already seen and heard about in the mainstream media, albeit in a new parodic light, laced with humor, sarcasm, and irony. Indeed, the popularity of *The Daily Show* may not be so much due to its writing and content as with the culture in which we find it. As Harries (2000) tells us, today's "culture is steeped in an ever-increasing level of irony" which he characterizes as society's state of "ironic supersaturation" (p. 3). He goes on to say that "with newer generations being fed a daily diet of ironic and parodic discourse in every type of media, one could even posit the threatened relevance of 'classic' canons to people in the not-too-distant future" (p. 3). But parody and irony are nothing new to television or to the media in general. Miller (1988) argues that "admen first deployed . . . irony during the Great Depression, in response to the rising distrust of big business" (p. 14). In fact, he argues, today's television protects itself against the disbelieving viewer by evincing endless amounts of irony via a process not unlike inoculation (see Pfau, 1992, 1995, 1997; Pfau and Burgoon, 1988). By co-opting a sense of irony, television appears to be an ally to the disbelieving public. So, by making fun of traditional television news *The Daily Show* endears itself to an audience already skeptical of traditional news sources.

Disjointed Aspects

An important element of the cultural influence of television is the disjointed and discontinuous barrage of information it displays. Television's disjointed nature comes from the way it combines signs and symbols in sometimes incongruous ways. Televisual imagery encourages a sense of discontinuity through its multiplicity of offerings often with images and stories with contrasting ideas. A news story of war, death, and famine is immediately followed by an upbeat human interest story about a litter of puppies, reports of imminent bad weather are followed by a victorious sports report, a story of a politician telling one truth is followed by another version of the truth, a commercial for breakfast cereal is followed by a spot for a lawyer seeking to smooth the way to bankruptcy. The writers for *The Daily Show* recognize the disjointed and contrasting nature of television and, using edited video clips, often mock commentators, politicians, and news reporters who contradict themselves. The June 21, 2010 episode provided one such example. In a story about the oil spilling into the Gulf of Mexico and President Obama's request that British Petroleum set up an escrow account to pay for the damages from this major industrial catastrophe, *The Daily Show* showed several clips of Republicans denigrating the President's actions. One clip from another network from June 15, 2010 showed Minnesota Republican representative Michele Bachman calling the President's plan "extortion," and "unconstitutional." Stewart then introduces a clip from a June 18 report showing Representative Bachman saying, "No one is saying that this fund shouldn't be set up . . ." Then, cut back to Stewart who sarcastically exclaims that, she was saying that! This sort of interplay of video clips and studio repartee is a common element of the show and a powerful way to ridicule public officials who, given the frequency such clips are used on *The Daily Show*, contradict themselves with startling regularity. The result is an enlightened viewer and, hopefully in the long run, a greater sense of accountability from our public officials. In the short term, however, bringing such contradiction to light may only make the public more cynical toward public officials and the television news shows that portray these contradictions. Again, the rate with which *The Daily Show* deploys this formula is a statement about the sheer amount of contradictory rhetoric public officials and others attempt to pass off to the public which they perceive to be lacking long-term memory. Through such visual displays, *The Daily Show* does much in the service of exposing the liars and con-men that lay claim to high levels of policy-making and decision-making.

Repetitiveness

In addition to the disjointedness it portrays, television is also highly repetitive (e.g., see Monaco, 1998). *The Daily Show* often uses repetition in its edited packages of images showing the same thing over and over. The result is a demonstration of a sort of silly mockery of the repetitive nature of television news and the people associated with it. For example in the June 23, 2010 program Stewart and "Senior Black Correspondent" Larry Wilmore discussed the nature of Presidential displays of emotion, in particular the angry reaction President Obama had to a *Rolling Stone* story in which General Stanley A. McChrystal was interviewed.[4] In the interview General McChrystal and his staff mocked civilian officials and stated their disappointment with President Obama's handling of the war in Afghanistan.[5] Inserted into Stewart and Wilmore's discussion of President Obama's emotional state was a series of six sound bites from other news shows such as Fox News and CNN. "Too cool," "too cool for school," "Mr. Cool," "cool, calm, collected President," and "no drama Obama," are some of the phrases uttered by commentators and news reporters with each segment lasting no more than a couple seconds then cutting back to Wilmore who sardonically puts down the Fox News and CNN reporters. *The Daily Show* regularly uses similarly edited collections of repetitive imagery. Such repetitive collections of images serve to poke fun at the mainstream media. They also conform to the parodic formula of the show.

Repetition is, in fact, a shaping characteristic for a lot of television fare. When something works in terms of attracting a large audience and television ratings, the formula is spun off and copied over and over again. Television news is no different and we see the repetitive nature of the traditional newscast look and visual style in *The Daily Show*.

Going back to the early forms of fake news, the cultural conventions noted here provide a general understanding of television and how *The Daily Show* fits into the overall "look" of the medium in terms of two aspects: disjointedness and repetition. The visual nature of *The Daily Show* emulates these aspects and uses television's disjointedness and repetitiveness as elements in its parodic performance. Let's now take a closer look at the visual conventions of *The Daily Show*.

A VISUAL AESTHETICS APPROACH

Visual aesthetics is the study of the variables used to construct images perceived by the human eye. The media have artistic qualities and by examining these qualities we can discover layers of meaning embedded within the visual messages that television conveys, intentional or not. But television is not typically thought of as an art form. In fact, Metallinos (1996) tells us that the influx of artistic standards into the design of televisual imagery was gradual. Likewise, Butler (2010) blames the dearth of television stylistic analysis on the television-as-transmission perspective which persists to this day. The television-as-transmission perspective narrowly defines television as the live broadcast of events that occur simultaneously with the time of viewing. In other words, according to this way of thinking, television is primarily a transmission device for showing events live, as they occur. As such, television is seen as a non-artistic conduit of events near and far. Over the years, several writers have remedied this situation and expanded our understanding of the aesthetic qualities of television (e.g., Tiemens, 1965; Newcomb, 1974; Baggaley and Duck, 1976; Fiske and Hartley, 1978; McCain, et al., 1977; Zettl, 1978, 2011; Baggaley, et al., 1980; Barker, 1985; Henderson and Mazzeo, 1990; Lorand, 2002; Lury, 2005). As aesthetic tools, television's production variables also have underlying meanings that add to the content being transmitted. In their discussion of television codes (as a kind of language of television), Fiske and Hartley (1978) tell us, "Aesthetic codes tend to . . . operate on both denotative and connotative levels of signification" (p.

61). This section examines the visual aesthetic codes of *The Daily Show* by again slicing out two components: Compositional elements and composite imagery. Singling out these two visual aspects comes at the expense of examining other production variables such as lighting, editing, the show's use of color and the myriad aspects of set design and graphic design. However, the compositional elements of *The Daily Show* are a microcosm for all the other production variables used to create the show. They are a microcosm in that they epitomize the ideas of mimicry and reproduction of the traditional news genre happening at all the various levels of production.

Compositional Elements

The Daily Show employs compositional techniques used on most mainstream network newscasts for framing shots of Jon Stewart, his guests, and news correspondents. As Stewart delivers the monologue, he is seen in the center of the television frame seated behind a desk in a medium- to medium close-up shot. When a box graphic appears screen left, the camera pans to frame Stewart off to the right-hand side of the frame.[6] The shots are not in an extreme close-up perspective as this would introduce too much drama and emotion into the show and potentially detract from the comedic element.[7] Rather the shots remain in a medium to medium close-up range throughout the show.[8] The use of the medium and medium close-up shots help television viewers identify with Stewart and the other people appearing on the show and gives the audience a clear view of expressive aspects of the face and hands. For a parody, such as *The Daily Show*, facial expressions are important. A subtly raised eyebrow, a knowing look, or a curled lip can make all the difference between drama and comedy. Chevy Chase, as the anchor for *Saturday Night Live's* news satire, "Weekend Update," was one of the masters at this technique. "Even if a joke wasn't working, he had a way of looking knowingly at viewers with an eyebrow raised that was totally disarming" (Hill and Weingrad, 1986, p. 132). Jon Stewart also employs facial expressions for comedic effect, but he often goes beyond the subtle to make exaggerated and outrageous facial expressions.

Slapstick is another visual form of comedy often seen on *The Daily Show* in which composition is important. Slapstick is a physical form of comedy that uses violence and exaggerated forms of physical interaction. Because the comedian usually uses his or her entire body, medium shots and long shots are typically used to portray slapstick routines. A spit-take is an exception. A spit-take is when someone spits a beverage from their mouth in reaction to a statement and is usually more effective in medium close-up shots than long shots. Stewart occasionally uses a spit-take as he did on the June 23, 2010 show when he reacted to a video clip of a reporter saying that her job was similar to that of the President of the United States. This rather base form of humor appeals to a less sophisticated audience, but used sparingly and in conjunction with satire, mimicry, and other more subtle comedic forms helps to inject a sense of raucous ridicule into the traditional news look.

When guests or "Special Correspondents" appear with Stewart on the set, a standard discussion style or interview technique is used. These include the staging of two or three people (usually Stewart and his guests) in conversation. The two-shot is as it sounds—both discussants are in the same shot. The main objective of this technique is to bring people closer to the viewer so that viewer interest in the conversation increases (paraphrased from Metallinos, 1996, p. 225). During a guest interview or a discussion with one of his correspondents, camera angles will vary between a two-shot, individual shots, and over-the-shoulder shots. Generally such segments start with a long shot showing Stewart and his guest or fellow correspondent (in a two shot). The image then cuts between individual shots of the discussion participants, the two-shot, and over-the-shoulder shots. An over-the-shoulder shot portrays one person facing the camera while the other is shot from behind and over the person's shoulder. Individual shots show either Stewart or his guest in a medium shot or medium close-up shot. While Stewart and correspondents address the television audience full face, i.e., directly addressing the audience by looking into the television camera, his guests during the interview segment never directly address the camera (even when seen in the over-the-shoulder shot the guest never looks directly into the camera lens even though we see him or her full face). Rather, guests are portrayed in profile, or half profile (except when shown in an over-the-shoulder shot). This is significant because the audience views the profile shot differently than direct address shots. "If a speaker is televised in half profile, the shot tends to be decoded as being of a more reliable and expert figure than if the same speaker is televised full face" (Fiske and Hartley, 1978, p. 62; also see Baggaley and Duck, 1976). There is nothing surprising or tricky about showing a guest in profile. Because they tend to be people invited to the show based on their expertise on some subject, the perception of their expertise is appropriate. And in fact the association between expertise and profile imagery may have evolved from television (and film to a certain extent). Since news and informational types of programs almost always portray experts in this way, the mass audience has over time come to associate profile images with expertise.[9] Now, simply showing someone in a profile shot can, all else being equal, add a sense of credibility to what they say or do. Subtle visual cues such as profile shots are important because we typically don't notice them, but their cumulative effect is significant and influences how people feel and think about what they see on television. This may be truer for parodic texts than other genres because it is these very techniques that come up for scrutiny in a parody.

As for *The Daily Show*, almost all the shots portray Stewart, the news correspondents, and guests in an eye-level shot, (i.e., the camera is positioned at about the same height as the people being shot). Such a shot places the audience at the same eye-level perspective as the people on television giving them an impartial point-of-view. Never (or at least very rarely) will the camera be positioned below or above the people it is shooting. This is typical of any traditional news show because high and low camera angles induce bias into the image, and in terms of traditional news production, bias should be minimized at all cost. High camera angles portray people as smaller, less authoritative, and less powerful, while low camera angles create the opposite effect. Objectivity is lost when these camera angles are used, so they are consciously avoided in traditional news productions. One might argue that since *The Daily Show* is not a traditional news show such camera angles could and should be used. However, because *The Daily Show* is a parody of traditional news, maintaining these production values (i.e., unbiased camera angles), is appropriate. They also lend an element of credibility to the show. Even though it is a parody with heavy use of ridicule and comedy elements, *The Daily Show* also exposes political and other forms of wrongdoing in the muckraking tradition. Thus, the show has an important social function beyond pure entertainment.

The other production elements of the show such as lighting, editing, graphic design, and set design also copy the professional standards laid out by the traditional television newscast genre. The lighting is diffuse and flat creating a bright and cheery appearance. The editing is of a standard style with cuts (instantaneous transitions) being the most common type of edit used. There is nothing special about the way the show is edited except to say that it follows the formula set out by traditional network news, showing the viewer what it needs to see when it needs to see it. The graphics and set design are professional and make the show look like a traditional news show. There are, of course, graphics that are designed to be outrageous and depict events and people in ways that can shock and shame, but are always slick and professional-looking. Thus, maintaining traditional television news production values helps to instill a sense of credibility within an overall parodic performance. The standardized production techniques also serve to legitimize *The Daily Show* as a source of information by depicting it as professionally produced. Thus, the rather staid appearance of the show, compositionally and otherwise (i.e., it looks a lot like a traditional network newscast) is appropriate.

Composite Imagery

Similar to collage and montage, composite imagery is created when parts of one image are cut out and pasted onto another image. One can do this simply with X-acto® knife and glue—for example, cutting the head of a horse out of one picture and gluing it to a person's body in another picture. Photomontage is an art form that utilizes the techniques of cutting and pasting photographic images together in various ways to create new meanings.

With today's computers, composite imagery can be a subtle and hard-to-detect process since digital cutting and pasting leaves little if any trace that anything has been cut or pasted. A recent example of this occurred when long-time staff reporter for the *Los Angeles Times*, Brain Walski digitally cut and pasted two striking images of Iraqi civilians being guarded by an American soldier to create a more dramatic image that was published in the newspaper.[10] A serious breach of photojournalistic ethics, he was fired when this manipulation was discovered. Back in the 1800s Mathew Brady's infamous photograph in which he cut a photograph of Abraham Lincoln's head and pasted it onto the body of John C. Calhoun provides an early example.

The Daily Show carries on the tradition of composite imagery to enhance its parodic performance. But more than that, I argue here that composite imagery or the idea of "composite-ness" is really another way to define *The Daily Show*. While the show uses composite images occasionally to depict people and events in outrageous ways, I argue that the show itself is a form of composite imagery.

A form of visual manipulation, composite photographs are nothing new to the fake news genre and *The Daily Show* uses them periodically for comedic effect. As mentioned above, you can trace the history of composite photography back to the very origins of the craft (see Rosenblum, 1989), but in terms of the news, the origins go back to one of the more notable early tabloids, the *New York Evening Graphic* that went so far as to present photographic documentation of the heavenly meeting of Rudolph Valentino and Enrico Caruso on the front page of its March 17, 1927 edition. Obviously fake, composite photography, or composographs boosted the *Evening Graphic*'s circulation. One such image, a fake image of Alice Jones Rhinelander baring her breast in court (part of the Kip Rhinelander divorce trial in 1925) is said to have boosted circulation by 100,000 copies (Pastepot Wonder, 1950). These early forms of photojournalistic manipulation presaged today's forms of fake news imagery. However, unlike other news outlets which attempt to hide the manipulative aspect of such images and present them as real, *The Daily Show* makes no attempt to deceive the audience. Rather, by pasting a group of Scottish Highlanders in kilts onto the back of a pick-up truck (to parody news about immigration from the July 8, 2010 episode), for example, the comedic element of such imagery is emphasized. Indeed, the sheer outrageousness of such images is cause for laughter.

Though common in the fake news genre, composite imagery is fairly rare in traditional television news. This difference, the use of composite imagery versus non-use, is an important distinction to make in terms of creating the parody that is *The Daily Show*. In fact, composite images are one of the more clear departures the show takes from the genre of traditional news that it parodies. It is this and similar points of departure from the normative news-cast that we find the elements of ridicule, sarcasm, and comedy. And as Harries (2000) indicates,

> This is the necessary oscillation between similarity to and difference from a target (in this cast traditional network news) that allows parody to maintain either the lexicon, syntax or style while manipulating others. By evoking and denying its selected target, parody becomes inevitably ironic—a quality that permeates all pa-rodic efforts. (p. 9; parentheses my addition) [11]

In other words, *The Daily Show* is always shifting between serious news (in a muckraking tradition) and comedy. This is done by upholding traditional new style and overall look while manipulating lexical elements like those in question here—composite imagery. Composite imagery is just one visual element of several that is manipulated. Others already discussed include facial displays and over-the-top kinds of interactions between characters that appear on the show.

In his examination of visual literacy, Messaris (1994) was keen to empha-size the importance of teaching and learning about forms of visual manipula-tion. Taking up Messaris's mantle then, we can look at the examples of the kinds of composite images used by the producers of *The Daily Show* and understand that the issue is not so much with the detection of the images as fake, as with understanding their purpose within the rubric of a parody. Since fun-making and frivolity at the expense of others such as politics, politicians, and media personalities, is an important element in the show, then such imagery might also play a key role in the parodic formula in general. Histori-cally, one can look to parodic narratives such as *Don Quixote* for analogous examples. In the story of Don Quixote we find a character that arguably is nothing more than a personality cut out of one time period and pasted into another much like a composite image cuts and pastes one image onto an-other. Borrowing ideas of chivalry from times past in books he'd read, Don Quixote and his befuddled squire Sancho Panza set out to defend the helpless and destroy the wicked. Taking up lance and sword upon his beleaguered and aged horse Rocinante, they set out on adventures in a time not acquainted with his chivalrous nature. So we see there is a tradition of the cut and paste method in parody and *The Daily Show* merely carries on this custom. [12]

Going a step further, we might analyze the entirety of *The Daily Show* as a composite image; i.e., in this way we might view the visual design of the show as a news set cut out and pasted onto a comedy. Indeed, tracing the history of parody from its ancient use "to describe the comic imitation and transformation of an epic verse" we find its modern manifestation in *The*

Daily Show (Rose, 1993, p. 280). Indeed, *The Daily Show* is seen here as having clear ties to the ancient use of parody if we understand the "epic verse" to be the traditional form of network newscasting and *The Daily Show* to be its comic imitation and transformation. Other definitions of parody include meanings such as resemblance, change slightly, imitation, replacement, and spuriousness (for example see Rose, 1993, pp 6–19). In the end, an examination of *The Daily Show* not only harkens back to ancient forms of parody, but also reveals new definitions of parody with the analysis of composite imagery leading one to question whether "cut and paste" isn't another way to understand the parodic method especially if we assume that replacement, copying, and mimicking are fundamental forms of parody.

CONCLUSIONS

This chapter is one of only a few studies that I have found which examine the visual nature of parody. With this in mind, I should mention that visual parody is nothing new. From costuming, makeup, and set design used for parody in the theater arts to Dadaism and other styles in the world of painting, sculpture, and related artwork, the artistic examination of parody as a visual phenomenon has a long record. A critical, academic examination of parody's visual aspects is, however, a fairly rare endeavor. So, I suspect that our understanding of parody's visual function and all of its nuances is still relatively undeveloped. Yet, understanding how parody is visually produced, disseminated, and digested by a viewing public is vital for today's society which is both increasingly visual and increasingly cynical. For example, a previous effort to examine *The Daily Show*, Jason Holt's edited volume, *The Daily Show and Philosophy* virtually ignores the visual aspects of the show. Moreover, most of the texts I examined on the topic of parody focus mainly on its verbal characteristics. But there is a performative aspect to parody (which implies visual features such as nonverbals and movements of different sorts) and a few studies cited throughout this chapter such as Dan Harries' (2000) work on film parody, address this. Scholars of parody such as Linda Hutcheon (1985) occasionally discuss the various aspects of visual parody in the art world as does Seymour Chatman (2001) who acknowledges the visual nature of parody when he mentions,

> a wonderful minimalist visual parody can be seen on enlightened automobile bumpers in America in recent years. Instead of . . . the fundamentalist Christian emblem of a fish referring to Christ, the Fisher of Souls, agnostics display a fish which has grown four stumpy legs with "Darwin" tattooed on its belly. (p. 29)

Such visual jokes are, however, according to Chatman (2001), "of little interest to students of the full complexities of idiosyncratic style imitation" (p. 29). In the area of visual literacy, Paul Messaris (1994) argues that visual parody is only possible if people are knowledgeable of the original work being parodied. Thus, one would conclude that the historical examination of key visual works such as *American Gothic*, the *Mona Lisa*, and *Whistler's Mother*, to name a few—paintings that are parodied over and over again—is an essential academic undertaking. Photographs such as Joe Rosenthal's 1945 image of the flag-raising at Iwo Jima are also widely parodied (see Edwards and Winkler, 1997; who rhetorically examine this image with a nod to parody).

As we see, research on the visual aspects of parody is widely scattered. Moreover, we find divergent approaches for examining this complex concept. The ways to examine the visual dimensions of *The Daily Show* are also many. This chapter devised a two-by-two method along historical/cultural and visual aesthetics dimensions. The analysis reveals some of the visual elements of parody that permeate the show, not only defining it, but it also offering a way to understand the visual nature of parody. There are many other ways in which parody manifests itself in *The Daily Show* and many more ways parody is visually depicted in other media formats. Thus, this study is one small node of research on the visual aspects of parody with much left to be done to understand the multi-dimensional aspects of its visual nature. Indeed, more study and intense critique of our parodic texts are necessary because, quoting Dwight Macdonald (1960), our culture is "suffused with parody. We are self-conscious, we have the historical sense, we look back on the past. We are backward-looking explorers and parody is a central expression of our times" (p. xv). As we look back, parody keeps evolving, creating new meanings for our culture and its mediated texts.

NOTES

1. It is true that one can also watch *The Daily Show* on a computer via the show's Internet site. The show is, however designed for the television medium and conforms to televisual production conventions and techniques.

2. Even the discussion of these two wide-ranging aspects is bound to be incomplete given the limited parameters of a single book chapter. Indeed almost any attempt to understand television in all of its nuances is bounded by several factors including author biases.

3. *Laugh-In* also included short "News Bulletins" and a segment called "News of the Future." The fake news bulletins had a War-of-the-Worlds-like moment when, after declaring, "Help! I'm being held prisoner in the news room!" a viewer in Springfield, Illinois, apparently not familiar with *Laugh-In's* format, took the bulletin seriously and soon the Springfield NBC affiliate was besieged by the local police department (see Erickson, 2000, p. 145).

4. McChrystal was Commander of U.S. Forces in Afghanistan until relieved of his command by President Obama.

5. General McChrystal was not quoted as being directly critical of the President's policies, but his aides discussed their perceptions of McChrystal's disappointment with the President (see Hastings, 2010).

6. I have not seen a box graphic appear anywhere else in a shot on *The Daily Show* other than screen left. Other news programs do use a box graphic on the right-hand side of the screen.

7. Close-ups are traditionally associated with emotion and dramatic imagery since they place the viewing audience at a close personal distance from the face of whoever is being photographed.

8. Medium shots and medium close-ups are less emotional than the close-up shot and provide the audience with a more objective viewpoint.

9. Conversely, shots in which the speaker is directly addressing the camera, i.e., he or she looks right into the camera lens and appears to be talking directly to the viewing audience, is perceived to be a spokesperson, or model, or someone reading from a script or teleprompter like a news anchor and is thus, not a true expert on the topic about which they are speaking.

10. There are many places you can find these images on the web including http://dvis-ible.com/2009/08/10/images-that-lie/.

11. Here lexicon is defined as the setting, characters and various props found in any television production. Syntax relates to the narrative structure of a text. In the case of *The Daily Show* the narrative is made up of the show's opening graphic segment, Stewart's introduction and subsequent monologue, correspondent segments, guest interview, and closing "Moment of Zen." The lexical elements operate within the overall syntax of the show. Style includes music, camera shots, dialogue elements which weave themselves "throughout the lexicon and syntax to add additional sets of expectations based on . . . the genre" (paraphrased from Harries, 2000, p. 8).

12. The related concept of pastiche, is a postmodern form of parody discussed for example by Dentith (2000).

REFERENCES

Allen, R.C. (1987). Introduction: Talking about television. In R. C. Allen (Ed.), *Channels of Discourse: Television and contemporary criticism* (pp. 1–16). Chapel Hill, NC: University of North Carolina Press.

Baggaley, J., and Duck, S. (1976). *The dynamics of television*. Farnborough, Hants: Saxon House.

Baggaley, J., Ferguson, M., and Brooks, P. (1980). *Psychology of the television image*. New York: Praeger.

Barker, D. (1985). Television production techniques as communication. *Critical Studies in Mass Communication, 2*, 234–246.

Baumgartner, J., and Morris, J.S. (2006). *The Daily Show* effect: Candidate evaluations, efficacy, and American youth. *American Politics Research, 34*(3), 341–367.

Baym, G. (2005). *The Daily Show*: Discursive integration and the reinvention of political journalism. *Political Communication, 22*, 259–276.

Berger, A.A. (1991). *Media USA: Process and effect* (2nd Ed.). New York: Longman.

Butler, J. G. (2010). *Television style*. New York: Routledge.

Chatman, S. (2001). Parody and style. *Poetics Today, 22*(1), 25–39.

Dentith, S. (2000). *Parody*. London: Routledge.

Edwards, J. L., and Winkler, J. C. (1997). Representative form and the visual ideograph: The Iwo Jima image in editorial cartoons. *Quarterly Journal of Speech, 83*, 289–310.

Erickson, H. (2000). *"From beautiful downtown Burbank:" A critical history of* Rowan and Martin's Laugh-In, *1968–1973*. Jefferson, NC: McFarland.

Fallon, P. K. (2009). *The metaphysics of media: Toward an end of postmodern cynicism and the construction of a virtuous reality*. Scranton, PA: University of Scranton Press.

Fiddy, D. (n.d.). That was the week that was. From the Museum of Broadcast Communications website. Retrieved from: http://www.museum.tv/eotvsection.php?entrycode=thatwasthe.

Fiske, J., and Hartley, J. (1978). *Reading television.* London: Methuen.
Gettings, M., (2007). The fake, the false, and the fictional: *The Daily Show* as news source. In J. Holt (Ed.), *The Daily Show and Philosophy* (pp. 16–27). Malden, MA: Blackwell.
Gitlin, T. (1987). Looking through the screen. In T. Gitlin (ed). *Watching Television: A Pantheon Guide to Popular Culture* (pp. 3–8). New York: Pantheon Books.
Harries, D. (2000). *Film parody.* London: British Film Institute.
Hastings, M. (2010, July 2–22). The runaway general. *Rolling Stone, 1108/1109*, 91–97, 120, 121.
Henderson, K. U., and Mazzeo, J. A. (1990). *Meanings of the medium: Perspectives on the art of television.* New York: Praeger.
Hill, D., and Weingrad, J. (1986). *Saturday Night: A backstage history of* Saturday Night Live. New York: Beech Tree Books.
Holt, J. (Ed.). (2007). *The Daily Show and philosophy.* Malden, MA: Blackwell.
Hutcheon, L. (1985). *A theory of parody: The teachings of twentieth-century art forms.* New York: Methuen.
Lorand, R. (2002). *Television: Aesthetic reflections.* New York: Peter Lang.
Lury, K. (2005). *Interpreting television.* New York: Oxford University Press.
Macdonald, D. (1960). *Parodies: An anthology from Chaucer to Beerbohm—and after.* New York: Random House.
McCain, T. A., Chilberg, J., and Wakshlag, J. (1977). The effect of camera angle on source credibility and attraction. *Journal of Broadcasting, 21*, 35–46.
Messaris, P. (1994). *Visual literacy: Image, mind, and reality.* Boulder, CO: Westview Press.
Metallinos, N. (1996). *Television aesthetics: Perceptual, cognitive, and compositional bases.* Mahwah, NJ: Lawrence Erlbaum.
Miller, M. C. (1988). *Boxed in: The culture of TV.* Evanston, IL: Northwestern University Press.
Monaco, P. (1998). *Understanding society, culture, and television.* Westport, CT: Praeger.
Newcomb, H. (1974). Toward a television aesthetic. In, Horace Newcomb (Ed.). *TV: The Most Popular Art* (pp. 478–494). New York: Doubleday.
Pastepot Wonder. (1950, Feb. 27). *Time.* Retrieved 6-7-10 from http://www.time.com/time/magazine/article/0,9171,812095,00.html.
Pfau, M. (1992). The potential of inoculation in promoting resistance to the effectiveness of comparative advertising messages. *Communication Quarterly, 40*, 26–44.
———. (1995). Designing messages for behavioral inoculation. In E. Maibach and R. L. Parrott (Eds.), *Designing Health Messages: Approaches from Communication Theory and Public Health Practice* (pp. 99–113). Newbury Park, CA: Sage.
———. (1997). The inoculation model of resistance to influence. In F. J. Boster and G. Barnett (Eds.), *Progress in Communication Sciences* (Vol. 13, pp. 133–171). Norwood, NJ: Ablex Publishing.
Pfau, M., and Burgoon, M. (1988). Inoculation in political campaign communication. *Human Communication Research, 15*, 91–111.
Postman, N., and Powers, S. (1992). *How to watch TV news.* New York: Penguin Books.
Rose, M. A. (1993). *Parody: Ancient, modern, and post-modern.* New York, NY: Cambridge University Press.
Rosenblum, N. (1989). *A world history of photography* (Revised Edition). New York: Cross River Press.
Tiemens, R. K. (1965). Some relationships of camera angle to communicator credibility. *Journal of Broadcasting, 14*, 483–490.
Wilson-Smith, A. (2004, Feb. 16). Making fun of the news. *McLeans.* 117(7). Online version retrieved 6-4-10 from Ebscohost.
Zettl, H. (1978). A rare case of television aesthetics. *Journal of the University Film Association, 30*(2), 3–8.
———. (2011). *Sight sound motion: Applied media aesthetics* (6th edition). Boston: Wadsworth.

IV

Issues

Chapter Eleven

Gaywatch: A Burkean Frame Analysis of *The Daily Show*'s Treatment of Queer Topics

C. Wesley Buerkle

When in September 2007 Iranian president Mahmoud Ahmadinejad denied the presence of homosexuals in Iran before an audience at Columbia University, *The Daily Show with Jon Stewart* aired the sound bite followed by Stewart, as news anchor, responding that the conservative movement in the United States was very similar in that it too has no homosexuals, merely men who have sex with each other (Bodow and O'Neill, 2007d). The pseudo-exchange between Ahmadinejad and Stewart represents a fairly typical response of *The Daily Show* to a noteworthy utterance referencing queerness: an individual outside of *The Daily Show* not supporting the rights—or existence—of gay persons and a witty *The Daily Show* reply to punish the rogue. As a self-purported fake-news show, the host and correspondents of *The Daily Show* give themselves carte blanche to provide news content with commentary and subjectivity. An event in the world of politics and news affecting queer-identified persons becomes a *cause célèbre* for *The Daily Show* news team. These efforts both provide coverage to topics that otherwise receive less attention from mainstream news outlets and seek equality for the gay community by using the electronic pulpit of cable television.

For all the fun of Stewart's rebuke above—and it is fun—there remains the question of the rhetorical effects of *The Daily Show*'s humor. The question I entertain here rests upon the symbolic consequences of the specific choices *The Daily Show* makes when covering issues of queer sexuality, most often instances of people thwarting or not sufficiently supporting gay rights. In the case of Ahmadinejad's denial that homosexuals live in Iran, for example, I ask about the logical connection and outcome of comparing the

Iranian president's remarks to a then-recent case of Larry Craig's—a straight-identified, anti-gay legislating U.S. senator—arrest for soliciting sex in a men's room. This particular instance punishes politicians across nationality for denying homosexuality and adds an exclamation mark to the reproof by offending conservatives in Iran and the United States with the image of gay-male sex. By doing so *The Daily Show* replicates the notion of homosexuality as a source of derision even if to advance queer acceptance. I do not mean that *The Daily Show* masks a homophobic position by espousing a pro-gay rights agenda, but rather their efforts promoting queer tolerance sometimes repeat the language of prejudice. In this example *The Daily Show* moves so swiftly to disabuse both Ahmadinejad and Republicans of their shared intolerance that the means to the end, and thus the rhetorical effects themselves, evade scrutiny. My interest, then, pertains to the specific ways in which *The Daily Show* provides coverage of GLBTQ topics to understand the value and pitfalls in their approach to supporting the gay community.

In this chapter I examine the eighty-two non-interview segments of *The Daily Show* discussing issues of homosexuality broadcast 2006–2009. Looking at segments presented as news reports or editorials rather than studio interviews enables me to concentrate on content over which *The Daily Show* writers and producers have complete creative control. Using Kenneth Burke's (1984a) discussion of poetic categories, I consider the ways in which *The Daily Show* frames gay rights and/or homosexuality itself by either offering correction to the queer-friendly when they err or totally denouncing those seen as enemies to the cause. In my analysis I see a fine yet harsh line delineating people as either friends or foes of gay rights. Additionally, the broad picture of *The Daily Show*'s treatment of queer topics suggests that though the show genuinely seeks the expansion of gay rights and acceptance in U.S. culture and abroad, the stock and trade in puerile humor sometimes clouds the issue and replicates the feel of homophobia it seeks to eliminate.

BEST F#@KING NEWS TEAM EVER

In the introduction to his third edition of *Attitudes Toward History*, Burke (1984a) sets as his goal the discussion of the various responses we have to events in our "political communities," the ways that we symbolically make sense and manage political struggles manifest in discourse. For that purpose Burke provides a set of poetic categories—otherwise called attitudes or frames—as the means to sort out our responses to socio-political turbulence. Differentiating the categories into frames of acceptance, rejection, and transition, Burke provides a vocabulary for describing our rhetorical responses to community unrest in terms of the attitudes assumed. Such an approach seems especially useful to understand *The Daily Show*'s rhetoric, as it seemingly exists to process for its viewers the various events of the day. Considering the combination of humor and serious news content, Geoffrey Baym (2005) argues that *The Daily Show* represents a new discursive mode that creates opportunities for alternative political engagement. Don Waisanen (2009) suggests that the political discussion *The Daily Show* participates in amounts to a form of rhetorical criticism, as supported by Jamie Warner (2007) who suggests *The Daily Show*'s humor provides an opportunity for audiences to critically engage in political discourse. The application of Burke's frames to *The Daily Show* rhetoric, then, seems especially well suited.

Before reviewing Burke's discussion of attitudes, I briefly outline here *The Daily Show*'s role and function in U.S. media and politics as late-night entertainment turned news and commentary outlet. Research on *The Daily Show* confirms that rather than common place late-night entertainment in the tradition of Johnny Carson, *The Daily Show* has created for itself a somewhat legitimate place in socio-political debates. Despite calling themselves fake news, *The Daily Show* has a deserved reputation for substantial reporting on the topics chosen for coverage. As a special case of "soft news (Baum, 2002), entertainment that incidentally informs, *The Daily Show* engages and educates its audience in ways sometimes comparable to mainstream news outlets thus contributing to a better informed electorate (Brewer and Marquardt, 2007; Harrington, 2008; National Annenberg, 2004). In comparison to mainstream news coverage, *The Daily Show* proves as substantive as its "real" counterparts (Fox, Koloen and Sahin, 2007) with the benefit of better length, depth, and contextual linkages (Baym, 2005). Beyond informing its viewers, research demonstrates that *The Daily Show* prepares its audience for intellectual engagement with current events (Baym, 2005) even as it peddles a cynicism that antagonizes viewers against government and mainstream news media (Hart and Hartelius, 2007). Such a move may help audiences to identify with *The Daily Show* as mutual outsiders (Burke, 1969, p. 55). Lauren Feldman (2007) suggests that connection empowers viewers feeling disaffected by the system to engage in an intellectual revolt, and with some noticeable effect (Baum, 2003; Baumgartner and Morris, 2006; Holbert, Lambe, Duido and Carlton, 2007). Even as *The Daily Show* engenders cynicism toward mainstream news media and the U.S. political system it fosters greater efficacy to engage in the political process (Baumgartner and Morris, 2006). Accordingly Robert Hariman (2007) and Lance Bennett (2007) suggest that *The Daily Show*'s cynicism creates the potential change through disrupting discourse-as-usual.

I offer this discussion of *The Daily Show*'s impact to suggest the importance of its contribution to the discussion of queer rights in terms of both content and tone. As soft news with credentials of legitimacy, *The Daily Show*'s commitment to provide content on cultural debates about sexual orientation makes an important contribution to the show's goal of social equality. First, a cursory examination suggests that the coverage of queer-relevant topics, in terms of frequency and depth, far exceed mainstream news outlets, consistent with earlier findings (Fox, Koloen and Sahin, 2007; Baym, 2005). In fact, in one instance *The Daily Show* criticizes mainstream news outlets for not covering a GLBTQ protest in the nation's capital and follows that with a segment providing the coverage (Bodow and O'Neill, 2009c). Second, the commentaries in those instances clearly aim to support gay rights efforts and move toward social equality for sexual minorities, which research (Baum, 2003; Baumgartner and Morris, 2006) suggests may actually affect viewers' opinions. Beyond mere coverage, *The Daily Show* assumes an ethical stance with the intent to change rather than merely observe the discursive scene (Darcy, 1994). The concern for queer rights advocates, however, may lie in the tone encouraged by *The Daily Show* in its coverage of topics relevant to the gay community and the hue it casts upon the discussion.

To understand the ways in which *The Daily Show* covers queer topics I use Burke's (1984a) description of poetic categories to sort out the various responses of *The Daily Show* to current events affecting homosexuals and how its framing of the events encourages viewers to engage the debate. Poetic categories (Burke,1984a) offer frames that serve as the rhetorical means by which we manage upsets in our daily life:

> He (sic) begins, we have said, with the "problem of evil." He (sic) finds good and evil elements intermingled. But he (sic) cannot leave matters at that. Exigencies of living require him to choose his (sic) alignments, by the devices of formal or "secular" prayer. (p. 106)

Examining coverage of queer topics means understanding how *The Daily Show* chooses to frame news events affecting the gay community. According to Burke (1984a) frames fall into one of three categories: acceptance, rejection, and transition frames. Each of these categories refer to a rhetor's move to deal with a moment of tension by labeling the conflict a flaw to be corrected for return to established customs, seizing upon the problem as a proof of a system we should reject, or stuck in transition between the status quo and something new. The subspecies of attitudes contained within each family of frames carry implications for how we should understand those implicated and the course of action that ought to follow. Though Burke (1984a) covers eight attitudes, I focus here on the three that emerge across my sample: comic, burlesque, and, occasionally, grotesque responses—an acceptance, rejection, and transition frame, respectively.

Acceptance frames consists of responses that understand moments of social unrest as the sign of a problem needing correction so the current system might resume its functioning, bettered by the experience. A comic response sees transgression against accepted norms as the product of stupidity rather than crime (Burke, 1984a, p. 41). Accordingly, comedy laughs—literally or figuratively—at a fool to offer redemption rather than seeking the destruction of the unsalvageable so long as the target of ridicule demonstrates worthiness of redemption. In so doing comedy provides the opportunity for all society to reconsider their own behavior (Duncan, 1962; Carlson, 1988). That we call a response comic does not require it be humorous, though it certainly may be. Sometimes comedy finds use in a conversion downward in which those who are high are made low (Burke, 1984b, p. 133), creating the opportunity for those with little social and political power to feel themselves a little more equal with those who enjoy greater influence in society (Brummett, 1984; Toker, 2002). The goal of conversion downward can attempt to move the citizenry to take a more engaged approach to the topic and question the wisdom of remaining silent to the (in)action of those in power. In the case of ACT UP, the group sought to educate the public about HIV and AIDS through demonstrations like a Ronald Reagan-driven quarantine-camp float during a gay pride parade or putting on a fashion show with hospital gowns as AIDS evening wear (Christiansen and Hanson, 1996). Therefore, the value of comic responses lies in the move for dialogue (Thompson and Palmeri, 1993).

In opposition to acceptance, rejection frames exploit a moment of discord in the system to justify denouncing the current order. In describing the nature of rejection Burke (1984a) says, "It takes its color from an attitude towards some reigning symbol of authority, stressing a *shift in the allegiance* to symbols of authority" (p. 21). The burlesque approach to rejection engages in *reductio ad absurdum* of the system by targeting a buffoon (Burke, 1984a). The buffoon, unlike the clown, receives no sympathy for wrongdoing, so banishment becomes the only option (Moore, 1992). The reductionism of the burlesque response dismisses the need to consider the motivation for bad behavior; it desires to see nothing more than the external features and exploits those flaws to their fullest. Second, the buffoon receives a much harsher treatment than the clown because the audience sees nothing of themselves in the victim and thereby feels free to mock the target with conscienceless abandon (Carlson, 1988). Case studies demonstrate that burlesque responses heighten foibles to make the case for lunacy more certain (Bostdorff, 1987; Appel, 1996) with the potential, at the extreme, to dehumanize a target (Hubbard, 1998).

Where the comic frame attempts maintenance of the current order and the burlesque frame seeks a break from the dominant mode, transitional frames identify problems in the system and wish a break from it but remain ambivalent in the quest for a new way. Grotesque responses, like that of the burlesque, have no sympathy for the offender who must leave the community (Burke, 1984a; Olbrys, 2006), but unlike the burlesque buffoon, the grotesque antagonist receives punishment and banishment while the system re-mains unchanged, making the loss of the character a hollow victory and the change incomplete (Watson, 1969; Boje, Luhman and Cunliffe, 2003; Buer-kle, 2010). The only value presented by a grotesque response may be the demonstration to others of what might happen to them for committing similar crimes (Chesebro and McMahan, 2006).

Rather than merely providing description, recognizing the different frames through which *The Daily Show* discusses queer topics facilitates a discussion of the implications for the various perspectives. To that end I examine *The Daily Show*'s GLBTQ rhetoric, looking at non-interview seg-ments from the years 2006 to 2009 that discuss or reference issues affecting the queer community. Using thedailyshow.com, which makes available and searchable by keyword or date nearly every segment of *The Daily Show* episodes since 1999, I have searched for segments tagged with the keywords "gay/homosexual" or similar during the years 2006–2009.[1] Immediately I excluded segment compilation videos that never aired and in-studio inter-views conducted by Jon Stewart, bringing the count of videos in the data pool to eighty-two. Then, focusing on my research question pertaining to *The Daily Show*'s coverage of queer topics, I kept only those that focus on an issue affecting the gay community (e.g., gay marriage laws) or otherwise dwell on issues of homosexuality (e.g., the accusation that evangelical preacher Ted Haggard had a relationship with a male prostitute), excluding segments possessing only a passing reference to homosexuality. These filters leave me with sixty-seven segments I categorize into their respective Burk-ean frames (Smith and Johnston, 1991; Kaylor, 2008). For my analysis I look at each application of the frame as best I can distinguish it to create a broad statement on how *The Daily Show* treats particular kinds of events and the actors who engage in them (Burke, 1984a, p. 57; Brummett, 1979).

NOW TO *DAILY SHOW* SENIOR RHETORICAL CORRESPONDENT, KENNETH BURKE

As the analysis that follows demonstrates, two frames emerge as dominant strategies for *The Daily Show* to manage the tension surrounding queer top-ics, the comic and the burlesque. Both of these strategies have proven highly amenable to humorous applications of themselves (Carlson, 1986; Bostdorff, 1987; Christiansen and Hanson, 1996; Buerkle, Mayer and Olson, 2003); *The Daily Show* merely extends that point. More importantly, of course, the in-stances in which the show turns to a comic or burlesque response demon-strate how the show manages conflicts by deciding to offer correction to some and seek the expulsion of others. As I illustrate, *The Daily Show* seems to most often offer comic correctives to those who do too little for gay rights or for those who become over-excited by issues surrounding homosexuality. In contrast, *The Daily Show* uses burlesque rejection of those who openly oppose gay rights or the general wellbeing of queer-identified persons. The sometimes fine line between *The Daily Show*'s strategies and targets evinces the volatile nature of its humor that can invite one person to turn back to the fold while tossing another from a moving train. Not all segments I analyze here fit in the comic or burlesque categories, though the vast majority do.

"The Gay After Tomorrow"[2]

In the manner of the comic frame, *The Daily Show* uses humor—often sarcasm—to show others where they have gone astray in their understanding of gay rights and the gay community, suggesting that if only they will recognize their own mistake everyone's lives would be improved. *The Daily Show*'s comic responses regularly travel one of two paths, 1) attempting to demonstrate the inconsistency of a stated view of gays and/or gay rights or 2) wanting to show the needlessness of homosexual panic resulting from the thought of gays improving their place in society. Many times, *The Daily Show* uses both of these strategies to help those who see homosexuality as foreign, and therefore dangerous, to either understand it as an experience not all that different from heterosexual life or to recognize heterosexuality itself as less sanctified than credited.

The Daily Show's comic theme of queer intolerance as inconsistent, or even hypocritical, takes as a given that a person unsupportive of gays shares with *The Daily Show* some common value about humanity and/or society. The jokes offered in this vein seek to build from their point of overlap to urge the fool to reconsider the matter in light of a common, established principle. An especially salient example comes from a segment on gay marriage, a favorite cause of *The Daily Show*. Covering a speech by President Bush in support of a constitutional amendment to ban gay marriage, Jon Stewart uses Bush's own words to show the president's inconsistencies. In one segment *The Daily Show* shows President Bush touting the virtue of the U.S. democracy as government not interfering with how citizens lead personal lives, a reference to the Republican goal of small government. Stewart then mockingly finishes Bush's sentence for him with the desire to thwart the marriage rights of gay people (Javerbaum and O'Neill, 2006a). The obvious contradiction quickly takes a key conservative philosophy of U.S. government and applies it to gay marriage, indicating that to be true to his principles on government Bush must reexamine his stance on same-sex unions. The demonstration of a logical contradiction in the absence of an insult for Bush's potential cruelty or hatred provides the hope for discussion and change.

In addition to demonstrating fools' hypocrisy, *The Daily Show* also seeks to correct errant community members by helping them see they unnecessarily suffer from homophobic panic. The clearest example of this comes when correspondent John Oliver investigates the term "radical gay agenda" at a gay pride parade. Parodying a journalist who has bought into homophobic panic, Oliver asks GLBTQ persons to state their agenda, which garners such innocuous yet vital rights as wanting their relationships with their partners recognized, wanting equal treatment, and visiting one's partner in the hospital (Bodow and O'Neill, 2009c). Covering President Obama's reluctance to act on his campaign promise to repeal the military's "Don't Ask, Don't Tell" policy, Stewart suggests the rationale for the public's reluctance to accept gays in the military as emanating from the fear Americans have of acknowledging humans' sexual dualism; after a brief pause, Stewart admits that description may just be for him (Bodow and O'Neill, 2009b). By making himself vulnerable and part of the joke, Stewart suggests the audience consider their homophobia as an unnecessary product of internal tension.

Two other segments featuring Lewis Black and Jason Jones, respectively, challenge the opponents of gay marriage that heterosexual marriages possess unique traits sufficient for protection from expanding the definition of legal unions. In response to U.S. Representative Phil Gingrey's claim that the love of heterosexuals deserves special status because it alone can produce a child, Black interjects that a loveless one-night stand involving alcohol and Quaaludes can also bear children (Javerbaum and O'Neill, 2006b). Reporting on the anti-gay marriage referendums approved by six states in 2006, Jason Jones further dispels the notion that heterosexual marriages, by nature, singularly possess something perfectly beautiful. Jones accomplishes this by parodying one who rejects honoring same-sex couples in committed relationships but accepts marriage as acceptable even when it includes arranged marriages, multiple marriages, and/or alcohol and violence infused marriages (Javerbaum and O'Neill, 2006e).The tactics used by Black and Jones both attempt to show that heterosexual marriages may not deserve quite the sacred pedestal they have been placed upon. Instead, Black and Jones suggest that legislators and voters reconsider the very premise that heterosexuality exists only in its most ideal forms and that same-sex couples differ greatly from heterosexual couples in the desire to enter into a union meant to recognize and honor mutual love.

The most poignant comic corrective offered by *The Daily Show* speaks directly to Ted Haggard who led the National Association of Evangelicals until Mike Jones came forward declaring he had a relationship with Haggard that involved sex and crystal methamphetamine. Ironically, Jones came forward because of Haggard's hypocrisy in supporting a Colorado gay marriage ban; as Stewart points out, a person has a problem when one loses credibility as forthright to a prostitute who deals drugs (Javerbaum and O'Neill, 2006d).

Using a familiar *The Daily Show* bit, "Meet me at camera three," Stewart decides to address Haggard directly.[3] Speaking mano-a-mano, Stewart chides Haggard for his self-hatred and denial, whose condemnations punish himself. Going on, Stewart explains that you cannot escape "gay," and that though you cannot "catch" homosexuality it will catch up with you even as you attempt to deny it. As reassurance, Stewart informs Haggard that accepting one's own homosexuality can make a person's world a more beautiful place, as TDS cuts to a shot of Stewart with a beautiful meadow behind him (Javerbaum and O'Neill, 2006d). The instance neatly captures the breadth of comic responses used by *The Daily Show* and the potential for their rhetoric to better the community. First, Stewart points to the obvious hypocrisy of denying a natural impulse Haggard, himself, cannot control. Second, Stewart attempts to talk Haggard off of his proverbial ledge to see that a happier life awaits him once he recognizes that queer sexuality holds the potential for joy and not destruction. Carlson (1986) clarifies that in order for any movement to be fully comic and have the greatest potential for social change it requires those wanting change and those who need to enact it must believe in the inherent value of our shared humanity. Stewart's outreach to Haggard, in the face of the show's opposition to Haggard's record against the gay community, works very much toward the goal of recognizing the humanity in others and urging Haggard to find it within himself. Though perhaps less heartfelt in tone, *The Daily Show* segments that engage a comic perspective by indicating contradictions or dispelling homophobic panic rely upon bringing out the shared decency of people to create a more humane society.

"You Have No Idea"[4]

To some of the very same issues addressed above (e.g., gay marriage) *The Daily Show* sometimes sees an offender without potential for salvation. In those situations in which people err greatly against norms of civility that support the queer community, they cut themselves off from change and deserve neither mercy nor acceptance back into the fold. *The Daily Show*'s use of burlesque responses help to depict those who oppose queer acceptance and rights as beyond comprehensibility and therefore not worthy of actual engagement. When *The Daily Show* chooses to burlesque someone, somewhat consistently the rejection focuses on the person or group's understanding of human sexuality rather than the position itself (e.g., attacking homosexuality rather than defending gay marriage bans). The following examples contrast starkly against those discussed as comic correctives, for in the cases below *The Daily Show* makes unreasonable and barely human buffoons of the offenders.

Coverage of President Bush's 2007 Surgeon General nominee's, James Holsinger, confirmation hearing provides a clear example of *The Daily Show* unable to imagine engaging another person on queer issues. Using a 1991 report Holsinger wrote for the United Methodist Church, *The Daily Show* identifies their inability to respect the man by quoting a pedantic report Holsinger wrote describing why anal sex is not natural, which Stewart describes as being the attempt to use science to justify an irrational fear of homosexuals (Bodow and O'Neill, 2007c). Nowhere in Stewart's response do we find a sense that the target merely needed to recognize his mistake. In fact, *The Daily Show* makes a point of demonstrating that Holsinger remains unrepentant by showing him before a Senate confirmation hearing dismissing his report as speaking to a different time (i.e., twenty years prior). In turn, Stewart dismisses Holsinger's excuse as inane for suggesting that people go through a phase "experimenting" with intolerance. The *sine qui non* of the burlesque response here lies in *The Daily Show* not offering Holsinger a moment of correction but instead showing pure intolerance for his mistakes. Deciding that Holsinger wrote out of ignorance and fails to fully grasp his mistake, *The Daily Show* decides he is a buffoon who cannot be engaged on the topic. Rejecting Hoslinger from the discussion of reasonable opinions serves to sideline him and those who would repeat his words and keep them from influencing the debate of ideas and policy direction.

A similar case of burlesquing a fool as simply beyond comprehension comes from a two-part segment on sexual reorientation featuring *The Daily Show* correspondent Jason Jones. Jones begins the segment by interviewing a man whose parents purchased sexual reorientation audio tapes for him to change his attraction to men. During the segment we hear clips from the tapes, which *The Daily Show* sees as hopelessly idiotic, such as telling the listener that ejaculating inside of a woman is pleasurable (Bodow and O'Neill, 2007a). To symbolize the sexual reorientation movement, Jones interviews Richard Cohen, certified sexual reorientation coach. Cohen attempts to illustrate the natural laws of heterosexuality by holding out the index finger of one and inserting it into a ring created by the fingers of his other hand, symbolizing a penis and vagina in coitus, explaining that this pairing works while two men—symbolized by bumping his two index fingers as metaphorical penises—does not. To show the coach's inanity, Jones replies dryly to Cohen that he doesn't believe that bumping penises into each other is how male-male sex works (Bodow and O'Neill, 2007a). As the scene progresses, *The Daily Show* provides clips of Cohen's unusual manners, including loudly belching and spontaneously engaging in stretching exercises. Later we see Cohen walking Jones through part of the reorientation process, Cohen holding Jones in his arms like a small child to recreate father-son bonding. The oddity of seeing one man swaddling another to expunge homoeroticism marks Cohen's practices as entirely odd. Jones, mockingly, attempts to use the technique acquired from Cohen to convert a gay man, whom we see at the segment's conclusion—a fictional six-month follow-up on the therapy offered—passionately kissing another man. This closing bit puts the exclamation point on *The Daily Show*'s burlesque rejection of sexual reorientation practices.

As with comic responses, *The Daily Show* regularly discusses stories surrounding gay marriage, but the burlesque responses suggest that the target has no potential for discussion. We see an example of this when four correspondents travel to the Republican national convention to interrogate the frequent use of the term "small town values." As the correspondents show, a commitment to marriage defined as a man and a woman serves as the only consistent and solid operationalization of the term among convention goers. The buffoonish words of one conventioneer explains that gay citizens can have rights the rights of straight citizens if only they would marry someone of the opposite sex because one's sexual preference is not justification for special rights (Bodow and O'Neill, 2008c). As this example shows, *The Daily Show*'s problem with "small town values" comes not from a lack of support for gay marriage but an unwillingness or inability to engage the topic in a rational manner (i.e., suggesting gays and lesbians become heterosexuals to gain equal rights).

In addition to a regular interest in stories related to gay marriage, *The Daily Show* also frequently covers stories related to the U.S. military's "Don't Ask, Don't Tell" policy. Two segments nicely demonstrate burlesque responses by focusing on terminally flawed notions about homosexuality. Discussing the case of Bleu Copas, an Arabic translator discharged from the military for being gay, *The Daily Show* interviews Paul Cameron, an anti-gay rights activist, to provide a buffoonish figure to embody the policy. Cameron fills the role nicely by discussing gay men as sexually obsessed and engaged in atypical acts, such as drinking one another's urine (Javerbaum and O'Neill, 2006c). Later, Cameron warns that gay men, naturally overcome by their desire for fellow soldiers, will assault the unsuspecting as they sleep by performing fellatio on them or penetrating their rectums (Javerbaum and O'Neill, 2006c). Using Cameron's views *The Daily Show* dismisses "Don't Ask, Don't Tell" by bringing out powerfully ignorant understandings of gay-male sexuality.

A second, similar example uses footage of a House of Representatives committee on the military's policy. Most powerfully, *The Daily Show* draws from the testimony of a former Army ranger who talks about the need to keep warm at night through skin-to-skin contact with other soldiers, which he fears would create sexual arousal for gay service members. Stewart rejects the retired officer's ridiculous beliefs that same-sex desire becomes so overwhelming it arises during the most inappropriate situations, suggesting that an erection from performing nighttime patrol speaks to a larger concern than sexual orientation (Bodow and O'Neill, 2008a). Here again *The Daily Show* denounces the policy by targeting the absurd assumptions about homosexuality implicit to the idea. Because the ideas expressed come across as incomprehensible, *The Daily Show* can refuse the commitment to dialogue that a comic approach engenders. The result means to deprive the targeted persons and ideas of any credibility or place in a serious discussion so as to reject the position all together.

JON STEWART, MEET ME AT CAMERA THREE

In the preceding analysis I argue that *The Daily Show* approaches most stories affecting GLBTQ persons through either a comic or burlesque perspective depending upon whether or not the show deems the persons in question capable of an intelligent, productive engagement. If the target seems only to violate a shared principle (e.g., equality) or posses an irrational fear, *The Daily Show* suggests that learning can occur and change made. By contrast, for those whom the show recognizes as too dull or hate filled for a reasonable discussion then change becomes impossible and rejection occurs. There are several cases from the sixty-plus segments in the analysis that do not fit within the comic or burlesque frames. These cases illuminate something about *The Daily Show* in general that merits discussion in the context of the specific segments and the breadth of the data analyzed here.

The Daily Show broadcast several segments dealing with queer topics that fall within the grotesque category. As a transitional frame, the grotesque attempts to reject the current way of doing but continues to cling to it. Consequently the response ejects a grotesque character while perpetuating that person's condemned traits. Several segments dedicated to U.S. Senator Larry Craig's arrest and guilty plea for soliciting sex in a Minneapolis airport men's room demonstrate a grotesque response by attempting to reject his stance against gay rights through making jokes in which his supposed homosexuality serves as the punch line (Buerkle, 2010). Likewise, during the 2008 Republican national convention in St. Paul, Minnesota, four male correspondents took part in protesting the Republican party's tradition of denying rights for the gay community by stating—with blatant references to Craig's arrest—that all Republicans are closeted homosexuals, as captured neatly by John Oliver who says that Republicans have come to Minnesota for secret, same-sex rendezvous. (Bodow and O'Neill, 2008b). As the bit continues we go into the staged site of Craig's arrest where men receive oral sex through holes in stall walls and half-naked men dance under a disco ball. The jokes here cut both ways, seeking to punish Republicans for intolerance by hoisting them on a homophobic petard yet operating at the expense of a homosexuality drawn as a caricature of sexual compulsiveness. The message becomes a muddled annoyance with Republicans for supposedly thinking the kinds of things about gay men *The Daily Show* depicts as a shared joke about gay men.

The grotesque example above proves instructive for a habit that occurs across a number of *The Daily Show* segments' coverage of queer topics, namely the use of hetero-masculine adolescent humor that giggles over the mere thought of same-sex contact among persons.[5] My own analysis of the comic and burlesque framing of those who do not fully support the needs of the gay community provides a *prima facie* case for *The Daily Show* as consistently protesting for queer citizens equal rights. That said, further examination demonstrates a tension in the show's rhetoric that ostensibly promotes equality but cannot divorce itself from the impulses of homophobia in their humor even as they challenge the same. As Burke (1984a) reminds us, frames do not exist in "chemical purity" (p. 57). Indeed, a number of segments evince a primary orientation that either accepts or rejects the primary actor of the story, yet the segments may include moments of homophobic humor that in isolation would suggest queer intolerance. In making a point about the silliness of those who support "Don't Ask, Don't Tell" based on a belief of gay person's sexual obsession, Jones begins a strip routine while Copas, a discharged Arabic linguist, attempts to translate a passage from Arabic to English (Javerbaum and O'Neill, 2006c). The laughter in that moment comes from Jones in his underwear, dancing under a disco ball to a techno beat while thrusting his pelvis and buttocks against Copas. The point about respecting same-sex desires gets lost under an adolescent joke about homoeroticism. Additionally, in a segment about hair-product producer Garnier Fructis sponsoring NASCAR driver Brian Vickers, correspondent Samantha Bee interviews an effeminate-appearing man about his disapproval of the Garnier sponsorship as unmanly. Bee makes a series of winking comments to the audience about his sexuality, causing studio audience laughter to peak when he confesses he use to have an attraction to men (Bodow and O'Neill, 2007b). Here, *The Daily Show* wants to make the point that homophobia comes from a person's own sexual insecurity, but the setup leaves us laughing at the man for his struggle to define himself sexually. The logical inconsistency of selective acceptance and rejection to promote gay rights then bears internal conflict with homoerotic desire as a punch line.

CONCLUSION

I raise the specter of *The Daily Show*'s occasional use of homophobic-tinged humor to highlight both a potential problem of the show's rhetoric and the complexities of the show's function in U.S. society. Fred Fejes and Kevin Petrich (1993) complain of heterosexually defined images of GLBTQ, a problem we can see persisting in U.S. representations of homosexuality (Battles and Hilton-Morrow, 2002; Raley and Lucas, 2006; Landau, 2009). Therefore, *The Daily Show*, as a queer-friendly site, requires further and ongoing discussion of how it attempts to speak for and about the gay community. As I discussed earlier, *The Daily Show* does encourage its audiences to critically engage in events of the day. Hariman (2008) suggests that in the final analysis *The Daily Show*'s political humor has the potential to redeem and seek the greater good even in the very moments it thrashes against decency. Perhaps so, but the thrashing itself has consequences in terms of the direction of discussion and the tone maintained. *The Daily Show*'s primary use of comic and burlesque responses ultimately seeks change through peaceful—though not necessarily cooperative—means. The comic frame, in its fullest, manifests a humane and evenhanded view of society (Carlson, 1986). Though a rejection strategy, the burlesque possesses some sense of mercy by neutralizing opponents (Appel, 2005) and rendering them too foolish to bother wasting any more energy on (Selby, 2005). Both approaches as used by Stewart and company seek to change the community for the better using humor. Even still, we must always interrogate humor for the ways in which it cuts off communication with those it disapproves of and sometimes makes collateral damage of the people it wishes to help (Smith and Windes, 1997).

In the final analysis, *The Daily Show* would seem to have a genuine interest and concern for promoting gay rights. Their use of grotesque tones vis-à-vis comic and burlesque responses suggest a lack of follow-through in their thinking rather than the sign of profiteers using whoever they can to sell a laugh for ad revenue's sake. The use of frames with sometimes homophobic overtones may speak most to the show's sense of desperation. The cynicism that research finds present in *The Daily Show* coverage and audience effects likely emanates from the show's own sense that they exist in a system where the struggle for equality is Sisyphean in nature. If a rhetor believes that the struggle will be without end, then desperation becomes inevitable. Between needing to make a joke work as well as possible for ratings' sake and focusing on producing the most potent content rather than the most strategic for equality's sake, we can expect to see homophobic humor, especially when produced by heterosexual-dominated outlets, persist in pro-gay messages. *The Daily Show* exists in a hetero-normative culture in which passing homophobic comments often go without note. Not surprisingly, the language and sentiment of homophobia even pervades the discourses meant to challenge sexual prejudice. That *The Daily Show* undercuts its own pro-gay rights message does not doom the message/goal to failure. Rather, my analysis indicates that *The Daily Show* must be more mindful of its rhetorical structure and that *The Daily Show* may be less innocent than it would prefer to consider itself when it comes to homophobia.

I want to complete my analysis of *The Daily Show* with mention of the singular example of the epic frame, the only other frame present across all cases studied. The epic frame focuses on a hero, as emblem of community ideals, who must endure great strife to vanquish those who would undo the status quo (Smith and Johnston, 1991; Buerkle, Mayer and Olson, 2003). *The Daily Show*'s example pertains to the story of a young schoolboy who engaged in civil disobedience by refusing to say the Pledge of Allegiance so long as gay citizens do not enjoy "liberty and justice for all" (Bodow and O'Neill, 2009d,). As the segment progresses the studio audience claps and cheers for the boy who challenges queer intolerance in the face of his schoolmates' homophobic jeers. The story is light on humor but sufficiently inspiring. Such stories won't consistently sell airtime; in fact, this story is the second half of a dual story segment—the first half mocking a man who feels discriminated against by a gay manager. For all the talk of *The Daily Show* as informing the electorate, encouraging political engagement, and keeping accountability, we must remember its primary role as revenue generator (Hart and Hartelius, 2007), which may sometimes trot out humor that slanders, inadvertently harms, or antagonizes friends and foes alike to serve capital needs while losing sight of loftier ends (Ramsey and Santiago, 2004). My analysis means to recognize *The Daily Show*'s contribution to the discussion of gay-rights and its potential detractions, neither to applaud nor condemn but encourage an ongoing comic conversation on the use of humor to serve humane ends.

NOTES

1. Specifically, terms included in the search were: bisexuality, gays, gays and lesbians, gay marriage, gay pride, gay pride parade, gay rights, gay sex, homophobia, homophobic, homosexual, homosexuality, homosexuals, lesbian, lesbians, and transsexual.

2. Taken from a segment of the same name.

3. Under the current circumstances the camera shot is filtered so that viewers can only see through a small hole in the middle of the screen to create the "glory hole cam." The effect of this particular choice contributes to homophobic-tinged humor I discuss in the concluding section.

4. Taken from a *The Daily Show* segment of the same name.

5. Ironically, *The Daily Show* specifically reproaches male-adolescent homophobia (Bodow and O'Neill, 2009a).

REFERENCES

Appel, E. C. (1996). Burlesque drama as rhetorical genre: The hudibrastic rhetoric of William F. Buckley, Jr. *Western Journal of Communication, 60*, 269–284.

————. (2005). Rush to judgment: Burlesque, tragedy, and hierarchical alchemy in the rhetoric of America's foremost political talk show host. *Southern Communication Journal, 68*, 217–230.

Battles, K. and Hilton-Morrow, W. (2002). Gay characters in conventional spaces: *Will and Grace* and the situation comedy genre. *Critical Studies in Media Communication, 19*, 87–105.

Baum, M. A. (2002). Sex, lies, and war: How soft news brings foreign policy to the inattentive public. *American Political Science Review*, 96, 91–109.

————. (2003). Soft news and political knowledge: Evidence of absence or absence of evidence? *Political Communication*, 20, 173–190.

Baumgartner, J. and Morris, J. S. (2006). *The Daily Show effect*: Candidate evaluations, efficacy, and American youth. *American Politics Research, 34*, 341–367.

Baym, G. (2005). The Daily Show: Discursive integration and the reinvention of political journalism. *Political Communication, 22*, 259–276.

Bennett, W. L. (2007). Relief in hard times: A defense of Jon Stewart's comedy in an age of media cynicism. *Critical Studies in Media Communication, 24*, 278–283.

Bodow, S. (Head Writer) and O'Neill, C. (Director). (2007a, March 19). [Television series episode]. In J. Stewart (Executive producer), *The Daily Show with Jon Stewart*. New York: Viacom.

————. (2007b, June 7). [Television series episode]. In J. Stewart (Executive producer), *The Daily Show with Jon Stewart*. New York: Viacom.

————. (2007c, July 17). [Television series episode]. In J. Stewart (Executive producer), *The Daily Show with Jon Stewart*. New York: Viacom.

————. (2007d, September 25). [Television series episode]. In J. Stewart (Executive producer), *The Daily Show with Jon Stewart*. New York: Viacom.

————. (2008a, July 28). [Television series episode]. In J. Stewart (Executive producer), *The Daily Show with Jon Stewart*. New York: Viacom.

————. (2008b, September 3). [Television series episode]. In J. Stewart (Executive producer), *The Daily Show with Jon Stewart*. New York: Viacom.

————. (2008c, September 5). [Television series episode]. In J. Stewart (Executive producer), *The Daily Show with Jon Stewart*. New York: Viacom.

————. (2009a, September 29). [Television series episode]. In J. Stewart (Executive producer), *The Daily Show with Jon Stewart*. New York: Viacom.

————. (2009b, October 6). [Television series episode]. In J. Stewart (Executive producer), *The Daily Show with Jon Stewart*. New York: Viacom.

————. (2009c, October 13). [Television series episode]. In J. Stewart (Executive producer), *The Daily Show with Jon Stewart*. New York: Viacom.

————. (2009d, November 19). [Television series episode]. In J. Stewart (Executive producer), *The Daily Show with Jon Stewart*. New York: Viacom.

Boje, D. M., Luhman, J. T., and Cunliffe, A. L. (2003). A dialectic perspective on the organization theatre metaphor. *American Communication Journal,* 6.2. Retrieved from http://www.acjournal.org/holdings/vol6/iss2/articles/boje.htm.

Bostdorff, D. (1987). Making light of James Watt: A Burkean approach to the form and attitude of political cartoons. *Quarterly Journal of Speech, 73*, 43–59.

Brewer, P. R. and Marquardt, E. (2007). Mock news and democracy: Analyzing *The Daily Show*. *Atlantic Journal of Communication*, 15, 249–267.

Brummett, B. (1979). A pentadic analysis of ideologies in two gay rights controversies. *Central States Speech Journal, 30*, 250–261.

————. (1984). Burkean comedy and tragedy, illustrated in the reactions to the arrest of John DeLorean. *Central States Speech Journal, 34*, 217–227.

Buerkle, C. W., Mayer. M. E., and Olson, C. D. (2003). Our hero the buffoon: Contradictory and concurrent Burkean framing of Arizona governor Evan Mecham. *Western Journal of Communication, 67*, 187–206.

Buerkle, C. W. (2010). *Cynics, hypocrites, and nasty boys: Senator Larry Craig and gay rights caught in the grotesque frame. Kenneth Burke Journal*, 7(1). Retrieved November 13, 2010 from http://www.kbjournal.org/buerkle.

Burke, K. (1969). *A Rhetoric of motives*. Berkeley: University of California Press.

———. (1984a). *Attitudes toward history* (3rd ed.). Berkeley: University of California Press.

———. (1984b). *Permanence and change* (3rd ed.). Berkeley: University of California Press.

Carlson, A. C. (1986). Gandhi and the comic frame. *Quarterly Journal of Speech, 72*, 446–455.

———. (1988). Limitations of the comic frame: Some witty American women of the nineteenth century. *Quarterly Journal of Speech, 74*, 310–322.

Chesebro, J. W. and McMahan, D. T. (2006). Media constructions of mass murder-suicides as drama: *The New York Times'* symbolic construction of mass murder-suicides. *Communication Quarterly, 54*, 407–425.

Christiansen, A. E. and Hanson, J. J. (1996). Comedy as the cure for tragedy: Act Up and the rhetoric of AIDS. *Quarterly Journal of Speech, 82*, 157–170.

Darcy, J. (1994). Die non: Gay liberation and the rhetoric of pure tolerance. In R. J. Ringer (Ed.), *Queer words, queers images: Communication and the construction of homosexuality* (45–76). New York: New York University Press.

Duncan, H. D. (1962). *Communication and social order*. New York: Bedminster.

Fejes, F. and Petrich, K. (1993). Invisibility, homophobia and heterosexism: Lesbians, gays, and the media. *Critical Studies in Mass Communication, 10*, 396–422.

Feldman, L. (2007). The news about comedy: Young audiences, The Daily Show, and evolving notions of journalism. *Journalism, 8*, 406–427.

Fox, J. R., Koloen, G., and Sahin, V. (2007). No joke: A comparison of substance in The Daily Show *with Jon Stewart* and broadcast network television coverage of the 2004 presidential election campaign. *Journal of Broadcasting and Electronic Media, 51*, 213–227.

Harrington, S. (2008). Popular news in the 21st century: Time for a new critical approach? *Journalism, 9*, 266–284.

Hariman, R. (2007). In defense of Jon Stewart. *Critical Studies in Media Communication, 24*, 273–277.

Hart, R. P. and Hartelius, E. J. (2007). The political sins of Jon Stewart. *Critical Studies in Media Communication, 24*, 263–272.

Holbert, R. L., Lambe, J, L., Dudo, A. D., and Carlton, K. A. (2007). Primacy effects of *The Daily Show* and national TV news viewing: Young viewers, political gratifications, and internal political self-efficacy. *Journal of Broadcasting and Electronic Media ,50*, 20–38.

Hubbard, B. (1998). Reassessing Truman, the bomb, and revisionism: The burlesque frame and entelechy in the decision to use atomic weapons against Japan. *Western Journal of Communication, 62*, 346–385.

Javerbaum, D. (Head Writer) and O'Neill, C. (Director). (2006a, June 6). [Television series episode]. In J. Stewart (Executive producer), *The Daily Show with Jon Stewart*. New York: Viacom.

——— . (2006b, July 26). [Television series episode]. In J. Stewart (Executive producer), *The Daily Show with Jon Stewart*. New York: Viacom.

———. (2006c, September 18). [Television series episode]. In J. Stewart (Executive producer), *The Daily Show with Jon Stewart*. New York: Viacom.

———. (2006d, November 6). [Television series episode]. In J. Stewart (Executive producer), *The Daily Show with Jon Stewart*. New York: Viacom.

———. (2006e, November 13). [Television series episode]. In J. Stewart (Executive producer), *The Daily Show with Jon Stewart*. New York: Viacom.

Kaylor, B. T. (2008). A Burkean poetic frame analysis of the 2004 presidential ads. *Communication Quarterly, 56*, 168–183.

Landau, J. (2009). Straightening out (the politics of) same-sex parenting: Representing gay families in U.S. print news stories and photographs. *Critical Studies in Media Communication, 26*, 80–100.

Moore, M. P. (1992). "The Quayle quagmire": Political campaigns in the poetic form of burlesque. *Western Journal of Communication, 56*, 108–124.

National Annenberg Election Survey (2004). *Daily Show* viewers knowledgeable about presidential campaign, National Annenberg Election Survey shows. Retrieved from http://www.annenbergpublicpolicycenter.org/Downloads/Political_Communication/naes/2004_03_late-night-knowledge-2_9-21_pr.pdf.

Olbrys, S. G. (2006). Disciplining the carnivalesque: Chris Farley's exotic dance. *Communication and Critical/Cultural Studies, 3*, 240-259.

Raley, A. B., and Lucas, J. L. (2006). Stereotypes or success? Prime-time television's portrayals of gay male, lesbian, and bisexual characters. *Journal of Homosexuality, 51(2)*, 19–38.

Ramsey, E. M. and Santiago, G. (2004). The conflation of male homosexuality and femininity in *Queer eye for the straight guy*. *Feminist Media Studies, 4*, 353–355.

Selby, G. S. (2005). Scoffing at the enemy: The burlesque frame in the rhetoric of Ralph David Abernathy. *Southern Communication Journal, 70*, 134–145.

Smith, L. D. and Johnston, A. (1991). Burke's sociological criticism applied to political advertising: An anecdotal taxonomy of presidential commercials. In F. Bioca (Ed.), *Television and Political Advertising*, Vol. 2 (115–131). Philadelphia: Lawrence Erlbaum.

Smith, R. R. and Windes, R. R. (1997). The progay and antigay issue culture: Interpretation, influence, and dissent. *Quarterly Journal of Speech, 83*, 28–48.

Thompson, T. N. and Palmeri, A. J. (1993). Attitudes toward counternature (with notes on nurturing a poetic psychosis). In J. W. Chesebro, *Extensions of the Burkeian system*. Tuscaloosa, AL: University of Alabama Press.

Toker, C. W. (2002). Debating "what ought to be": The comic frame and public moral argument. *Western Journal of Communication, 66*, 53–83.

Waisanen, D. J. (2009). A citizens guide to democracy inaction: Jon Stewart and Stephen Colbert's comic rhetorical criticism. *Southern Communication Journal, 74*, 119–140.

Warner, J. (2007). Political culture jamming: The dissident humor of The Daily Showwith Jon Stewart. *Popular Communication, 5*, 17–36.

Watson, E. A. (1969). Incongruity without laughter: Kenneth Burke's theory of the grotesque. *University of Windsor Review, 4.2*, 28–36.

Chapter Twelve

Modern Hebrew Prophets? *The Daily Show* and Religious Satire

Brian T. Kaylor

When the Reverend Jim Wallis appeared on *The Daily Show* on January 18, 2005, he told Jon Stewart, "The Hebrew prophets used humor and truth-telling to make their point, which I think you do very well so maybe you're one of the prophets." Wallis has reiterated the point, even featuring the Jewish comedian on the cover of his Christian magazine *Sojourners* and as a key example in his book *Rediscovering Values*. In the interview with Stewart for the July 2009 *Sojourners* cover story entitled "The Truth Smirks," Wallis started by making his prophet comparison again, but this time added "satire" to the list of characteristics that Stewart shared with the Hebrew prophets (Wallis, 2009b, par. 1). On other occasions, Wallis has further explained his argument. Following Stewart's interview of CNBC's Jim Cramer in March of 2009, Wallis wrote on his "God's Politics" blog, "Last night, millions of Americans went to Sunday school, or more accurately, Sunday school came to them through Comedy Central" (Wallis, 2009a, par. 1). He added that in the midst of an economic crisis that is also "a moral crisis," the program "sounded like a mix between a confession and a good old values lessons" (Wallis, 2009a, par. 1–2). Wallis concluded, "I hope pastors and Sunday school teachers across the country watch this show and take notes because what's needed from our pulpits is being preached by a comedian" (Wallis, 2009a, par. 5). The following Sunday, Wallis preached at the National Cathedral in Washington, D.C., and referred to Stewart's interview of Cramer when discussing Jesus kicking the money changers out of the temple. Wallis called Stewart's effort "a modern enactment of that parable" (Wallis, 2009b, par. 10). Wallis is clearly a proponent of Stewart's prophet status.

Although Stewart and his correspondents frequently make jokes about religious individuals and leaders—just like they do about politicians and celebrities—could such humor actually be compared the discourse of a prophet as Wallis contends? Can satire be a form of prophetic discourse, which is rhetoric designed to help bring people closer to God and the way God desires people to live? This study will consider those questions by rhetorically analyzing *The Daily Show*'s religious coverage. Despite the growing body of research focused on considering Stewart's program, little research has considered the religious rhetoric of Stewart and his show. Additionally, although rhetorical scholars have examined prophetic discourse, such efforts have primarily focused on the jeremiad or similar rhetorical forms that focus on exhorting the people to return to following the covenant or face negative consequences. However, such messages do not cover the breadth of prophetic techniques utilized by the Hebrew prophets in their quest to change how the people thought and lived. Thus, this chapter will propose a genre of prophetic discourse—based upon the work of biblical scholar Walter Brueggemann—that differs substantially from the jeremiad and related covenant-focused forms. *The Daily Show*'s coverage of religious topics will be compared to the dramatic and imaginative messages used by some Old Testament Hebrew prophets, and then will be used to develop the generic characteristics of this unique but important rhetorical form. As Wallis has identified, Stewart—and his correspondents—serves as an excellent modern exemplar of this understudied type of prophetic discourse. Implications from this analysis concern both the importance of identifying and understanding this rhetorical form of the "imaginative prophet" and how Stewart uses this approach to advance his view of how religious individuals should behave.

PROPHETIC DISCOURSE

Although scholars have examined various forms of prophetic discourse, none of them captures the essence of the religious rhetoric of *The Daily Show* nor has the breadth of prophetic rhetoric been captured by scholars. Garnering the most scholarly attention is the jeremiadic genre (e.g., Buehler, 1998; Johannesen, 1985, 1986; Johnson, 2004; Jones and Rowland, 2005; Leeman, 2006; Murphy, 1990; Ritter, 1980), which is a rhetorical form derived from Puritan speakers of the seventeenth and eighteenth centuries. With this form, the speaker both criticizes the people for sinning and encourages them as the "chosen" people. Bercovitch (1978) described the structure of Puritan speakers, or "the political sermon, as the New England Puritans sometimes called this genre" (p. xiv):

... first, a precedent from Scripture that sets out the communal norms; then, a series
of condemnations that details the actual state of the community (at the same time
insinuating the covenantal promises that ensure success); and finally a prophetic
vision that unveils the promises, announces the good things to come, and explains
away the gap between fact and ideal. (p. 16)

With this form, "God's punishments were corrective, not destructive" and
God's "vengeance was a sign of love, a father's rod used to improve the
errant child" (Bercovitch, 1978, p. 8). Although the modern jeremiad is a
more secular version of the Puritan form, modern jeremiahs still focus on the
need to repent and reform to avoid disaster.

Despite being the most common prophetic genre considered by rhetorical
scholars, the jeremiad does not accurately capture the rhetoric of *The Daily
Show*, although Stewart and his correspondents do usually address religion to
condemn the actions of religious individuals. The critiques, however, are
usually not framed within the covenant or as coming from a messenger of
God. In fact, Stewart rejects Wallis's claim that he is a modern prophet
(Wallis, 2009b). Since the jeremiad is offered by a member of the community being judged (DeSantis, 1990), it would be difficult for the Jewish
Stewart to play the part of a modern Jeremiah when criticizing Christianity.
Stewart and his correspondents often cover topics concerning religious communities in which they are not a faithful member, although some—most
notably former correspondent Stephen Colbert—are actually active within
their faith. Additionally, the use of satire, parody, and overly dramatic exag-
gerations suggest that something else is occurring besides a traditional stoic
jeremiad.

A few other prophetic forms have also been proposed by scholars. Jones
and Rowland (2005) dealt with an augmented version of the jeremiad, which
they labeled a "Covenant-affirming jeremiad," where a speaker does not
actually charge the audience with having broken the covenant. Instead, they
are warned not to break the covenant while being affirmed for upholding it.
Additionally, this version of the jeremiad argues that continuing to remain
faithful to the covenant will fix society's problems. Such rhetoric modifies
the "jeremiadic form to transform a fundamentally negative message into a
positive one" (p. 170). This form fails in capturing the tone of *The Daily
Show* since the covenant-affirming jeremiad is from a member of the community and does not include the judging tone of *The Daily Show* or the
traditional jeremiad. Bostdorff (2003) explored the form of a "covenant renewal" speech, which she proposed involves declaring that the people are
blessed, warning about threats coming from outside forces, urging the next
generation to adopt the covenant, speaking about the current crisis as tests to
pass, and encouraging good works. Thus, this "discourse depicted a more
benevolent God than jeremiads had" by pointing to "external evil" instead of

"communal sin" as the reason for the current problems (p. 297). Bostdorrff argued that this form, like the jeremiad, was utilized by Puritan speakers, but she did not note the biblical antecedents for the form that existed in the Old Testament with rhetors like Moses and Joshua. With a removal of the focus on the sin of the people, this form also provides little similarity with the approach of *The Daily Show*.

Finally, DeSantis (1990) proposed what he called the "Amostic" speech. A rhetor utilizing this form is more in the tradition of the Old Testament prophet Amos than Jeremiah. Yet, it is a speech similar to the jeremiad with a focus on sin, impending punishment, and necessary repentance (although with a more specific organizational pattern than the jeremiad). However, the critical difference is that unlike with the jeremiadic tradition, the speaker is not from the community being addressed but is an outsider. Although given by an outsider, this form includes a rigid form that *The Daily Show* does not generally follow and the Amostic form does not capture the more satirical aspects of the program. Each of these rhetorical forms traces a type of prophetic discourse where the rhetor attempts to tell the people how they should be living.

Although scholars have not identified a rhetorical genre of prophetic discourse that matches the religious coverage of *The Daily Show*, there are antecedents in the biblical corpus for a prophetic form that relies heavily on satire, parody, and gross exaggeration. Jeremiah had himself tied to a large wooden yoke to symbolize Judea's oppression under the Babylonians and Ahijah cut his garment into twelve pieces and presented King Jeroboam with ten of them to symbolize that God was tearing away ten of the twelve tribes of Israel as the nation split; Stewart often utilizes props—including clothing items like a hat and a monocle—to dramatize his points and criticize the nation's elites. Isaiah walked naked through Jerusalem for three years to demonstrate what happened to Egyptians and Ethiopians taken captive by the Assyrians; Stewart often offers bleeped cock jokes, his correspondents occasionally strip down to their pixelated naked selves, and his book *America (The Book)* included photoshopped naked photos of the Supreme Court justices. Ezekiel lay on his left side for 390 straight days and then on his right side for 40 to represent the guilt of Israel and Judah respectively, baked bread over burning animal dung to symbolize the unclean food the people will eat as exiles, and burned, chopped, and scattered most of his hair to represent the scattering of the people with only a few to be saved during the exile; Stewart often acts out skits to make a point, and makes numerous jokes about feces. Hosea married a prostitute to represent how Israel had been unfaithful to God and even the names he gave to his children were part of the prophetic messages; Stewart's team frequently assume a character in the real world beyond the studio, and Stewart gives them all special titles—such as "Senior Child Molestation Expert," "Senior Gay Correspondent," and "Senior PlayStationologist"—to add to their points. Clearly, the gags and parodies of *The Daily Show* fit within the persuasive tactics of the often outlandish biblical prophets.

However, dramatic and exaggerated satire is not necessarily prophetic. The message that Stewart and his correspondents offer must also align with prophetic discourse. Although *The Daily Show* might not match established rhetorical genres of prophetic discourse, it resonates closely with the work of biblical scholar Walter Brueggemann, a prolific author and former Old Testament professor at Columbia Theological Seminary. In his classic 1978 tome *The Prophetic Imagination*—which was updated in a 2001 edition—Brueggemann explained his reading of a prophetic approach often ignored by scholars. He argued that rather than merely holding to "the old confrontational [prophetic] approach," we must view the prophetic as "more cunning and more nuanced and perhaps more ironic" (Brueggmann, 2001, p. xii). To those who hold the positions of dominance being challenged (such as Pharaoh and the kings in the Bible), "the prophetic alternative is a bad joke either to be squelched by force or ignored in satiation" and followers of such a prophet "are a haunted people because we believe the bad joke is rooted in the character of God himself" (p. 36). Thus, he argued that the "prophetic must be imaginative because it is urgently out beyond the ordinary and the reasonable" (p. xv). Brueggemann traced this prophetic form in the actions and teachings of biblical leaders such as Moses, Jeremiah, Isaiah, Amos, and even Jesus. Although Brueggemann does not propose a specific rhetorical genre or trace this type of discourse in non-biblical discourse, he does describe key characteristics of the rhetoric of biblical prophets that can easily serve as a model for considering the works of other rhetors.

The imaginative prophetic approach both criticizes the dominant perspective and energizes an alternative community. This prophetic style is characterized by public critique of the powers that attempt to squash imagination and alternative views. As Brueggemann (2001) explained, "It is the vocation of the prophet to keep alive the ministry of imagination, to keep on conjuring and proposing futures alternative to the single one the king wants to urge as the only thinkable one" (p. 40). To the "royal consciousness," "imagination is a danger" and '[t]hus every totalitarian regime is frightened of the artist" (p. 40). Chief among the critical targets for those utilizing the imaginative prophetic style is consumerism and its consequences. To accomplish these critiques, the imaginative prophet must work to provide powerful symbols to activate the consciousness of the people and to provide metaphors to help provide a clear understanding of God.

Another key characteristic of this style of prophetic discourse is the public grieving as a tool for criticizing and energizing. Individuals who adopt the imaginative prophetic style are essentially artists who grieve the present as a way of drawing critical attention to the mistakes of the past and energizing action to create a more hopeful future. The issue is not about a covenant to return to, or even a promise that God will again bless the people. Rather, the imaginative prophet is trying to create an alternative community and consciousness that exists within the shadow of the dominant interests. Those forces will likely not be redeemed or corrected but God's remnant can carve out a faithful way of living despite the oppression and corruption. It is about destroying the "numbness" of the people that has them living in denial in hopes of helping them recognize reality rather than change it (Brueggemann, 2001, p. 42). Thus, it is about pointing out what the dominant perspective wishes to ignore, especially in regards to the potential ending of their power and lives. The imaginative prophet must "cut through the numbness, to penetrate the self-deception, so that the God of endings is confessed as Lord" (p. 45). It is, in essence, to declare that the emperor has no clothes so that the people will finally see the nakedness for what it is and quit submitting to the emperor.

THE GOSPEL ACCORDING TO *THE DAILY SHOW*

Despite the popularity and influence of *The Daily Show*, few scholars have considered the religious rhetoric of the program. Philosophers Lopresti (2007) and Frazier (2007) both considered *The Daily Show*'s now basically defunct sketch "This Week in God," arguing, respectively, that it promoted pluralism and was an anti-fundamentalist approach to understanding God. Among communication scholarship, Kaylor and Compton (2009) included *The Daily Show* in their textual examination of how late night comics treated the death of John Paul II. The authors noted that *The Daily Show* went further than most programs by including more risqué jokes that could offend faithful Catholics. However, Kaylor and Compton concluded that *The Daily Show* and the other late night comics paid homage to the Pope in their own unique way, with jokes about Catholics and others designed to prod people to be more like John Paul II. However, no rhetorical examination of *The Daily Show*'s broader religious themes exists.

Utilizing *The Daily Show*'s (Karlin and Stewart, 1996) online video database, this chapter analyzes videos with religious search terms—and thus focused on religious individuals or issues. Tags examined included: Religion, Christian, Christianity, Judaism, God, Jesus, Bible, and This Week in God. Videos were examined for a five-year period (May 2005–April 2010) to provide a long-term view of the show's religious discourse. The focus of the analysis, which involved repeated viewing and comparison to the imaginative prophetic approach, was to determine the tone Stewart and his correspondents took toward religion and religious issues. Are they primarily mocking them and making light of religious beliefs? Or are they—as Wallis argued—using satire to call religious individuals toward better fulfilling their religious teachings and objectives?

Critiquing the Dominant Perspective

Brueggemann (2001) noted that the imaginative prophetic approach involves the critique of "royal consciousness"—which he also called the "false consciousness" or "dominant consciousness"—that represents the positions and interests of the privileged class. For the prophet, "The dominant consciousness must be radically criticized and the dominant community must be finally dismantled" (p. 81). He added, "The task of prophetic ministry is to nurture, nourish, and evoke a consciousness and perception alternative to the consciousness and perception of the dominant culture around us" (p. 3). The prophetic must help nurture an "alternative consciousness" that has been "co-opted and domesticated" by the "dominant" perspective (p. 3). Before the people can be energized toward more completely following God, the stranglehold of the dominant consciousness must be broken. Thus, the target of the imaginative prophet's criticism is the powers that be. This is not an address to the people, but to those in position of authority and privilege—politically, economically, and religiously.

One area where the dominant consciousness is repeatedly challenged on *The Daily Show* is when prominent religious leaders declare God's wrath in violent terms. During the September 26, 2005 "This Week in God" segment, correspondent Stephen Colbert noted that some Christian leaders claimed God sent Hurricane Katrina as punishment for homosexuality. Colbert then showed on a map that although the French Quarter was not flooded, the sections of the city next to it were. Thus, he concluded with prophetic tongue firmly in check that this means "God loves gays, but hates the gay-adjacent." At the end of the segment, Colbert offered the opposing theory of "a sect known as meteorologists." This critique was designed to call out the religious leaders for their false claims by pointing out the absurdity through absurdity. In a similar manner, during the August 11, 2005 "This Week in God" segment, Colbert critiqued Pat Robertson for praying for the deaths of Supreme Court justices (so that they could be replaced by more conservative justices that would rule how he wanted). Thus, Colbert critiqued the famed televangelist for making comments that seemed so obviously unchristian.

Other correspondents also tackled this problem of religious leaders adding to the oppression. After a pastor told Jason Jones during the February 24, 2009 broadcast that President Barack Obama was "exhibiting signs of the antichrist," Jones looked confused and asked for clarification. When the pastor repeated his claim, Jones chuckled and started looking around, asking where Ashton Kutcher was and asking if he was "being punked." Jones then spoke with another pastor who declared Obama to be "the next Hitler." After the pastor explained his comparison, Jones pointed at the man and joked that he was impressed if the man was Howie Mandel in a disguise. When the pastor making the Hitler claim added that Obama was also bisexual, Jones asked for evidence. After the pastor said he had no "empirical evidence," Jones quickly asked the man if he thought before he spoke. Rather than offering stern condemnation of these pastors, Jones attempted to spark an alternative consciousness by noting the absurdity of their claims. Jones then continued this effort in dramatic satirical fashion by going to the streets with a megaphone and a street preacher-like sign that read "Obama is the Anti-christ and/or Hitler!" As Jones preached this message, he turned around to reveal that the back of his sandwich board sign read "Suits Suits Suits 50% Off." With that, the religious emperors are shown to have no clothes.

The other dominant topic where *The Daily Show* challenges the dominant religious consciousness concerns the use of religion in politics. In a May 17, 2006 "Back in Black" segment, Lewis Black critiqued the over-politicization of evangelical Protestants. Black noted that if one is not willing to declare they have accepted Jesus "as your personal Lord and Savior" then that person is "probably not in politics." Black criticized politicians like Democrat Howard Dean for going on Pat Robertson's show in quest of votes. After showing a clip of Dean attempting to woo evangelicals to the Democratic Party, Black quipped that although Dean was "on his knees" it did not seem like he was praying. This crude innuendo serves to undress the façade of the political and religious leaders. Similarly, after showing a clip on June 22, 2005 of a congressman decrying "the long war on Christianity," Stewart mockingly declared that he hoped one day America might be a nation "where Christians can worship freely" and that "there could even be an openly Christian president." Stewart quickly added that it would especially be nice if there could be "forty-three of them, consecutively." Through parody, Stewart attempts to awake the consciousness of his viewers and reject the dominant consciousness where the individuals actually controlling the political and religious systems use complaints of victimhood to maintain their power over the true victims.

In both of these areas, Stewart and his correspondents critiqued religious and political leaders for misusing and misrepresenting God—and were therefore practically calling the established leaders "false prophets." As Brueggemann (2001) noted, "much caricatured prophetic speech serves only to encourage the suppression rather than to end it" (p. 45). Thus, the imaginative prophets of *The Daily Show* must undermine the claims of such would-be prophets. Stewart and his correspondents must demonstrate how the dominant religious leaders are not upholding their own religious values. For instance, during a December 15, 2005 "This Week in God" segment, correspondent Rob Corddry noted a new Vatican policy cracking down on priests who might be sexual predators. Corddry summed it up by saying a priest is supposed "to love Jesus" but must keep their "filthy paws off Jesus (Hey-Seuss)." The critique with this quip is not an attack on religion or God but rather an attempt to demonstrate how far from that standard the leaders have fallen. As imaginative prophets, *The Daily Show*'s crew attempts to expose the nakedness of the nation's religious and political leaders.

Criticizing Consumerism

One primary target for the imaginative prophet is consumerism and its dangerous consequences. The problem with consumerism is that it numbs the spirit and creates complacency that leads people to trust the royal consciousness over God. Brueggemann (2001) explained, "The contemporary American church is so largely enculturated to the American ethos of consumerism that it has little power to believe or to act. . . . Our consciousness has been claimed by false fields of perception and idolatrous systems of language and rhetoric" (p. 1). The imaginative prophet must help free the people from the allure of consumerism since—as Jesus taught—one cannot serve both God and mammon. When consumerism dominates a culture, the voice of God—and those of God's prophets—can easily be lost. As Brueggemann argued, "It is not so easy in our electronic environment of consumerism to imagine prophetic discourse and prophetic action, but such consumerism is nonetheless likely the foremost circumstance of prophetic faith in the United States" (pp. xvii–xviii). Although consumerism makes it difficult for the prophetic voice to arise, it is also what makes such a voice so necessary in the first place.

The Daily Show's prophets often turn their sights upon society's obscene quest for religious profits. During the June 6, 2005 "This Week in God" segment, Stephen Colbert noted that "if you can do it, eat, or smell it, you can do it, eat it, or smell it for Christ's sake." The segment critiqued the growing market of "Christian" goods. For instance, he noted a new candle that claimed to be the scent of Jesus as described in a Bible verse. Colbert joked that it gave the perfect "subtle spiritual scent" to mask the smell of "that burrito you just cast into the porcelain abyss." Similarly, during the July 31, 2006 "This Week in God," Rob Corddry critiqued the Christian video game *Left Behind* for being as violent and graphic as secular video games. *The Daily Show* not only critiques kitsch religious products, but also uses such critique to try and remind people how far consumerism is taking them from the true religious message. For example, Corddry exclaimed during the November 10, 2005 "The Week in God," that people should not "lose faith" since Christmas was near. Thus, everyone needed to remember the "inspirational" saying, "no Jesus, no Xbox." Similarly, after showing footage of holiday shoppers tackling each other to get into a store at the start of the

Christmas shopping season, Stewart declared during the November 28, 2005 episode that "the spirit of Christmas is alive" since people were willing to show their love for "the baby Jesus" by being willing "to kick another man's nads in for an iPod!" By satirically describing the consumeristic actions as acts of religious devotions, Corddry and Stewart attempt spark an alternative consciousness and remove the numbness that comes from mindlessly consuming more and more.

Brueggemann (2001) argued that a key characteristic of the royal consciousness is when we join "in an economics of affluence in which we are so well off that pain is not noticed and we can eat our way around it" (p. 36). Because consumerism pushes critical questions about death and God out of our minds, the royal consciousness promotes it. This "religion of optimism" teaches that "God has no business other than to maintain our standard of living, " which actually helps the privileged king in "ensuring his own place in his palace" (p. 37). Thus, the imaginative prophet must battle the god of consumerism in the quest to create an alternative consciousness. Only by freeing religion from the consumeristic temptations of the almighty dollar can the prophet lead the people to a deeper relationship with the Almighty God.

Redemptive Symbols

Brueggemann (2001) offered that the imaginative prophet's task included three rhetorical functions. First, the prophet must "offer symbols that are adequate to confront the horror and massiveness of the experience that evokes numbness and requires denial" (p. 45). This does not mean inventing symbols but rather "that the prophet is to reactivate out of our historical past symbols that always have been vehicles for redemptive honesty" (p. 45). Second, the prophet must "bring to public expression those very fears and terrors that have been denied so long and suppressed so deeply that we do not know they are there" (p. 45). Finally, the prophet must "speak metaphorically but concretely" about these matters (p. 45). The imaginative prophet, thus, is an artist seeking to bring truth to the public square through the use of powerful symbols and metaphors.

Much of the work of *The Daily Show*'s prophets seemed designed to reclaim religion—and its holy symbols—from the extremists and the powerful. On March 14, 2006, Stewart interviewed biblical scholar Bart Ehrman, who explained how to interpret the Bible and more fully and accurately understand Jesus. Stewart responded that Ehrman's approach made the Bible "seem almost more godly." Similarly, on August 16, 2009, Stewart interviewed Jeff Sharlet, author of *The Family*, a book about a semi-secret powerful Christian group in Washington, D.C., with many political connections. During the interview, the two talked about how other Christians—including other fundamentalist Christians—have denounced the teachings of the group as being in opposition to the teachings of Jesus and the Bible. The two sought to distance the religious beliefs of this group of Christians from both mainstream Christianity and the teachings of the Bible. Thus, one of the goals of Stewart, Ehrman, and Sharlet was to reclaim the sacred teachings from the political and religious elites. Stewart continued this effort in an October 2, 2007 segment entitled "Is that really necessary?" Stewart critiqued Republican presidential hopeful John McCain for pandering to conservative Christians just to win the presidency. Stewart noted that McCain went from a "principled" critique of Reverend Jerry Falwell during the 2000 campaign to speaking at Falwell's Liberty University and strongly advocating the positions of conservative Christians. Stewart argued that McCain's religious rhetoric during the 2008 campaign seemed insincere and therefore would not actually help McCain win over voters. Stewart similarly criticized politicians using religion—claiming they would face "a judgment day" at some point—during his December 5, 2006 interview with former Republican Senator and Episcopalian priest John Danforth. With the increased mixing of religion and politics, Stewart attempted to divorce the two in a quest of reestablishing the power of the religious symbols and texts.

Perhaps the most obvious effort to reclaim a powerful symbol occurred on the April 17, 2007 show. During a segment about the effort to fire a city manager in Florida because he decided to undergo a sex change, one of the individuals testifying at a public hearing declared that Jesus would want the transgender manager "terminated." At that point, correspondent Rob Riggle said it matched the story from the Bible when Jesus—who was depicted on screen of having the hair and voice of Donald Trump—said to "the thirteenth apostle" that he should not have removed his "genitalia" and thus was "fired!" This satirical response was the only rebuttal given to the Jesus comment, but it served to distance Jesus from the condemning claim shown in the video. Rather than mock Jesus, this segment was actually mocking the image of Jesus the man in the video was presenting—an image that *The Daily Show*'s prophets believed to be contrary to the way Jesus was presented in the Bible. The goal was to reclaim Jesus as a powerful symbol for redemption.

By reclaiming symbols—even through the use of parody or humor—the imaginative prophet attempts to show what is actually real. As Brueggemann (2001) explained:

> And so the offering of symbols is a job not for a timid clerk who simply shares the inventory but for people who know something different and are prepared, out of their own anguish and amazement, to know that the closed world of managed reality is false. (p. 64)

When combined with public expression of the very things that have been suppressed, the role of the imaginative prophet is to proclaim God's faithfulness even to the point of using "absurd practice" and "subversive activity" (p. 65). The prophet reclaims the symbols to clearly present reality. By publicly expressing hope for a new way and speaking of the very things the royal consciousness would like to deny, the absurd prophet brings hope with the powerful symbols. As Stewart proclaimed during a March 19, 2007 interview with author Stephen Prothero that it seemed that "the people controlling the agenda" were disengaged from "the overwhelming majority of reasonable Americans." In such a situation, the imaginative prophet must reclaim the religious symbols to nurture an alternative consciousness for reasonable majority.

Public Grieving

At the heart of the imaginative prophet's approach is public grieving, which serves to both criticize the royal consciousness and to energize the creation of an alternative consciousness. Brueggemann (2001) posited that "the real criticism begins in the capacity to grieve because that is the most visceral announcement that things are not right" and because "[o]nly in the empire are we pressed and urged and invited to pretend that things are all right" (p. 11). He explained that crying out "also functions for the official filing of a legal complaint" (p. 11). The imaginative prophetic style publicly laments how things are as a way of indicting how things got that way. Rather than the stern prophet that stands from a distance and condemns, this prophetic style sits among the oppressed and grieves. Rather than pointing the judgmental index finger with condemnation, this prophetic approach holds up the middle finger with anguish.

Stewart at times offers this public anguish when he tires of politicians using religion to cover up their sin. For instance, during the June 29, 2009 episode, Stewart played a clip of disgraced South Carolina Governor Mark Sanford, who had recently admitted to having an affair with an Argentinean woman, invoking the biblical King David to explain why he would not resign as governor. Stewart then chided Sanford for using the story for political cover. Stewart complained that Sanford only decided to "go Old Testament" because he "[bleeped] up!" During his rant, Stewart pulled out a Bible and started reading New Testament passages about being righteous and condemning adulterers. After reading several, Stewart puts the book away sheepishly as if he was reenacting Sanford's attempt to deal with the scandal. Then Stewart pulled out another book and declared it was time to "go Old Testament!" Stewart's irritation with Sanford's use of the text for cover drove him to offer this public lament that sacred scriptures were being used to cover up obscene behavior that the Bible actually strongly condemns.

More often, such laments are offered to religious leaders for not living up to the standards of their faiths. During the April 7, 2010 show, Stewart played a news clip about the allegations that Pope Benedict XVI had previously passed on punishing a priest who sexually abused young boys. After the clip ended, Stewart responded with, "[bleeped] [bleeped] [bleeped]!" and then announced he had vomited inside his head. Later in the segment, Stewart added that the Church was not showing enough contrition and he yelled that "[f]or God's sakes" Dominos appeared much more apologetic for making "[bleeped] pizza" that tasted bad. The grief expressed through expletives clearly marks how far the Church had fallen from where it should have been. Similarly, during the April 22, 2010 episode, Stewart criticized the Muslim radicals that sent death threats to South Park creators. Joined by a robed church choir, Stewart repeatedly sang out that the radicals should "[g]o [bleeped]" themselves. By doing so, he expressed in the only way he knew possible his grief that a New York-based group could take such an action against fellow artists at his New York comedy station—with expletives. Such is the way of the imaginative prophet.

Perhaps the clearest example of Stewart as the prophet of public laments occurred during the January 14, 2010 show. Stewart showed a clip of Pat Robertson's declaring that God was punishing Haiti with the recent devastating earthquake. Afterward, Stewart responded with telling Roberston to "[s]hut your pie hole." Stewart then complained that Robertson should have used his "religion to bring comfort to a devastated people and region." After pulling out a large Bible, Stewart flipped through and emphatically read several passages about God caring for people and being there to help them through difficult times. Stewart then attacked Robertson for ignoring those passages and instead deciding "to go with tough titties devil folk." With expletives, Stewart questioned if Robertson had even read the Bible and urged people to "put aside ideology for a second." Ironically, the non-devout Jewish Stewart seemed to understand Robertson's sacred texts better than the Reverend Robertson did. Yet, this is what happens in the world of the imaginative prophet. This is the world in which such a prophet is needed. And when the dominant consciousness—as represented by Robertson—strays so far from the biblical mandate, the best response seems to be for an absurd prophet to publicly cry out in disbelief.

Brueggemann (2001) argued that public lament was the key tactic of the imaginative prophet. He explained, "Bringing hurt to public expression is an important first step in the dismantling criticism that permits a new reality, theological and social, to emerge" (p. 12). Crying out is the first step to showing that the dominant consciousness is wrong. It is also an effort to provide hope by acknowledging that religion can and should be better. Public grieving is not an act of self-pity but rather a revolutionary act designed to criticize and energize.

CONCLUSION

Although the proposition that Stewart and his sarcastic correspondents are prophets might strike many as absurd—and even appear to some as sacrilegious—this analysis makes clear that there is much truth in the claims made by Jim Wallis. The comedians on *The Daily Show* are not Jeremiahs warning of doom and gloom unless the people return to the covenant. But, that was never the only style of prophetic discourse, and, according to Brueggemann (2001), is not even the dominant approach used by Jeremiah and the other prophets. Rhetorical scholars, therefore, must expand the consideration of prophetic genres to include approaches such as those employed by what I have termed the "imaginative prophet" that is based on Brueggemann's work on *The Prophetic Imagination*. This prophetic style—no less significant or appropriate than the more traditional prophetic approaches—seems particularly well suited for artists like the cast of *The Daily Show*. Perhaps other such dramatic and satirical modern day imaginative prophets could be identified (such as Reverend Billy). Yet, Stewart and his correspondents seem to perfectly embody this unique rhetorical style. More attention should be given to this type of prophetic discourse that might not fit into more traditional rhetorical forms but which impacts the people view religion. Although many Americans attend religious services on the weekend, many tune in four nights a week to listen to sermons of Stewart, Bee, Oliver, and others at the church of *The Daily Show*. Without an understanding of the discourse of the imaginative prophet, such parodic messages would not be properly understood or appreciated.

Some might view *The Daily Show* as anti-religious or sacrilegious—and some of their jokes clearly lend credence to such a view—but a closer examination reveals that most their religious jokes are not actually mocking the religious beliefs and ideals. Rather, Stewart and his correspondents are lamenting when religious leaders misuse religion or fail to live up to their own teachings. As Stewart told Wallis during the *Sojourners* interview, "Religion makes sense to me. I have trouble with dogma more than I have trouble with religion. I think the best thing religion does is give people a sense of place, purpose, and compassion" (Wallis, 2009b, par. 27). This public grieving "is the beginning of criticism" that works to make "clear that things are not as they should be, not as they were promised, and not as they must be and will be" (Brueggemann, 2001, p. 12). Echoing this sentiment, Stewart told Wallis during the *Sojourners* interview, "What we're trying to do is square our reality with the reality of what we're seeing. It's just trying to line up worlds" (Wallis, 2009b, par. 44). The critique is not about religion but rather the gap between religious claims and religious practice.

When even those who should be our prophets have fallen, it takes a different kind of prophet to bring attention to reality. As Brueggemann (2001) explained, "This denying and deceiving kind of numbness is broken only by the embrace of negativity, by the public articulation that we are fearful and ashamed of the future we have chosen" (p. 56). Stewart's jokes might seem negative and even harsh, but that is only because of the negative and harsh reality we find ourselves in. When such numbness abounds, the truth will inherently seem absurd and harsh. But, it is important to remember that such crying out is needed to carve out an alternative consciousness: "Without anguish the new song is likely to be strident and just more royal fakery" (Brueggemann, 2001, p. 79). In an age where news seems fake, it takes a fake news team to bring the truth. And in an age where religion seems fake, it takes fake prophets to proclaim God's truth. Clearly, the comedians on *The Daily Show* are modern prophets working in their own unique way to change the way people think and live in hopes of creating a better and even more godly society. Perhaps, then, Stewart was correct when he declared during the January 4, 2010 program that his team of corresponds was "the best [bleeped] theological team on the planet."

REFERENCES

Bercovitch, S. (1978). *The American jeremiad.* Madison, WI: University of Wisconsin Press.

Bostdorff, D. M. (2003). George W. Bush's post-September 11 rhetoric of covenant renewal: Upholding the faith of the greatest generation. *Quarterly Journal of Speech, 89,* 293–319.

Brueggemann, W. (2001). *The prophetic imagination* (2nd edition). Minneapolis: Fortress Press.

Buehler, D. O. (1998). Permanence and change in Theodore Roosevelt's conservation jeremiad. *Western Journal of Communication, 62,* 439–458.

DeSantis, A. D. (1990). An Amostic prophecy: Frederick Douglass' The meaning of July Fourth for the negro. *Journal of Communication and Religion, 22,* 65–92.

Frazier, B. (2007). Contingency, irony, and "This Week in God." In J. Holt (Ed.), *The Daily Show and Philosophy: Moments of Zen in The Art Of Fake News* (pp. 175–189). Malden, MA: Blackwell Publishing.

Johannesen, R. L. (1985). The jeremiad and Jenkin Lloyd Jones. *Communication Monographs, 52,* 156–172.

———. (1986). Ronald Reagan's economic jeremiad. *Central States Speech Journal, 37,* 79–89.

Johnson, D. (2004). The rhetoric of Huey P. Newton. *Southern Communication Journal, 70,* 15–30.

Jones, J. M., and Rowland, R. C. (2005). A covenant-affirming jeremiad: The post-presidential ideological appeals of Ronald Wilson Reagan. *Communication Studies, 56,* 157–174.

Karlin, B., and Stewart, J. (Executive Producers). (1996). *The Daily Show with Jon Stewart* [Television broadcast]. New York: Comedy Central.

Kaylor, B. T., and Compton, J. (2009). Papal punchlines: Late night comedic treatment of Pope John Paul II. In J. R. Blaney and J. P. Zompetti (eds). *The rhetoric of Pope John Paul II* (pp. 3–22). Lanham, MD: Lexington Books.

Leeman, R. W. (2006). Speaking as Jeremiah: Henry McNeal Turner's "I claim the rights of a man." *Howard Journal of Communicatoin, 17,* 223–242.

Lopresti, M .S. (2007). The challenge of religious diversity in "This Week in God." In J. Holt (Ed.), *The Daily Show and Philosophy: Moments of Zen in the art of fake news* (pp. 161–174). Malden, MA: Blackwell Publishing.

Murphy, J. (1990). "A time of shame and sorrow": Robert F. Kennedy and the American jeremiad. *Quarterly Journal of Speech, 76*, 401–414.

Ritter, K. W. (1980). American political rhetoric and the jeremiad tradition: Presidential nomination acceptance addresses, 1960–1976. *Central States Speech Journal, 31*, 153–171.

Wallis, J. (2009a, March 13). "Sunday school with Jon Stewart." *God's Politics*. Retrieved April 24, 2010 from http://blog.sojo.net/2009/03/13/sunday-school-with-jon-stewart.

———. (2009b, July). "The truth smirks." *Sojourners*. Retrieved from http://www.sojo.net/index.cfm?action=magazine.articleandissue=soj0907andarticle=the-truth-smirksand0907_webextra=Extended percent20Formatandcookies_enabled=false.

Chapter Thirteen

The Daily Show and Barack Obama's Comic Critique of Whiteness: An Intersection of Popular and Political Rhetoric

Stephanie M. Purtle and Timothy R. Steffensmeier

Bill Moyers (2003) asserts, "You simply can't understand American politics in the new millennium without *The Daily Show*." If *The Daily Show with Jon Stewart* is imperative to an understanding of contemporary American politics, an examination of the intersection of political and popular discourse is warranted for those hoping to understand the rhetoric of *The Daily Show with Jon Stewart*. Barry Brummett's (2004) *Rhetorical Homologies* offers critics a path to examine the intersection of political and popular rhetoric via the concept of homology. A rhetorical homology is a formal resemblance that can be found among disparate texts that functions to manage meaning. An analysis of homologies shared by *The Daily Show with Jon Stewart* and presidential rhetoric provides insight into the possibility of these seemingly disparate rhetorics to reveal power structures and offer a new path toward the progressive pursuit of a more perfect union.

A provocative place to begin such an analysis is with the Rev. Jeremiah Wright controversy of the 2008 U.S. presidential election. The controversy was unique for a presidential campaign in that it did not involve the actions of the candidate; rather, it was a controversy derived from the sermons of the candidate's pastor (Dumm, 2008). The Wright controversy is a complex site of hegemonic struggle in which we can observe whiteness, "*a historical systemic structural* race-based superiority" (Wander, Martin and Nakayama, 1999, p. 15), in contemporary discourse. Barack Obama addressed this controversy on March 18, 2008, in his speech titled "A More Perfect Union."

Subsequently, *The Daily Show with Jon Stewart* covered the controversy and Obama's speech in multiple segments. By analyzing both Obama's speech and *The Daily Show with Jon Stewart*'s reactions, the critic can locate a shared homology that emerges at the intersection of the discourses. This analysis reveals that the comic frame is the predominant homology that offers a way for both Obama and *The Daily Show with Jon Stewart* to critique the Wright controversy while simultaneously subverting whiteness.

When analyzing homologies, critics should consider "the political or ideological interests served by ordering a rhetorical transaction in a certain way" (Brummett, 1991, p. 98). In this chapter, it will be argued that constructing the rhetoric of Obama and *The Daily Show with Jon Stewart* with the comic frame serves the ideological interests of those who are advocating for social justice and working to subvert whiteness by calling attention to its privilege. The comic frame is applicable particularly for a presidential candidate and *The Daily Show with Jon Stewart* who must address whiteness yet still rely, in part, on the support of white voters and viewers. The chapter will argue that the rhetoric of Obama and *The Daily Show with Jon Stewart* is motivated by a contemporary appetite for a comic frame, while simultaneously increasing people's expectation for this frame in political discourse. An analysis of Barack Obama's "A More Perfect Union," and *The Daily Show with Jon Stewart*'s reactions to Obama's speech, will provide insight into the ways in which the comic frame can be utilized to address whiteness. First, this chapter will perform a rhetorical analysis of Obama's speech via the homology of the comic frame. Then, the comic frame is applied to the rhetoric of *The Daily Show with Jon Stewart* so as to explore the intersection of political and popular discourse.

RHETORICAL HOMOLOGIES AND THE COMIC FRAME

Brummett's (2004) *Rhetorical Homologies* explains that homology is a pattern found to be ordering certain features in disparate texts (p. 1). A *rhetorical* homology "is a special case of formal resemblance, grounded in discursive properties, that facilitates the work of political and social rhetoric, or influence" (Brummett, 2004, p. 3). If we consider certain texts individually we may overlook the ways in which the texts are understood together by individuals experiencing the texts in the moment. Searching for a rhetorical homology allows the critic "to track lines of rhetorical influence that might otherwise be obscured" (Brummett, 2004, p. 3). Homologies are powerful in that they can make one text vulnerable to the rhetorical influence of other texts. "Vulnerability is but another way of saying that one experience may have rhetorical effects on how people perceive and order another experience or group of experiences if they are formally linked" (Brummett, 2004, p. 41). Each study of homology should contribute to our understanding of how rhetorical texts are connected and interact, as well as expand our understanding of "how power is created, managed, or refused rhetorically in human affairs" (Brummett, 2004, p. 3). The project is not complete once a homology has been identified; rather, the critic must explore who benefits from the homology and how power is being managed rhetorically.

According to Brummett (2004), Kenneth Burke "explores the intersection between politics and art, which is in and of itself suggestive of homologies linking disparate orders of experience" (p. 21). Central to Burke's work is the idea that common poetic categories are also found in non-literary discourse, and humans use these forms as a "code of names by which they simplify or interpret reality. These names shape our relations with our fellows. They prepare us *for* some functions and *against* others, *for* or *against* the persons representing these functions" (Burke, 1984, p. 4). Furthermore, such names function to tell us "*how* you shall be for or against" something (Burke, 1984, p. 4). Thus, these literary forms guide us as we work to understand a text, and its formal characteristics are clues as to the assumptions of the text and how it wants to be read.

The comic frame is a species of the poetic form, which differs from the tragic and heroic frames not in subject matter but in the frame's "depiction of the human role in affecting social outcomes" (Christiansen and Hanson, 1996, p. 159). The tragic frame depicts man as evil or the villain, whereas the comic frame depicts man as mistaken and foolish. "Rather than reducing social tensions through mystification, scapegoating, or banishment, rhetoric in the comic frame humorously points out failings in the status quo and urges society to correct them through thoughtful action rather than tragic victimage" (Christiansen and Hanson, 1996, p. 161). These failings of the status quo are embodied in the "creation and castigation of a 'clown'" (Carlson, 1988, p. 312). People can address societal ills by directing their energy toward correcting the clown. "The clown is created not to serve as an enemy, as in tragedy, but as an example" (Carlson, 1988, p. 312). The clown resonates with humans because "people are *necessarily* mistaken . . . *all* people are exposed to situations in which they must act as fools . . . *every* insight contains its own special kind of blindness" (Burke, 1984, p. 41). In this way, the comic frame is a humane response to imperfection in the social order. "When the clown is punished, a dialogue can begin, eventually leading to a rapprochement. Clown and society remerge in a newly repaired social order" (Carlson, 1988, p. 312). The process of improving society does not necessitate tropes of *villain* or *evil* once an imperfect human condition is acknowledged.

Perspective through incongruity is the means by which the clown is corrected, wherein the rhetor intentionally uses uncommon associations to disrupt normal patterns or orders, and by doing so misnames the issue according to the language of hierarchy. Burke (1984) explains perspective by incongruity is "a method for gauging situations by verbal 'atom cracking.' That is, a word belongs by custom to a certain category—and by rational planning you wrench it loose and metaphorically apply it to a different category" (p. 308). Such incongruity exposes agents to new meaning that transcends the limitations of the current situation. Such incongruity exposes both clowns and audiences to new meanings that transcend the limitations of the status quo.

The comic frame allows consideration for the complexity of the situation by placing it within a larger context. The comic frame, Burke (1984) argues, is more realistic than the epic or tragic frames because "it takes up the slack between the momentousness of the situation and the feebleness of those in the situation by *dwarfing the situation*" (p. 43). For example, in the comic perspective crimes are not rooted in evil, rather rooted in human error. "In sum, the comic frame should enable people *to be observers of themselves, while acting*. Its ultimate would not be *passiveness,* but *maximum consciousness*" (Burke, 1984, p. 171). Rather than turning to a scapegoat, the comic frame asks readers to care about and identify with the clown; this requires cognitive complexity to consider the situation within a larger context.

The comic frame emphasizes unity through shared identification, yet provides the tools necessary for changing the social order. The comic frame is an effective means of altering the system as long as the order is "presented as capable of accommodating the needs of the out group" (Carlson, 1988, p. 319). This chapter will argue the comic frame is a particularly important frame for addressing issues such as whiteness. Whereas traditional conceptions of racism assume intentional racist acts on the part of an individual, the concept of whiteness addresses the subconscious and unintentional ways in which oppression persists systemically in contemporary society (Simpson, 2008). "Whiteness is a state of being that carries with it many attendant privileges and yet is also cloaked in a discourse of normalcy such that attitudes, behaviors, experiences, cultural norms, and taboos that are more reflective of the experience of European Americans become generalized and accepted as normal, natural, right, and just" (Simpson, 2008, p. 147). The inability of some whites to recognize the way in which they are privileged by skin color would be better understood in the comic frame with the white person being a clown rather than a tragic scapegoat. As Carlson (1988) explains, "The clown is not an evil person, although s/he may do evil through ignorance" (p. 312). It is imperative to note: the comic frame's ability to avoid scapegoating does not absolve people of personal responsibility for participating in racism but instead leaves room for individuals to reject and subvert whiteness.

"A MORE PERFECT UNION"

The Rev. Jeremiah Wright controversy was a pivotal moment in the 2008 presidential campaign that created a significant event for *The Daily Show with Jon Stewart* to cover. "Sometimes there are unscripted moments in American presidential races that condense important themes of the campaign," such as the Kennedy-Nixon debates "when image first trumped substance" (Dumm, 2008, p. 317). Yet the Wright controversy is distinctly different as "the video clip... shows no candidate blunder, dissembling, or dramatically revealing an otherwise hidden aspect of their 'character.' Instead, a video clip culled from many hours of sermons . . . has had the greatest impact on the shape of this race" (Dumm, 2008, p. 317). Sound bites of Wright professing "God damn America," claiming the attacks of September 11 were the result of United States foreign policy, and asserting that the United States deliberately spread AIDS in Africa were looped incessantly across media networks. "The clips . . . highlighted the black-white breach in public opinion. A poll taken by the Pew Research Center showed that 58 percent of white Americans were personally offended by Wright's sermons, compared with 29 percent of black Americans" (Fraser, 2009, p. 31).

The sound bites of Wright's sermons were part of the racialization of Obama's candidacy. Despite the campaign's attempts to portray Obama as a highly qualified candidate "who happened to be black," the campaign was racialized through the persistent media focus on race, such as the Bradley Effect and other signs of fearful whites (Fraser, 2009). Obama faced a double standard, "White Republican candidates have not faced similar pressures to repudiate views of other politically vocal conservative Christian leaders, such as Pat Robertson and the late Jerry Falwell" (Bennett, 2008, para. 12). This double standard "in America requires a member of a minority group to dissociate him or herself from fellow 'troublemakers' in ways not expected of whites" (Bennett, 2008, para. 10). The mass media focused on the relationship between Obama and Wright, which reinforces a white perspective that views Wright's rhetoric as offensive. The repetition of the sound bites allowed for many to scapegoat Wright as racist or evil, while simultaneously ignoring perspectives that would have shed light on Wright's intended message.

Typically, it would behoove the candidate to reject the controversial figure outright and move on with the campaign. However, to do so would be to reject Trinity church, "A major center for social justice ministry" (Marable, 2009, p. 8). To reject Trinity would be seen as a rejection of black theology, and by extension a rejection of those who fought in the civil rights movement and made his candidacy possible. Such a rejection would function to reinforce the universalization of whiteness. Obama faced a conundrum: he could not outright reject or accept Rev. Wright. Obama's speech would have to manage this rhetorical problem and bridge the potential division. The epic and tragic frames would not suffice because the rhetorical problem was one of scapegoating Wright as evil or racist. The comic frame, however, is particularly effective for dealing with this problem because "it warns against too great reliance upon the conveniences of moral indignation," and instead promotes "forensic complexity" by taking into consideration context (Burke, 1984, p. 174). Because Obama could neither completely reject nor accept Rev. Wright, Obama would need the benefit of context that the comic frame provides.

Obama uses the comic frame within the first eight paragraphs of the speech when he places the Wright controversy within the larger American context. Obama opens with the famous first line of the preamble to the Constitution: "We the people, in order to form a more perfect union." After establishing this theme, Obama constructs the context by taking the audience back 221 years to the nation's conception, setting the scene for the American creation myth. From this specific moment of the nation's inception, Obama widens the scope and exposes the flaws and imperfections within the Constitution, which was "unfinished" due to America's "original sin of slavery, a question that divided the colonies and brought the convention to a stalemate until the founders chose to allow the slave trade to continue . . . to leave any final resolution to future generations." The Founding Fathers and Constitution are typically idealized as heroic, but Obama goes beyond the fictitious images of the epic frame to a more realistic image of America's conception within the comic frame. Obama avoids magnifying the Founding Fathers as god-like figures; instead, he portrays them as humans who were undoubtedly far from perfect.

Despite the seemingly tragic imperfections of slavery that plagued the nation and Founding Fathers, Obama reassures his audience that the system is in fact capable of accommodating the necessary changes. Obama says, " . . . the answer to the slavery question was already embedded within our Constitution; a Constitution that had at its very core the ideal of equal citizenship . . . a union that could be and should be perfected over time." From the American creation myth, Obama identifies the nation's imperfections and locates the means of transcendence as built into the Constitution. Yet, Obama's fourth paragraph even contextualizes the Constitution: just "words on a parchment" that alone are not going to solve problems. For the system to truly be changed it requires the hard work and dedication of the citizens to fight for what is right. Through acts of "protests and struggles, on the streets and in the courts, through a civil war and civil disobedience, and always at great risk" generations of Americans have worked "to narrow the gap between the promise of our ideals and the reality of their time." The feebleness of humans is established as an inevitable problem. Obama utilizes the comic frame to place the Founding Fathers within context; Obama does not magnify the Founding Fathers as heroes, rather as human. Through the comic frame Obama establishes the nation's ultimate purpose: a journey towards perfection, impossible without the social movements that make such generational changes a reality. The rhetoric places America's creation and the Constitution in context, avoiding the magnification of America as perfection, which is necessary for the performance of the comic frame.

After Obama establishes these contexts, he contextualizes his own campaign: "This was one of the tasks we set forth at the beginning of this campaign: to continue the long march of those who came before us, a march for a more just, more equal, more free, more caring and more prosperous America." Although many would-be voters had built up Obama as hero, he avoids such magnification by positioning his campaign as but one leg of a much larger American journey towards "a more perfect union."

The rhetorical exigency for this speech was the demonization of Wright in morally absolute terms, but how has Obama established the good and/or bad? As James Darsey (2009) explains, the *journey* is Obama's archetypical metaphor. To handle the rhetorical problem of moral absolutes, Obama's rhetoric makes the ultimate "good" the act of striving for perfection but not the perfection itself. The anaphora Obama uses in "a march for a *more*just, *more*equal, *more*free . . . [italics added]" establishes his campaign as part of such goodness. Such a framing of the American story reinforces the comic frame which views "man as eternal journeyman" (Burke, 1984, p. 170).

Obama states that the public's desire for unity and change was successfully focusing the campaign on the more important issues, until the recent "divisive turn." Here, Obama establishes the ultimate negative as divisiveness. Divisiveness distracts Americans from the important policy issues at hand. Obama never bothers to question the justification for visceral outrage over Wright's statements; instead, he works from the premise that people are justified to feel alienated by Wright's language because it is divisive. Wright was speaking from a tragic frame. Obama is careful to "condemn" Wright's language but not the man, because the words were harming America at a time when it needed identification and unification. Obama castigates the behaviors and ideas of Wright that are socially unacceptable to the majority, while carefully avoiding tragic victimage. Obama says that the real foible of Wright is that his words insinuated that the country was static, "as if no progress has been made; as if this country . . . is still irrevocably bound to a tragic past." Wright's mistake was viewing America in a tragic frame; whereas, Obama encourages audiences to use a comic frame.

Obama further encourages the audience to adopt the comic frame by providing the context necessary for understanding Wright's anger expressed in those sound bites: "For the men and women of Rev. Wright's generation, the memories of humiliation and doubt and fear have not gone away; nor has the anger and the bitterness of those years." While the anger is understandable, Obama recognizes that this anger can be problematic and can inhibit progress: ". . . it keeps us from squarely facing our own complicity in our condition, and prevents the African-American community from forging the alliances it needs to bring about real change." Obama legitimizes the anger as real and says to ignore it will only "widen the chasm of misunderstanding that exists between the races." To provide further context, Obama goes beyond legitimizing the anger of the black community, and he voices the white perspective: ". . . a similar anger exists within segments of the white community. Most working- and middle-class white Americans don't feel that they have been particularly privileged by their race." Obama says to call white anger racist without context also inhibits understanding between groups. For perhaps the first time in America, a presidential candidate addressed the conflicting black and white perspectives that contain both truth and fiction (Marable, 2009; Fraser, 2009). Obama constructs an account of reality that does not allow colorblind norms to reinforce whiteness, and instead allows a new understanding of reality that can accommodate the new information. But Obama warns the ultimate danger we face is allowing the divisive racialization of politics, the media searching for polarization as all such strategies serve to distract us from the important bigger issues that actually keep all types of Americans disadvantaged. Obama emphasizes the need for context, rejects the demonization of individuals or groups, and as a result reinforces the comic frame as a viable means by which we can understand contemporary society.

Obama utilizes perspective through incongruity with the retelling of his biography narrative. He reminds the audience that he is the son of a white mother from Kansas and a father who was an immigrant from Kenya. He went on to Harvard and now is running for president. Obama then repeats a sentiment often heard in America, "I will never forget that in no other country on Earth is my story even possible." The *American dream* mythos is not typically about biracial couples and immigrants who entered the country in places other than Ellis Island, yet Obama's story fulfills the myth, almost. The incongruity housed within Obama's version of the *American dream* mythos reveals the whiteness of the traditional *American dream* mythos. Obama acknowledges this incongruity when he says in reference to his personal story, "It's a story that hasn't made me the most conventional candidate. But it is a story that has seared into my genetic makeup the idea that this nation is more than the sum of its parts—that out of many, we are truly one." Despite his story not fitting the typical *American Dream* myth, Obama deliberately recharacterizes the mythos so that his story emerges as an exemplar of the "American dream."

Obama makes it clear that it is the audience's choice to utilize the comic frame, or else suffer a tragic fate. "For we have a choice in this country. We can accept a politics that breeds division, and conflict, and cynicism." Or, Obama says, we can choose the path towards perfection, which "requires all Americans to realize that your dreams do not have to come at the expense of my dreams." Obama says when he begins "feeling doubtful or cynical about this possibility, what gives me the most hope is the next generation: the young people whose attitudes and beliefs and openness to change have already made history in this election." Obama's speech illustrates the fallibility of humans, for even Obama succumbs to cynicism and doubt at times, allowing for identification. Further identification with the audience in forged when Obama says things such as, "my unyielding faith in the decency and generosity of the American people." Obama's speech reframes the Wright controversy in a way that rejects the tragic frame that made the speech exigent, emphasizing a common identification as imperfect humans. The rhetoric encourages agents to maximum consciousness so they can participate in a social movement towards a more perfection union. It is not that America currently lacks those qualities; rather, the rhetoric acknowledges that the United States continues to strive for *more* of that which Americans value.

The overarching theme of Obama's speech "A More Perfect Union" is the comic frame, which functions to ameliorate the Wright controversy and salvage the Obama campaign. Burke (1984) says the comic frame "might mitigate somewhat the difficulties in engineering a shift to new symbols of authority, as required by the new social relationships that the revolutions of historic environment have made necessary" (p. 173). Obama has to mitigate the anxiety in predominately white America over a black president, and he has to translate Wright into a reality that is not threatening to voters. Obama uses the comic frame to "provide important cues for the composition of one's life, which demands accommodation to the structuring of others' lives" (Burke, 1984, pp. 173–174).

THE DAILY SHOW WITH JON STEWART

Obama contends that distraction is the ultimate danger for the American people, a distraction from important social issues that must be addressed to make a more perfect union. And it is not too far-fetched to presume that *The Daily Show with Jon Stewart*'s comical reaction to Obama's speech would only fuel the distraction of the Wright controversy. However, the analysis of *The Daily Show with Jon Stewart* reveals that the "fake news" and Obama's political speech are homologically connected by a comic frame. This assertion is revealed through the analysis of three clips addressing the Rev. Wright controversy. Each segment is representative of the three major segments featured on *The Daily Show with Jon Stewart*: the headlines, Stewart interviewing a senior correspondent, and the guest interview segment.

The first segment on March 18, 2008 signifies that *The Daily Show with Jon Stewart* values Obama's speech based on the title of the segment: "Barack's Wright Response." The play on Wright/right implies an approval of Obama's handling of the exigency (Bodow and O'Neill, 2008a). Stewart places the Wright controversy in a specific context, explaining that throughout Obama's campaign there had been an undercurrent of fear. Obama is the Other, manifested in claims that Obama is a Muslim. Stewart announces the positive news is that we can now know with confidence Obama is a Christian, however, the down side is that Wright is his pastor. The scene cuts from Stewart to the frequently aired sound bites of Rev. Wright, then cuts back to Stewart who appears scared of Wright's anger. Stewart then plays news clips from cable networks repeatedly saying that these Wright sound bites will scare white voters. Stewart sarcastically agrees with the clips by asking why Wright had to be so threatening to whites. Then Stewart explicitly says that this controversy is actually about race, not religion. Stewart places the Wright controversy within the larger context of Obama's campaign, which is vital to enactment of the comic frame.

After building the context, Stewart then addresses Obama's speech. Stewart adopts the role of the clown in the segment, representing a white perspective Obama acknowledged in the speech, one that is unfamiliar with black anger and harboring their own feelings of anger and fear. Yet, Stewart performs as a clown the audience already adores and sees as a credible person. Stewart's willingness to perform as a white clown that is ignorant of black anger or black perspectives discourages the audience from scapegoating similarly ignorant whites, but instead encourages the adoption of the comic frame. Also, white audience members can identify with Stewart, thus beginning to recognize how their own whiteness structures their perceptions of Wright. This segment uses perspective through incongruity. One of the reasons Wright was alienating for whites was the angry nature of his statements. When Obama says that black anger is real and legitimate, Stewart is surprised to find out that there is still black anger. Stewart then pulls out car keys and pretends to use the remote to lock his desk. The beeping of a car alarm makes Stewart's desk formally vulnerable to the image of a scared white driver in a predominately black neighborhood. Stewart braces himself to hear an angry diatribe against white America, but that diatribe does not come. Instead Obama acknowledges the legitimate anger that whites experience. Stewart is pleasantly surprised and feels safe enough to unlock his desk.

Surprised by Obama's acknowledgement of white anger, Stewart again utilizes perspective through incongruity when he asks two men in white Ku Klux Klan sheets their perspective on the speech. The KKK member says he did not expect to hear that from Obama. Obviously, real KKK members would never be so thoughtful about Obama's speech. The KKK members are incongruous with the whiteness that average whites typically reinforce in society, which, does not take the form of white sheets and burning crosses, rather manifests through the subconscious and unintentional preferences for whites in contemporary culture. This incongruity makes it clear that Obama's audiences are not the people we typically think of as "racist," but rather average whites who unintentionally perpetuate whiteness.

Finally, Stewart closes the segment with an earnest and powerful line announcing that for the first time a politician addressed the public about the issue of race in a way that was not patronizing. This line was genuine praise for a politician, an endorsement Stewart rarely provides. Such an incongruous statement with typical *The Daily Show with Jon Stewart* humor makes it clear that the speech, in Stewart's opinion, was a rare moment in which a politician addressed race in America without the patronizing simplicity that comes with scapegoating and the tragic frame. This line is not a punch line; rather, the power lies in the statement's ability to catch the audience off guard and reveal a deeper meaning about the significance of Obama's speech.

"Barack's Wright Response" leads directly into the second segment from March 18, 2008 titled "Open Dialogue." Stewart has a dialogue with senior black correspondent, Larry Wilmore. According to Stewart, the dialogue was inspired by Obama's speech (Bodow and O'Neill, 2008a). First, the clip establishes the identification of both Jon Stewart and Larry Wilmore as individuals as well as representative of their respective races. The two men use us/them language, such as Wilmore complaining that whites have a tendency to take great music and ruin it (such as Kenny G's contributions to jazz), and Stewart who says blacks tend to play their stereos too loud and that whites are uncomfortable asking blacks to turn them down. While Wilmore and Stewart have yet to find common ground, the two men build identification with their respective races in the audience. Because both men are offering issues they have with the other group, they share characteristics that are seen as funny, humbling because all humans are fallible. This context removes the politics of a presidential campaign, and instead places Obama's speech in the context of two largely normal guys performing the message of Obama's speech by having a dialogue on race.

Stewart and Wilmore are able to address white privilege via perspective through incongruity. When Wilmore complains that despite his hard work and the success he has achieved, he is sometimes followed in stores as if he is going to steal. Stewart acknowledges this is unfair, but attempts to be positive by saying at least America is a country where one can work hard and become successful. This comment makes Wilmore defensive. The rugged individual mythos does not ring true for everyone, especially many African

Americans. Wilmore rejects this narrative on the grounds that it does not acknowledge the persistence of racism. Wilmore asks if his success somehow makes it okay that he still experiences racism. Wilmore rejects and disrupts the cultural norm and insists there is more progress to be made. Stewart acts offended and performs a common white sentiment, one voiced by Obama as well. Stewart argues that his family worked hard too, as taxi cab drivers, etc. Wilmore responds by reminding Stewart that Stewart's people were given the choice to immigrate to America, which leaves us with the undeniable reality of the forced immigration of Africans via slavery. The mythos of America's European immigrants and the melting pot metaphor is disrupted by the harsh reality of slavery, another instance of perspective through incongruity. Stewart, at this point in the dialogue, is incredibly uncomfortable with Wilmore's frank statement, and this leads Stewart to again lock his desk out of fear of Wilmore's anger. Stewart again performs as a clown, representing the white foible of fearing the frustrations and anger of blacks as exposed by the performance of Obama's speech.

The men struggle to find something to say after the conflict, until one of them mentions *Starsky and Hutch*. The two men are able to find common ground with a television show. It is reminiscent of the narrative Obama ends his speech with. Obama tells of a moment of recognition between a young white girl and an older black man is not enough to fix our problems, but it is where we begin a process of healing. Similarly, the common ground between Stewart and Wilmore is not enough to heal the tensions revealed in the exchange, but it is a good place to start. The lesson here is the racial divide still needs to be bridged, but common ground is possible. It is just a matter of trying hard enough to find or create it.

Finally, the last segment of *The Daily Show with Jon Stewart* is the May 13th, 2008 interview with Bill Moyers, the host of *Bill Moyer's Journal* and author of *On Democracy*. Although this segment airs over a month after Obama's speech, the controversy had been rekindled by the media and subsequent statements made by Reverend Wright, including ones made during an interview on *Bill Moyers Journal*.

Promoting Moyer's book in the interview quickly becomes a transition into a discussion about the Wright controversy (Bodow and O'Neill, 2008b). Stewart asks Moyers why he compiled his old speeches into a book if he has his own television show. Moyers says he has developed a more nuanced and complex understanding of democracy than he can effectively discuss on his television program. Stewart feigns surprise, and he asks if it is because television overuses sound bites. Moyers agrees and quickly offers Jeremiah Wright as exemplar of the damage that can be done with sound bites. Moyers and Stewart then begin discussing the problems of a sound bite obsessed medium by providing context. Stewart mentions Moyers' interview with Wright, and he asks if Moyers thinks Wright is a thoughtful man or the cartoon-like figure the media portrayed him to be. Stewart's loaded question signals his perspective on the matter: Wright is not the person implied in the sound bites. Moyers said he has been asked how Wright could sound so reasonable on his show, yet so angry in subsequent media appearances. Moyers admits that he does not know the answer for he is not a psychologist and he cannot know for certain what another person thinks and feels. This statement disrupts the tendency to make tragic assumptions about individuals as either evil or good. However, because he mentioned his interview with Wright, it establishes the source of Moyer's limited expert opinion about Wright. Moyers says he thinks Wright was angry because his thirty-six years at Trinity were reduced by the media to sound bites in an attempt to wound Obama's campaign. Moyers attributes the folly of sound bites to the media that endlessly loops the statements, and he compares Wright to someone who steps out on his front porch to get the paper and is swept up in a cyclone. Moyers provides context in this dialogue that reprimands the clowns in the media for the foible of sound bites.

The argument that it was unfair to summarize Wright's work into sound bites, thus failing to understand Wright's context, had been made by Obama and others. However, Stewart provides a challenge to this argument by saying that some of Wright's statements, even in context some people found offensive, and Stewart asks if Wright seemed to recognize his statements were abrasive to the mainstream. Moyers makes a disclaimer and says he does not make excuses for his guests. However, Moyers emphasizes the fallibility of humans, in that, we have all said things we regret. Moyers is working to build identification. Moyers said he did not get the chance to ask Wright about his claims the government spread HIV; however, he explained the anger and paranoia blacks justly feel because of things like the Tuskegee experiments. Many Americans of all races and ages have never learned about these atrocities. Consideration of perspective and context are necessary for the comic frame and are integral to the rhetoric of Stewart and Moyers.

Stewart and Moyers end the segment with an optimistic conclusion. Stewart asks Moyers if he is more dispirited than he has been in the past, to which Moyers says democracy has a long history of overcoming threats to the system. According to comic frame, the threat is from the detrimental actions of clowns. Moyers says he sometimes wonders if his optimism is justified, but he thinks that Obama's primary wins after the Wright controversy are indicative of the public's ability to manage the problems of our society. However, Moyers fears that his grandchildren and Stewart's audience will not have equality of opportunity which is a fundamental value of American democracy. Stewart agrees, but optimistically asserts that he believes the younger generation, once they recognize the disparity, will embrace the movement and continue the American journey towards a more perfect union.

The interview concludes by reinforcing the message of Obama's speech, as well as reinforcing the value of adopting the comic frame.

CONCLUSION

In order to shed light on the intersection of political and popular discourse the analysis uncovered the homology of the comic frame linking the discourse of Obama and *The Daily Show with Jon Stewart*. However, Brummett states, "The critic is not a mere jigsaw puzzle worker who is satisfied once a coherence is identified, but must ask *why* a certain homology could have obtained in a situation" (Brummett, 1991, p. 98). The project must explore how the homology of the comic frame *may* serve as equipment for living for individuals experiencing the Wright controversy, Obama's rhetoric, and *The Daily Show with Jon Stewart* discourse. The critic must ask: who benefits from the homology? Whose interests are served?

First, the comic frame is a rhetorical homology that can further attempts to expose and subvert racism and whiteness. "Race relations itself has been such a complicated, difficult, and painful issue for so many Americans for so long that free and open discussion of racial matters may be difficult for people" (Brummett, 2008, p. 3). Indeed, Obama faced a difficult task in addressing whiteness and racism while maintaining a generally positive persona many white voters would appreciate. If Obama would have allowed the media reports and critics to demonize Wright for the sake of his winning the election, he would have contradicted the "change" he purported to represent. The comic frame was a vehicle through which Obama could successfully address such a complex and thorny rhetorical task. As Burke (1984) argues, the names we give things will impact the ways in which we act towards the individuals representing those names. The term "racist" has become such a socially stigmatized label, it alienates and scapegoats anyone to which it is applied. As highlighted in the clip "Barack's Wright Response," KKK racism is not the racism Obama or *The Daily Show with Jon Stewart* aims to address. Such racism employs a tragic frame. The tragic term "racist" prepares us *against* the individual who is deemed racist, especially those who do not reflect the racism of the KKK, rather than *against* the behaviors that are harmful and result in oppression. However, the comic frame *reveals* whiteness and offers an alternative shared sense of identification that moves beyond racial and ethnic boundaries. The comic frame is an attitudinizing frame that allows for the correction of behaviors that perpetuate inequalities while recognizing human fallibility. It promotes a consideration of perspective and context. The comic frame's potential to address issues of whiteness is the power of Obama's rhetoric. The comic frame's ability to avoid scapegoating does not absolve whites of personal responsibility for participating in racism, rather it makes the process of accepting personal responsibility less painful and more likely. The homology of the comic frame serves as equipment for living for those who must reveal and address whiteness in contemporary society.

The benefits of addressing race via the comic frame make the benefits for Obama's speech obvious. However, what does it mean that *The Daily Show with Jon Stewart* also uses the comic frame when addressing the Wright controversy? *The Daily Show with Jon Stewart* could have demonized the mass media or those white voters alienated by the sound bites. Yet, *The Daily Show with Jon Stewart* seems to convey the ideology of Obama's rhetoric. In this way, *The Daily Show with Jon Stewart* can be seen as an accurate reporting of Obama's speech, more so than the relentless looping of Wright's sound bites by the mass media. Indeed such a report would be a complex and informative commentary. Such a reading would support the argument that *The Daily Show with Jon Stewart* "can be better understood not as 'fake news' but as an alternative journalism" (Baym, 2005, p. 261). However, *The Daily Show with Jon Stewart* has routinely used the comic frame outside of the Wright controversy (Hariman, 2007). Furthermore, the conclusion that *The Daily Show with Jon Stewart* is reporting on Obama's ideological message delimits our understanding of the show to the realm of journalism, whether "fake" or "alternative." To label *The Daily Show with Jon Stewart* as journalism requires a more robust notion of the form and function of political news, for the show utilizes a comic frame that traditional news media are discouraged from using. *The Daily Show with Jon Stewart* does not aim to *inform* the audience about something, it provides equipment for living. The "Open Dialogue" segment performs for the audience a method in which they can enact Obama's message. *The Daily Show with Jon Stewart* reinforces Obama's rhetoric not because they want to support the candidate; rather the show employs the homology of the comic frame as a tool for living in this contemporary political climate. And it is this shared homology of the comic frame that we find throughout the rhetoric of Obama's campaign.

The popularity and cultural power of *The Daily Show with Jon Stewart* is the result of their masterful use of the comic frame. Baym is right when he says *The Daily Show with Jon Stewart* "is a product of a specific historical moment, fueled both by the post-September 11 dissuasion of open inquiry and the particular talents of its current host" (Baym, 2005, p. 274). Furthermore, Obama's campaign was similarly fueled by the talents of the candidate and the historical moment. The historical exigency of *The Daily Show with Jon Stewart* and Obama's rhetoric was a thirst for alternatives to the tragic status quo, such as the demonization of Wright and a political discourse that is determined by sound bites. It seems that their use of the comic frame is not a reaction to the specific exigency of the Wright controversy; rather it is

Obama and *The Daily Show with Jon Stewart*'s ideology that has been cultivated from their own life experiences and used to address contemporary exigencies. Their popularity is evidence of an appetite for the comic frame at this moment in time, and their rhetoric further enhances this taste for the comic frame as an alternative to a tragic one. Perhaps this homology is indicative of a distinct type of social movement rhetoric, and scholars may find it fruitful to open homology and the rhetoric of Obama and *The Daily Show with Jon Stewart* to the study of social movements.

In today's world where digital rhetoric can easily be circulated, audiences are less dependent on traditional media to frame political rhetoric. In the case of Obama's "A More Perfect Union," people bypassed traditional political commentary and watched Obama's address on YouTube or followed the Wright controversy through *The Daily Show with Jon Stewart* ("Barack Obama's race speech," 2008). Brummett's concept of rhetorical homologies is precisely the method to address this new landscape that intersects political and popular discourses.

According to our analysis, Moyers gets it right: "You simply can't understand American politics in the new millennium without *The Daily Show*" (2003). The analysis of political and popular discourse expands our understanding of how these discourses intersect. The homology of the comic frame links the disparate texts of Obama and *The Daily Show with Jon Stewart*, and their use of the frame is perhaps indicative of a cultural shift from a tragic to a comic frame. The changing landscape of racism and whiteness in contemporary American culture necessitates this shift in homologies, as the comic frame is particularly useful in disrupting power structures. The comic frame offers a rhetorical form to address whiteness by focusing on shared identification, performing as clown, and using context to dwarf the situation. It offers an alternative way for both political and popular discourse to address whiteness in the pursuit of the progressive journey to a more perfect union.

NOTE

This chapter is derived from Stephanie Purtle's master's thesis titled *Barack Obama and* The Daily Show*'s comic critique of whiteness: The intersection of popular and political discourse.* Timothy Steffensmeier was the major professor. A copy of the thesis can be found at: http://hdl.handle.net/2097/2160.

REFERENCES

Barack Obama's race speech an online video hit. (2008, March 21). *Agence France-Presse* Retrieved from http://afp.google.com/article/ALeqM5hk5k_4GTjX1jadJTk23xAnxcxYUA.

Baym, G. (2005). *The Daily Show*: Discursive Integration and the Reinvention of Political Journalism. *Political Communication, 11*, 259–276.

Bennett, J. (2008, March 20). Obama's pastor's words ring uncomfortably true. *San Jose Mercury News*. Retrieved from http://www.webcitation.org/5WcldcmR8.

Bodow, S. (Head Writer) and O'Neill, C. (Director). (2008a, March 18). [Television series episode]. In J. Stewart (Executive producer), *The Daily Show with Jon Stewart*. New York: Viacom.

———. (2008b, May 13). [Television series episode]. In J. Stewart (Executive producer), *The Daily Show with Jon Stewart*. New York: Viacom.

Brummett, B. (1991). *Rhetorical Dimensions of Popular Culture*. Tuscaloosa: The University of Alabama Press.

———. (2004). *Rhetorical Homologies*. Tuscaloosa: The University of Alabama Press.

———. (2008). *Uncovering Hidden Rhetorics: Social Issues in Disguise*. Los Angeles: Sage Publications.

Burke, K. (1984). *Attitudes Toward History*. (3rd Ed.). Berkeley: University of California Press.

Carlson, C. (1988). Limitations on the comic frame: some witty American women of the nineteenth century. *Quarterly Journal of Speech, 74*, 310–322.

Christiansen, A. and Hanson, J. (1996). Comedy as cure for tragedy: Act Up and the rhetoric of AIDS. *Quarterly Journal of Speech, 82*, 157–170.

Darsey, J. (2009). Barack Obama and America's journey. *Southern Communication Journal, 74*(1), 88–103.

Dumm, T. (2008). Barack Obama and the souls of white folk. *Communication and Critical/Cultural Studies, 5*(3), 317–320.

Fraser, C. (2009). Race, post-black politics, and the Democratic presidential candidacy of Barack Obama. *Souls, 11*(1), 1–15.

Hariman, R. (2007). In defense of Jon Stewart. *Critical Studies in Media Communication, 24*(3), 273–277.

Marable, M. (2009). Racializing Obama: the enigma of post-black politics and leadership. *Souls, 11*(1), 1–15.

Moyers, B. (2003, July 11). Transcript: Bill Moyers Interviews Jon Stewart. *NOW*. [Television news program].Retrieved from http://www.pbs.org/now/printable/transcript_stewart_print.html.

Obama, B. (2008, March 18). A More Perfect Union (Transcript). *American Rhetoric*. Retrieved March 11, 2009 from http://www.americanrhetoric.com/speeches/barackobamaperfectunion.htm.

Simpson, J. (2008). The color-blind double bind: whiteness and the (im)possibility of dialogue. *Communication Theory, 18*(1), 139–159.

Wander, P. W., Martin, T. N., and Nakayama, T. K. (1999). Whiteness and beyond: Sociohistorical foundations of Whiteness and contemporary challenges. In T. K. Nakayama and J. N. Martin (Eds.), *Whiteness: The communication of social identity* (pp. 13–26). Thousand Oaks, CA: Sage Publications.

Index

ABC, 139; News, 10, 11, Sunday talk show, 37
abortion, 77
academic world, praise of *Daily Show*, 131
accident, as evasion tactic, 44
actors. *See* political actors
ACT UP, 192
agon (encounter), 79, 80, 83, 89
Ahmadinejad, Mahmoud, 189
AIDS/HIV, 192, 227, 235
All in the Family, 38n1
America (The Book): A Citizen's Guide to Democracy Inaction (The Writers of The Daily Show), 85, 94, 95
American Gothic, 183
Amostle speech, 210
Anderson, K. K., 54
anger: Aristotle on, 13; black, 232, 233, 235; confederate audience's, 71; at injustice/hypocrisy, 14; Limbaugh and O'Reilly's trade in, 14; at Massa scandal, 63; satirical argument's link to, 71; Stewart's, 14, 71; white, 232; Wilmore's, 233; Wright's, 229, 232
Anti-Oedipus (Foucault), 35–36
Apple, 121
Archie Bunker (fictional character), 38n1
Arendt, Hannah, 80, 90
arete (excellence, virtue), 6, 6, 17. *See also* good moral character

arguments: anger's link to satirical, 71; carnivalesque self-parody, 93–110; rhetoric with issues strategies and, xi–xiii; staff writers' strategies with, 106; Stewart's political, xii. *See also* humorous arguments; political arguments; public arguments
argument scheme: carnivalesque as, 102–108; carnivalesque self-parody as, 93–110; comedy v. "news" and, 106–108; premise of carnival and, 102–104; self-parody, puppets making crank phone calls and, 104–106
Aristotle, 82; on anger, 13; *Daily Show* ethos from perspective of, xii, 3–17; humor types of, 13; persuasion defined by, 5; rhetoric defined by, xi, 5; wittiness defined by, 13. *See also* ethos
Atlantic, 153
AT&T, 121
attacking the accuser, 44, 51
Attitudes Toward History (Burke), 190
audiences: comic framing informing, xiii; of *Daily Show* as most informed population, 4; demographic of *Daily Show*'s, 29; humor types for educated/ ignorant, 13; jester living up to expectations of, 33; judgment of source's character from viewpoint of, 5; speaker's ethos inspiring trust in, 7

cable news: clip remediation with, 10;
feud, xii, 19, 27, 27–29
Calhoun, John C., 180
Cameron, David, 23
Cameron, Paul, 199
Canadian Broadcasting Company (CBC),
173
Cao, X., xi
Card, Andy, 84
Carell, Steve, 94, 161, 162
Carlin, George, 35
Carlson, A. C., 196
Carlson, C., 226
Carlson, Tucker, 94, 106, 135; criticism of
Stewart, 36; criticized by Stewart, 14,
85, 96, 104–105; interviewing Stewart,
85–86
Carnahan, Russ, 77
carnivalesque, 21
carnivalesque self-parody: as argument
scheme, 93–110; carnivalesque and,
99–100; comedy v. "news" with,
106–108; conclusion, 109–110;
explanation of, 93; Perelman's starting
points with, 97–99; premise of carnival
with, 102–104; puppets making crank
phone calls and, 104–106; self-parody
at carnival and, 101; targets of radical
critique with, 94–96
carnival theory: responsibility with, 21. *See
also* carnivalesque self-parody
Carson, Johnny, 191
cartoons. *See* political cartoons
Caruso, Enrico, 180
Catalus, 106
catharsis, 71, 72
CBC. *See* Canadian Broadcasting
Company
CBO. *See* Congressional Budget Office
celebrity reworking rules of, 86
Cenac, Wyatt, 23
Central Intelligence Agency (CIA), 10,
39n8, 30. *See also* Tenet George
Chase, Chevy, 177
Chatman, Seymour, 182
Cheney, Dick, 140
Cheney, Lynne, 84, 89
China, 138
Chung, Connie, 160

Chvasta, M., 100
chyrons, 150n3
CIA. *See* Central Intelligence Agency
Clancy, Jim, Blitzer's interview with,
143–144
clarification, as rhetorical function of
humor, 61, 62
Clinton, Bill, 84
clip remediation: drawn from other media
exhibiting good sense, 8, 10–11; as
media criticism, 11; as method of
accountability, 11, 12
clips, edited for brevity/clarity and
changed meanings, 10
clowns. *See* jesters
CNBC, xii, 28, 33; Stewart's
characterization of Cramer and, 43–55
CNN, 39n6, 37, 51, 105
Coburn, Tom, 77
Cohen, Richard, 198
Colbert, Stephen, 20, 37, 102, 209, 213; on
being characterized as conservative,
38n1; criticized by mainstream media,
30, 30; in "Even Stevphen", 94, 162;
fabricated personality of, 23; *Fresh
Air*'s description of, 22; interview style
of, 34; ironic strategy employed by, 24,
32; occupying space of comic and
journalist, 22–23; roasting of Bush by,
29–30; satire and irony as infinite with,
31; speech at 2006 Press Club Dinner,
29–31, 32
The Colbert Report, 38n3, 22; genesis of,
23. *See also* Colbert, Stephen
Colebrook, Claire, 21–22, 24
Colletta, L., 8
Comcast, 139
comedians: Colbert occupying space of
journalist and, 22–23; jokes employed
by political, 19; Stewart as self-
described, 8, 39n6, 33, 34. *See also
specific comedians*
comedy: difference between satire and, 8;
"news" v., 106–108
Comedy Central, 28
comically profane language, 20
comic framing: audience's perceptions of
media/politics with, xiii; coined by
Burke, 136; of Obama's speech and

About the Contributors

Jonathan E. Barbur holds a master's degree from Oregon State University. Currently, he is reworking his master's thesis on Nobel Peace Prize speeches for publication. He hopes to begin law school in the next year.

C. Wesley Buerkle, PhD, is assistant professor of communication at East Tennessee State University. His research focuses on the representation of gender and sexuality, primarily focusing on issues related to masculinity, such as studies of masculinity and meat consumption (*Text and Performance Quarterly*, 2009) and masturbation discourse in *Seinfeld* (*Sexualized Bodies*, 2011).

Josh Compton (PhD, University of Oklahoma) is an award-winning speech professor and public speaker. He is a recipient of the National Speakers Association Professor of the Year award, and his teaching has earned honors from the Instructional Division of the International Communication Association and the Pi Kappa Delta National Honorary. Josh has earned research recognitions from Pi Kappa Delta, the Central States Communication Association, the International Communication Association, and the National Communication Association. His research has appeared in journals such as *Human Communication Research*, *Communication Quarterly*, *Journal of Applied Communication Research*, *Communication Yearbook*, and *Health Communication*. His writings about political humor effects appear in *Laughing Matters: Humor and American Politics in the Media Age*. Josh is senior lecturer in speech at the Institute for Writing and Rhetoric at Dartmouth College.

Trischa Goodnow (PhD, University of Pittsburgh) is an associate professor in the Department of Speech Communication at Oregon State University. Her primary teaching area is rhetoric where she teaches courses in rhetorical theory and criticism, popular culture and visual rhetoric. She has published numerous articles and book chapters in outlets such as *Visual Communication Quarterly, The Handbook of Visual Communication* and a forthcoming essay in *American Behavioral Scientist.*

Aaron Hess (PhD, 2008, Arizona State University) is assistant professor of rhetoric at Indiana University-Purdue University, Fort Wayne. His research program follows the dual lines of rhetoric and qualitative inquiry, focusing largely on new media contexts. His work has been featured in premier journals of the field, including *Media, Culture & Society* and *Critical Studies in Media Communication.* This project is, in part, an outgrowth of his master's thesis from California State University, Chico, which was recognized as the Outstanding Thesis of the Year in 2003.

Brian T. Kaylor (PhD, University of Missouri) is an assistant professor of communication studies at James Madison University. His research focuses primarily on religious and political rhetoric. He authored—along with a co-author—a chapter in *The Rhetoric of Pope John Paul II* that textually analyzed how late night comics covered the death of John Paul II, arguing that Stewart and the other comics used humor to offer their unique type of eulogies. Kaylor has won several top paper awards and recently received the top dissertation awards from both the Religious Communication Association and the University of Missouri.

Ryan McGeough is a PhD student in rhetorical studies in the Department of Communication Studies at Louisiana State University. He currently serves as the editorial assistant for the Kenneth Burke Journal. He has published essays and book reviews in the edited collection *Concerning Argument*, the *Kenneth Burke Journal*, and the *Quarterly Journal of Speech.*

Lawrence J. Mullen (PhD, University of Iowa) is professor of media studies in the Hank Greenspun School of Journalism and Media Studies at the University of Nevada, Las Vegas. He is the author of numerous journal articles including publications in *Visual Communication Quarterly, Communication Studies, Communication Yearbook* and *Critical Studies in Mass Communication.* He is also author of the book *Las Vegas: Media and Myth.*

Stephanie M. Purtle received her BS in speech communication at Northwest Missouri State University and her MA in communication studies at

Kansas State University. She currently resides in Eugene, Oregon, and has a job that in no way pertains to either popular or political discourse.

John W. Self (PhD, University of Kansas) is an associate professor of communication at Truman State University teaching classes in rhetoric, political communication and even a class about the art and science of humor. The use of humor as argument became an interest during the 2000 presidential election and has been researching it ever since. His other main research interest is the negotiation of presidential debates.

Robert N. Spicer is an instructor of communication at DeSales University in Allentown, PA. He is currently working on his PhD in media studies at the School of Communication and Information at Rutgers University. His forthcoming chapter "The Obama Mass: Barack Obama, image and fear of the crowd," will be appearing in the anthology *The Obama Effect*.

Timothy R. Steffensmeier (PhD, University of Texas) is assistant professor of communication studies at Kansas State University. He has co-published a textbook on argumentation and essays focused on deliberative democracy and community development.

Penina Wiesman is a doctoral candidate in media studies at Rutgers University. She received her MFA in film studies from Boston University. Her current work focuses on both entertainment media forms as well as news and political communication in the context of media literacy education.

Kelly Wilz's (PhD, Indiana University, Bloomington) research focuses on rhetorical constructions of gender, violence, and dissent within the context of U.S. war culture. Specifically, she is guided by issues of how dissent and a re-articulation of dominant narratives function as a response to pro-war rhetoric. Related topics of interest include how dehumanizing and demonizing rhetoric extend beyond war to issues of social violence based on discourses of race, gender, sexual orientation, ethnicity and other identity markers. She earned her doctoral degree in communication and culture with a doctoral minor in religious studies from Indiana University, Bloomington. She teaches at the University of Wisconsin-Marshfield/Wood County in the Department of Communication and Theatre Arts and in the Department of Women's Studies.